LOVE

LOVE

Traversing Its Peaks and Valleys

Published under the auspices of
ISAPZURICH
(International School of
Analytical Psychology Zürich)
AGAP Post-Graduate Jungian Training

Series Editors
Stacy Wirth, Isabelle Meier, and John Hill

Consulting Editor
Nancy Cater

Spring Journal Books
New Orleans, Louisiana

Published by
Spring Journal, Inc.
627 Ursulines Street #7
New Orleans, Louisiana 70116
www.springjournalandbooks.com

Spring Journal™, Spring: A Journal of Archetype and Culture™, Spring Books™, Spring Journal Books,™ Spring Journal and Books™, and Spring Journal Publications™ are all trademarks of Spring Journal Incorporated. All Rights Reserved.

Cover Photograph:
Hotel Paxmontana © Courtesy of Hotel Paxmontana
Flüeli-Ranft, Switzerland

Cover design and typography:
Northern Graphic Design and Publishing
info@ncarto.com

Text printed on acid-free paper

Library of Congress Cataloging-in-Publication Data Pending

Grateful acknowledgement is made to the respective publishers, institutions, and/or individuals for permission to reprint as follows:

Val di Campo by Samuel Langmeier, photograph, © 2008 Samuel Langemeier, reproduced by permission of Samuel Langemeier.

Stable in the Mountains by Andreas Schweizer, photograph, © 2012 Andreas Schweizer, reproduced by permission of Andreas Schweizer.

"Please Call Me By My True Name" by Thich Nhat Hanh, in *Call Me By My True Name: The Collected Poems of Thich Nhat Hanh*, © 1999 Parallax Press, reprinted by permission of Parallax Press, Berkeley, California.

"Crowned Passion" by Zayra Yves, in *Crowned Compassion: Poetry Collection by Zayra Yves* [label unsigned], Audio CD, © 2006 by Zayra Yves, reprinted by permission of Zayra Yves.

"Nicholas of Flüe," Artist Unknown, in Petrus Hugo, *Nicolai von der Flüe Leben dess weitberühmten Br. Clausens, Einsidels und Landtmans zu Vnderwalden, Leben und Wandel* (Luzern: [publisher not named], 1684/1705), p. 159, digital image provided and reproduced by the kind permission of the Graphics Collection of the Zentralbibliothek Zürich.

Dedication

*This volume is dedicated to all who undertake
the journey of soul, in particular to the students, analysts,
and visitors of ISAPZURICH who gathered from all over the
world in Flüeli-Ranft to explore love's peaks and valleys.*

Contents

Acknowledgements

Our gratitude goes as ever to Nancy Cater of Spring Journal Books. Not only has she continued to endorse the Jungian Odyssey Series as well as the retreat itself. As the years go by, she stands by increasingly as an intimate consultant to our undertaking. In doing all of this, she helps to make of the Jungian Odyssey a widely known event that welcomes exchange among participants from a wide variety of cultural and professional backgrounds.

The Odyssey's rich program and smooth running relies always on the finely synchronized talents of many individuals. We appreciate and wish to especially recognize our colleagues, too many to name here, who conduct the afternoon seminars and workshops. Unfortunately, limits of space prevent the inclusion of their contributions in the Jungian Odyssey Series. For leading the Flüeli-Ranft tour, "Walking in the Footsteps of Brother Klaus," we heartily thank Josef Marty, Jungian analyst and former president of the *Schweizerische Gesellschaft für Analytische Psychologie* [Swiss Society for Analytical Psychology].

As ever, we are grateful to Helga Kopecky, ISAPZURICH's librarian, for keeping us well supplied with titles for our bookshop. Mary Tomlinson, an analyst and ISAP graduate (2011), continued to manage the individual course preferences. Andrew Fellows, also an analyst and ISAP graduate (2009) again provided music and acted as DJ for our closing evening. ISAP candidates, too, held forth with remarkable dedication: Isolde Kunerth, David Markus Schmid, and Katarzyna Wach provided technical support throughout. Susanne Bucher and Rose Nicol managed book sales. Margareta Ehnberg once again documented the whole week with her exquisite photography, which can be viewed at: http://s.ehnberg.net/JO2012.

These acknowledgements would be incomplete without an expression of deepest, heartfelt thanks to two colleagues who stepped down in 2012 as members of the Jungian Odyssey Committee. John Hill originally envisioned the Jungian Odyssey as a traveling conference and retreat that would draw inspiration from each *genius loci*. He began to serve as Academic Chair already in 2004 when the idea was still emerging. As if with a final tip of his hat, it was John who had the idea to return to our first venue, Flüeli-Ranft, and he who discerned in this landscape the topic of love. Isabelle Meier joined the committee at the conclusion of the first Jungian Odyssey in 2006, to serve as Co-Chair for six successive events. Managing a complex array of administrative demands behind the scenes, Isabelle brought to each Odyssey her warm heart and laughing spirit. John and Isabelle will both be missed, while their well welcomed successors have already begun to prepare Odysseys to come: Ursula Wirtz (Academic Chair) and Deborah Egger-Biniores (Co-Chair).

Stacy Wirth
Co-Chair, Jungian Odyssey Committee
Zürich, 2013

Introduction

Love:
Traversing Its
Peaks and Valleys

Stacy Wirth, Isabelle Meier, John Hill

T he seventh Jungian Odyssey, and these essays ensuing from
the retreat, were inspired by the *genius loci* emanating from
Flüeli-Ranft, a tiny agricultural village at the opening of the
great Melch Valley in the central Swiss Alps. "Flüeli," as the village is
fondly known, lies at the center of a magnificent *temenos* of valleys,
rivers, lakes, and woodlands encircled by breath-taking snow-topped
mountain peaks. Our venue's name, Paxmontana—mountain
peace—, alludes to its hilltop perch and healing serenity.

Built in 1896 in Art Nouveau style, Paxmontana was recently
restored and certified as a protected historic site. Originally it was a
sanatorium, founded by the entrepreneurial Franz Hess-Michel. Hess-
Michel also maintained an agricultural business, raising cows, horses,
pigs, and bees, and running a creamery, a bakery, an apple press, and
a sawmill. It was Hess-Michel who, for the benefit of the sanatorium
guests, designed the area's first network of walking trails and plotted
them on the first excursion maps. Still surrounded by the old trails,

Paxmontana remains like a fairy-tale castle, its proud turrets adorned with wraparound balconies, its mansard roof embellished with gabled windows, its gardens lush with flowers. And it still resonates the intimate hospitality—one might say the *agape*, the unconditional love—that once served the sanatorium's purpose, the healing of body and soul.

From Flüeli-Ranft the arc of our *genius loci* reaches across the valley to the numinously daunting Mount Pilatus, whose snowy peak juts to some 7,000 feet (2,133 meters). The daring among Odyssey participants took a trip to this mountain, which is named after the Roman governor Pontius Pilate, himself touted by legend to be buried here. Medieval belief held that magical healing dragons inhabit the mountain's rugged clefts and crevices. As we learn from C.G. Jung himself:

> On a high pasture of Mount Pilatus, which is particularly notorious for spooks—it is said to this day that Wotan practices his magic arts there—[Rennward] Cysat, while climbing the mountain, was disturbed by a procession of men who poured past his hut on both sides, playing music and singing . . . .
>
> The next morning Cysat asked the herdsman with whom he had spent the night what could have been the meaning of it. The man already had an explanation: Those must be the departed souls . . . namely, Wotan's army of blessed souls. These, he said, were in the habit of walking abroad and showing themselves.[1]

Among its esteemed visitors Flüeli counts Pope John Paul II, who spoke here in 1984. Indeed already in the 15th century, Flüeli-Ranft began to gain renown as a place of pilgrimage, for it was home to the hermit and mystic Brother Klaus. Born in 1417, Klaus was a family man, farmer, soldier, and member of the village council—that is, until he abandoned his beloved wife and ten children to become a mendicant monk. On the way, he received a number of disturbing visions. In one of them he saw Mount Pilatus tremble, collapse, and sink into the ground—and there followed a profound revelation of God's love for humankind. Thus, Klaus came to spend his last twenty years living in a tiny cell, which remains today, nestled into the steep gorge beneath

Paxmontana and overlooking the rushing Melch River. Klaus's unorthodox biography and religious visions have been studied by many scholars, including C.G. Jung.[2]

The spirit of this place subtly permeates the essays in this volume on love's peaks and valleys. The authors illuminate love in its many forms and manifestations—from the oh-so-human to the divine—from its joys to its risks and ravages. They contribute insight from the analytic consulting room, and draw as well on theology, folk song, legend, myth, theater, and the visual arts. Jungian analyst Ann Ulanov, the Odyssey keynote speaker, picks up the thread that runs throughout:

> To love a particular someone, a definite idea, a distinct place, a principal symbol, or notion of the psyche, opens us to loss with all its searing pain. The other who once loved us, opened to us a chance to find and live a new I-ness we had not known before, may stop loving us. Was it all fake then? Can we sustain our own loving, still owning the preciousness of what happened, not wreck it out of grief?[3]

Readers of this volume will find encouragement, but no easy answers. In the end, the authors might be said to concur with Jung, who frankly confesses, "… I have again and again been faced with the mystery of love and have never been able to explain what it is."[4]

NOTES

[1] C.G. Jung, *Memories, Dreams, Reflections*, ed. Marie-Louise von Franz, trans. Richard and Clara Wilson (New York: Vintage 1989), p. 230. Rennward Cysat was the author of the 17th century Lucerne Chronicle, in which Jung discovered the spooky story of the procession on Mt. Pilatus.

[2] See for instance C.G. Jung, "Brother Klaus" (1933), in *Psychology and Religion: West and East*, Vol. 11 of *The Collected Works of C.G. Jung*, eds. Sir Herbert Read, Michael Fordham, Gerhard Adler, William McGuire, trans. R.F.C. Hull (Princeton, N.J.: Princeton University Press, 1977). See also Franz-Xaver Jans-Scheidegger, "Brother Klaus

of Flüe and the Prayer of the Heart: A Map of Individuation," in *Unwrapping Swiss Culture, Spring: A Journal of Archetype and Culture,* Vol. 86 (2011). In the current volume see Isabelle Meier, "Brother Klaus and His Love of God."

[3] Ann Ulanov, "The Particularity of Love," in this volume.

[4] Jung, *Memories,* p. 353.

1

The Particularity of Love

Ann Ulanov

My focus on the particularity of love recognizes the risks and joys that love brings. "Particular" stems from an Indo-European base of Latin *pars*—to procure, produce, prepare—and from Hittite *pars-*, *parsiya*, to break, divide, from which derives particular, a little part.[1] Hence we, a little part, differentiated (divided), open to another distinct part, responding to a connection that if lived, calls us into our own, into our world, into the real.

The risk lies in the particularity—to love this person, this line of a Matisse drawing, this sound of Mozart's aria "Dove Sono" of lost love. We have all worked with people for whom a specific beach at the edge of the sea spells the location of the *axis mundi* for them. This so-called object of love we experience as a subject in its own right, a beingness, a presence, a coming forth of the unique embodied real. Through the wide-eyed looking of this child, through this dog's unfailing glad wagging when we arrive, through the national music of this country, the force of love catches our breath.

These are not exchangeable objects, and therein lies the profound risk of loving them. For opening our heart, and body, exposes us to their loss, their vanishing through neglecting or rejecting us, their disappearing from tangible presence through death. We know in our own vernacular the abstract language of Martin Heidegger when he says death individualizes you. We feel the lurking punctuation of the period put to the end of the arc of a life, the life you risked loving all-out. Loving, then, opens us to mourning, to grief at having this particular other no more in the flesh. Or, opened to a hurt so deep, through our being cast aside, that we vow never to love again. We seal up against the danger. Worse still, is the audible buzz people report when trauma at the hand of another strikes into them like an electric current; they can hear it pierce through their being and jolt them toward ruin.

Love is mysterious in its choices, like the small girl who leaves aside the hippo blanket her mother lovingly chose to delight her daughter, in favor of the scruffy elephant one that belongs to her brother, who, equally mysteriously, yields it to her. This singular form signals to us and we reach for it. We utterly destroy other forms imposed on us, albeit in kindness, like the small boy who tore up the paper cutouts his mother painstakingly assembled for him to find when he awoke the next day.

To follow what triggers our longing means we, too, dare to come into distinct embodied form, particular in our limits as well as potencies. Can we chance such loving in this body, not some ideal one, but this actual one, adhering to the boundaries of this time and space? The inexchangeable objects of our loving, and we ourselves in our inexchangeable body, thrust us into the contingencies of life, usher us to the borders of death.

THE MEETING SPACE

We do not love in general but in particular. We can dodge its risks by going general to avoid all the hazards of loving this particular man or woman, this particular neighbor, this particular enemy. This is not the ideal dog but the smelly one who tracks mud and sheds hairs; not the ideal lover but the one who gets tired and says not now; not the ideal child of fantasy but the one who shows such a different body pace and imaginal rhythm that we wonder where did this child come from?

Loving in particular ushers us into a meeting space of conflict, congress, endless invitation to translate the ineffable into the flesh of everyday living; it commands our radical attentiveness. Right away it opens the world to us and us to the world. We shrink, protesting too much! too demanding this work of love!

On the one hand, love announces inaugural instants, and through its particularity of feeling or impulse we reach toward this specific other. It is as if the wholeness of the whole opens to us. For such a grand theme, I like the translation of Anaximander of Miletus (pupil of Thales) of *arche* and thus of archetype as what he understood of the originative essence as the wide openness *to apeiron* that emphasizes the indeterminate origin of things, not reducible to fixed definitions of symbolization. As beginning and fount of all things, the cause of coming to be and destruction of the world, not reducible to any of the elements, the Indeterminate is source.[2] We feel we love the All through this particular, the universal through the individual, the many through this one who draws us out of our confined ego stance into unprejudiced seeing, indeed, to otherness, to life. Vladimir Solovyev says, for example, sexual love alone trumps our egoism.[3] Pulled out of ourselves, across from ego territory, we open to the other. That opening replicates the stranger's generosity to the person who lost their train ticket. In America at Christmas, the news reported that more than a few times a stranger walked into Kmart store presenting cash to pay off an outstanding bill of some unknown person: an offering.

On the other hand, the particular is just that, small, not the All but a little part, through which the sacred becomes visible, smellable, through just this image or odor. I have worked with analysands for whom love stole in, and with it the wide world, through their dog and thrummed for years in their devoted care, changing their lives to accommodate this wonderful creature who offers encounter with the mysteries of loving, giving all out without reserve to meet this endearing other.

In this meeting space of the All and the small, we are exposed to everything that will come in. Hence we risk destructiveness, loss, contraction of this space to nothing, and, as well, its opposite danger of expansion of space into gap, abyss into which we fall, swallowed up. In analytical sessions, we return to what was lost, given up, wrecked, to open that space again, to find the personal purchase points outside trauma. If the work goes well enough, a disposition to receive again slowly emerges in the space of relationship between analyst and analysand, and within the analysand to find again personal response to what was lost and destroyed.

For the meeting space to be a space and not a gap of dissolution, we must respond to create it, like a knock on the door we must open, or that we may ignore, refuse, shut up against. We know from our analytical sessions the idiosyncratic style of how a person does this opening. I can hear the music one person brought when she finally consented to being in the analysis. She brought a song that she played with the question, will you be my witness, meaning the one who hears and knows the me that I am reaching for. We feel sorrow when a person exposes there is no me (even though that confession is the beginning of a me observing there is no me). One man remembered setting up a pretend store as a boy. With great care he assembled desk, pencils, papers, only to uncover he had no starting point, no place from which to live, nothing to offer from the store.

Our particular personal response is necessary to find and create that meeting space between the All and the small, the Vast and the specific, the beyond and the here and now. We supply the warmth of personal living, that pulsing of the blood, recognition of one person to another that infuses seeing with being seen, circulating a human warmth that Origen says was lost in the Fall. Hence redemption, any kind of saving, means warmth coming in.

We can err with lack of personal response to these seminal moments, not noticing, not caring if we do notice, not saying Yes or a vigorous "No," which is also a response. I think of those words in the Gospel of Luke (7.32), "I piped and you would not dance, I wept and you would not mourn, so I spit you out of my mouth." We can overdo awe of the All, of the universal, praying to love the whole, not just our little part, but humankind, not our estranged relative or friend. The All floods in with its expansive reality, its infinite possibilities, its utter otherness, and we wash out to sea, not able to drink a cup of it and be nourished. Overcome by suffering in the world, by injustice even of our justice systems, by indiscriminate appearances of beauty, we just pale and do not give body to the real.

I think of the remarkable symbol of Chora, the matrix before and beneath even images, let alone concepts of conscious or unconscious, "the nurse of all becoming and change" as Plato says in Timaeus (49-51), behind the meeting of the personal and universal, the All and the small.[4] Its generative capacity displays an emptiness, a huge space, before anything is made of it, before the advent of the new. In an Istanbul church, Chora is pictured as mother and child, titled, "The Container of the Uncontainable." That instantiation of All and particular symbolizes the necessity for human holding that makes the space into a meeting.

Yet we can err by overdoing the particular too, so we fall into a subjectivist captivity, unable to see through to the dot of light in the midst of shattering darkness of trauma. What is needed is seeing through the particular to the glimpses of the whole, reckoning the weight of the dead-making depression, the blitzing of anxiety, the fog of confusion that make us feel we go out of our minds—to see through in this suffering to the something else that holds when we fall apart, whether that be the relation to the analyst, the fact we dream, the unexpected touch and kindness, hope for what is on the other side of pain.

The meeting space that love opens requires both the particular and the All and our human capacity to translate between them. But on the way to learning that translating, we meet challenges. In the particular story a person tells us in analysis, we hear the background of human story. We need to hear both; both stories are necessary lest the person's I-ness gets swallowed up in the universal—oh that is your mother complex, or other archetypal signatures. The person's particular cultural location and language also tell the specificity, the detail, the scrap of the whole that makes this narrative come alive. Yet, again, one can get so stuck into the distinct object relations and cultural language that we lose the larger sweep of suffering, what human angle this person is working on and from which will contribute to all the rest of us. The notion of Jung's objective psyche helps us see afresh that what you or I do with our own suffering, even as suffering contributes to the whole. Like an underground river, we work on our patch and facilitate the flow of the whole that irrigates the problem for everyone. The challenges, however, are real and to those I now turn.

VIOLENCE

The first challenge is violence. That space of meeting generates claims that veer into a concreteness so extreme they collapse the space.

What circulates between self and other, as if bespeaking that Chora space before, beneath, beyond what becomes visible, not yet stepping over into actual forms, caves in on itself. Instead of love generating particularities of idea, insight, affection, claims of utmost concretization get asserted into rigid reifications. We confound our tribe with the sacred and then promote our point of view as the only truth. It must obtain or catastrophe ensues. We override all reflection, consultation, mediating impulse, concern for neighboring views and people. We prosecute our view over their mangled feelings and sometimes even bodies.

In analysis, violence erupts from the grip of a complex. The patient is convinced the analyst must do the vital thing—be it sex this instant, money refunds, confession of mistake, multi-sessions or phone calls. Failing that required proof, dire consequences threaten—suicide, report to authorities, brutal attack on the treatment, rage acted out. The meeting space implodes; fundamentalistic thinking and symbolic equation take over.[5] Sometimes the analyst gets extraordinary luck, a grace of bursting through opposites, like a Koan, into a moment of enlightenment. The analyst says a word or gives a surprising response that breaks up the fanatic captivity. The analyst is up against what Michael Fordham called defenses of the self that he would continue to interpret, but Ann Cannon said no, that only inflames, and recent trauma theory suggests instead only a kind of witnessing may help.[6] But nonetheless it is a dire moment and the analyst is deeply grateful if a way opens through it.

The violence can come from the analyst too who cannot see through the holes in his theory, but persists from the vantage point of knowing better, of trying to match analysand to theory instead of the other way round. This causes rage and craziness in response.

Another source of violence is blindness to the fact that every appearance of the new, every stranger, is not necessarily divine or positive. This other may be a monster. More beguiling and confusing still is a person captive to their own complex and unconscious of it, who presents themselves to themselves as innocent, commendable, reasonable. Nonetheless, they insert poison from a place kept secret from consciousness, or exert an emotional abandonment while believing themselves loving. Such mixed impact provokes violence in the recipient, either to themselves as feeling crazy, or in enraged outbursts that seem crazy to others. The importance of reflection, discernment in the midst of openness to loving, differentiating fantasies of merger from a space of meeting, are part of bringing all of ourselves to the new, to the other.

Loving some one, some thing, some bit of the real means everything comes in, the negative too, which means we must find a place for destructiveness in living and in loving.[7] We may escape violence but not if we do not find where destructiveness belongs. This leads to a second challenge that takes us deeper still in what defies loving.

Loss, Death, Nothing

To love a particular someone, a definite idea, a distinct place, a principal symbol, or notion of the psyche opens us to loss with all its searing pain. The other who once loved us, opened to us a chance to find and live a new I-ness we had not known before, may stop loving us. Was it all fake then? Can we sustain our own loving, still owning the preciousness of what happened, not wreck it out of grief?

The lost good object becomes the dreaded object, like an infected tooth, or worse, an infection in the whole body that inflicts pain and threat of ruin. We defend ourselves with reasoning about shifting loyalties, about seeing other aspects of the idea or the person that compromise the full-out goodness we once experienced. Other ideas exist in the world, other paths of faith, other people; we use the general to protect against the wound of the particular. This whole subject arouses our defenses.

For behind loss, rejection, fading of goodness and of connection to the life-giving relation to the particular other stands death, the ultimate rubbing out of whatever particularity of love graced our life. The mother the woman describes as full of light has gone to the darkness of her grave. The beloved mate, so unique in giving interest to our own I-ness, so recognizing and enjoying our uniqueness, is dead and lives on as irreplaceable. Felled by grief, whom shall we tell? Even believing in an afterlife does not bring that other here, now, in the immediate flesh with its sights, sounds, and scents. The one who would want to know our reaction to music just heard and how it recalls a brother we love who though alive is all but dead, living inside a thick-walled castle inside a moat. Whom shall we tell? A lost gladness, a lost faith, we now say we outgrew that primary wonder, that all-out response; now categorize it as youthful, unconscious, full of projections, as if we created what was there instead of finding it. Places in nature—the waterfall, the rock, the greenness sprouting in the winter grasses, the wide sky, the mountain—all gone to developers, to job-makers. Is love as strong as death (Song of Songs 8:6)? Or, as we say in America, is that just whistling Dixie?

The punctuation of death must be reckoned with, or we dare not risk the particularity of love. But particularity of love also risks the nothing place opening wide within us while we are still alive.[8] In this nothing place inside us, that space of meeting of the All and the particular does not get started, or started does not sustain, or sustained, inevitably falls into a gap. For none of our constructed precious forms of loving—of science, for example, or the reality of books, or the new wonders of computer connections across the globe—and none of our formulations for the reality of psyche, the bridges symbols make to the unknown, ever replace the unknown. God-images are real images but not the real God. All our constructions fail, falter, turn to dust, because the small shoe cannot enclose the big foot, the incomprehensible cannot fit into comprehending human premises. The Vast bursts all containers we make, and we fall into a gap. We fear not just that the particulars we love will vanish, but that we, ourselves, have disappeared already.

A hole, a crack, a fissure, a breach in human-made certainties, deranges our knowing, destroys our certainties and hopes. We dread we will become the lost object that left us, the one who abandons others. Right here at this point of space becoming gap, we face the mystery of where destructiveness belongs in life and in our own living. If not through violence, then how? How do we align with this destroying energy?

We succumb in part to the gap.[9] Our certainties empty out, tumble into silence. We discover what particular form destructiveness takes for us—abandonment? betrayal? blind fate crushing us? obliterating rage? hopelessness that sears through every nub of hoping? Each of us will have her or his particular fear that accompanies their particular loving. The boy with the store and nothing to sell besets the grown man, who earns a living in a creative profession, dreads at bottom he has no starting point, no place to begin from. A woman says she fears no-thing inside me, no inner vision, just borrowing from others and expecting to be disregarded. Another woman says anything she produces in work is drivel and she wants to lay waste to the whole thing.

These examples show how we each reach our distinct wreckage, our form of alternating between presence and absence. We arrive at a "'nothingness,' an act of self-dispossession from the familiar habituated ego."[10] There we suffer repeated attack by reductionist forces that dismiss our efforts to make something out of what happens to us, disdain constructions we build of ideas or job possibilities or new attitudes to neighbors. With contempt that withers our seedling hopes, the great reductionist questions level any new venture that we might dare. We hear, so what? This has been said by others before you, and better. Who do you think you are with your idea instead of traditions? How selfish can you get, holding so adamantly to what is life-giving for you? You should be serving others, not thinking of yourself. And so on.

In this pivotal struggle we seek points of purchase outside reductionist attacks. But these reductions make us see the particular forms of destructiveness that flatten us. We must fight back. Here are ways people have found: One woman goes straight into the abysmal fear she can do nothing, is nothing, nothing but webs, confetti. She goes far down and down further into herself, saying, "I feel winnowed down to the small nub of I am, this tiny bit; I must speak from that central point. Winnowed down to origin, genesis, taproot." I was struck by the word "winnow" that means to free of chaff, to clear out or away, to refuse falsehood, to sort, and, to fan with wings, deriving from wind.[11] I thought of spirit as blowing from we know not where, stirring new life.

Another person through a searing experience found in the loss of something that was sacred to him a way to hold to his ownmost self as sacred. Through the loss of the representing symbol of the sacred, he found a path to what it symbolized. He imagined himself from thenceforth holding onto to this symbol, clutching it, not allowing himself to be made into a dismissible item in the world. Still another person was caught by a friend's invitation to embark on a physical venture, a kind of hiking trip. Could she do it? Would it be beyond her physical powers? The possibility glowed in her; she saw it conveyed a deeper attitude—that she could risk asserting herself with all her vulnerability, giving energy to stepping forth against reductionist thinking toward the new.

All these examples require great expenditure of energy and determination to set forth, to persist, to destroy or at least quell reductionist forces. We accept the gap of emptiness, the loss of certainties. This effort uses destructive energy toward living, recognizing the sacred and holding to it, accepting the contingencies of human life, the indeterminacies, *to apeiron* again, that, once seen, convicts us of the gap between our formulations and the real they try to represent. Hence we destroy our notions of any final summing up, any totality of answers. We destroy our notion of banishment of the bad, the meaningless, daring instead to give them a seat at the table. We stay open to reconfiguring again the central points of origin in our lives, expressed in the particularity of our loving.

What then do we love? Where does it turn up and with whom? The gap returns again to the spaces of meeting; the emptiness bespeaks Chora containing all the uncontainables from which particular lovings emerge.

ANALYTIC LOVE

Chief among these big "uncontainables" is analytic love, love in analysis. Can we think about it, speak about love for our patients, their love for us, our love for each other? In the background is our love for psyche, on which we meditate daily, giving to it our radical attentiveness, in session after session. How lucky are we to have found work so exciting, for each analysis is a venture into the unknown. We do not know where it will lead. As Wilfred Bion reminds us, the presenting problem is the cover story. No one comes into analysis saying, "I don't know how to love." But that is the animal in the thicket, the emotional truth we have yet to find.

First among many issues is, what is the analyst's relation to love? Not what the analysand's loving transference is, but what experiences do we analysts bring to the analytic field, before anything awakens in the analysand? Where have we loved, or failed to do so, or been unable to do so? What happened when we loved a particular one, or someone loved us, or a singular poem or scientific insight or wooly pet signaled to us, summoned our full-out heart's response? Did we flee? Pounce?

Swoon? Pretend it did not happen? Or was not really important? Did we perjure our experience by reducing it all to our early object relations, or to "mere" sex, or "only" to projection? Did we fall into inertia, away from the jazz beat of life fully alive? Or did we secure a solid relationship to the particular one, the specific vocation, the principal idea, or unique value, full of aliveness to this day?

As clinicians we need to know where we are with love. What are the chinks where we are still unlived, still to be lived, still willing to be surprised and live more? Where are the young, undeveloped parts of ourselves that might spontaneously pour out to another who prizes our subjectivity? Where has love mixed with Eros for us? For Eros in the body is sexuality, and where does that come in analysis? Love includes Eros but is not equated with it, and Eros in our body shows in sexual moving toward culmination, even ecstasy, in actual congress with another, or in climax of getting the idea in just the right words, or the stroke of white in our painting that sheds light throughout the canvas.

Eros is the function of psychic relatedness urging us to get involved with, poke into, get inside of, not to abstract and theorize but to invest energy, endow libido. Relatedness does not mean relationship; that requires conscious participating, development of feeling toward the other and toward what psychic responses the other elicits in us, our psychic stuff. The pull of the erotic is more bawdy, lusty, ardent, passionate, personified by Cupid shooting his arrows that arouse us to lavish libido on objects, be they sexual conquests, fine fabrics, businesses. Eros is like a huge spark that ignites our passion and confronts us with how we live with this fire in ordinary space and time.

Marion Milner says of D.W. Winnicott that he was "on excellent terms with his primary process; it was an inner marriage to which there was very little impediment."[12] C.G. Jung's images of the union of king and queen, sun and moon, lover and beloved, matter and spirit, constructing the *lapis,* the stone symbolizing the center of the person and of finite and infinite reality itself, convey the momentousness of anyone who dares to love and to respond to it wherever it is found. The complexity of such a constellation in analysis shows in the jumble of relationships between the consciousness of both analyst and analysand, and also each one's unconscious to the other's consciousness, and of both their unconsciousnesses to each other.

We experience the jumble of love and Eros in analysis in
different ways. Sigmund Freud says "the 'Eros' of the philosopher
Plato coincides exactly with the libido of psychoanalysis;" he also
remarks to Jung, "the cure is effected by love." Hans W. Loewald
writes of loving the analysand "whose truth we want to discover,"
and Medard Boss says the analyst must be imbued with *agape* love
to do the work. What Ogden describes as private conversations we
analysts have with ourselves, as reverie stirred by our analysand's
unconscious that issue in interpretations, are, I believe, a form of
love of our own subjectivity.[13]

Love in analysis, especially in an analysand, brings an opening of
self, even a pouring out to another who sees us, recognizes who we are
in our I amness, that mirrors the momentous words announced to
Moses when he asked what is your name? Who shall I say sent me?
God says, "I AM WHO I AM" sent you (Exodus 3:14).

Love also includes that purposive drive of Eros to make unities,
wholes, a sense of going somewhere that feels important, that matters,
enlists body, soul, and spirit. It is that sense of purposiveness that makes
people betray, break vows, fall into messes, as well as sell all they have
to find and pursue the pearl of great price. I think of young Matisse
in the hospital after his psychological collapse, where his roommate
suggests he take up painting to help his convalescence. Matisse's mother
brings him a paintbox, and he says of it: "From the moment I held
the box of colors in my hand, I knew this was my life. Like an animal
that plunges headlong towards what it loves, I dived in…It was a
tremendous attraction, a sort of Paradise Found in which I was
completely free, alone, at peace."[14]

Love between analyst and analysand, love in the room, happens
in specific ways with each person. Do we fear it? Can we recognize it?
Can we endorse this space of meeting that allows us to experience, in
some instances for the first time, an all-out loving of an other that we
can look into and explore, protected by the boundaries of analysis that
eschew acting it out in behavior or in prolix wordiness knowing all
about it?[15] Here a person can dare a dependence they have held
themselves up from before entering analysis. A space of safety, of feeling
cherished, that there is nothing wrong with me, I can lean my full
weight and find out my responses to what I experience without editing.
The rush of gladness, of gratitude, of discovery, feels like loving.

Yet the nature of love is to want all, to explore the full range of human emotions. That stirs up fear—this will be too hot, or too frustrating because we are not going to have an affair, or because I recognize the analyst's life separate from mine with its own validity and loyalties which I do not want to hurt.

In seeking all that is there to be felt, even to the edges, love disturbs: it calls forth destructiveness because that exists too. Negatives awaken—the need to be the special one, envy of others, to inflict vengeance out of hurt, terminal stupidity, attack on the reality of this connection, indeed all the infamous sins that express our captivity in the nothing place. We are landed in conflicting opposites that tear us apart, as well as having awakened all the flotsam and jetsam of what we have not experienced but could and should—Bion's beta elements, Stern's unformulated experience, Jung's *Red Book* injunction to follow your path, live all of your life. In short, that unlived life steps to the front of the line of consciousness and says, experience me. It is a crowded scene.

Do we flee through abstract theorizing, taking, for example, transference love, valid as idea, but use it to turn our particular feeling into a generality? Do we blunt our perception of a patient's love for us by calling it transference? Or our own love for them with the name countertransference? We flee to the abstract from the personal, from the particular instantiation of the infinite coming into finite livable form of love for another to evade what it arouses. We ask, but is this real love? What am I putting into it that is more about me than the other? Of course we do that, any one loving does that, for emotional longings, spiritual intuitions, bodily impulses toward health hiding in dreadful trauma come forward when love is touched.[16]

To see our psychic contributions to our image of the other, our projections, to use the official word, does not reduce the experience. To say something includes psychic bits of us does not mean it does not exist in itself also. But we can misuse theory, here of projection, forgetting Jung's seminal contribution to theory of projection. In addition to being a defense, a hurling outward what we cannot yet own, as defense against psychic pain, projection is a normal way we become conscious of something that belongs to us. We dream from what is between us; we individuate in relation to others, we find our other side in "you" and together are both parts of "a transcendent unity."[17]

Analytical love is very vulnerable to reductionistic forces. The "so what?" questions bombard confidence in this space of meeting. How can this love be real if we are not having sex? So what if we love each other or love dwells here in the analysis, my life is still a mess? Do you have this with all your patients? We are tempted to close off the space, let it collapse through the weight of our reductive questions, or because we cannot concretize this attachment.

But love is a mystery and turns up in many places and spaces, including analysis. If consented to, accepted, the space enlarges; it opens to love of psyche that sustains the work. We love the snake of the person; we love the snake of ourself. Something generative happens in sessions for both people, issuing in new insights, deeper unknowings, accumulating some sort of ground? weight? air? from which we live, which supplies dark nutriment to the risk of living all out. We experience this space as amplitude, as plenty: we live from it. We gain elbow room to respond to questions put to our lives. Ego tasks present themselves and differentiate from self tasks, so we live at once in the here and now of finite space and time and as a citizen of the ages, contributing our widow's mite to the whole offering.[18] I have seen this shift happen, and it remains mysterious to me, moving from enacting in transference what cannot be rescued yet into dream image or words, and then it can, and the enactment dissolves, just fades away. A shift happens from madness to perception, from fracture to finding the missing pieces to add up to a whole number, a whole person. A coagulation holds.

When we see the shift that just shifts, without any announcement or bugle sounds, when the invisible crosses to the visible, another task faces us in our particular loves. How to translate them into living?

TRANSLATING

Translating means taking from one language into another, carrying across from one context into a new one. In the loving that turns up in analysis, translating brings the snake we discover in our depths into the ordinary day of homework, doing taxes, laundry, groceries, talking on the phone or computer, cleaning the house, showing up at our job and getting work done, all the particularities of living. Then the infinite finds its particular form of attitude, glance, recognition in the finite detail, a person's particular idiosyncratic living of the real, alone and with others.

We discover an inner secret essence peculiar to a specific person, or text, political event, business, that incarnates into an individual style of working, writing, dreaming, making love, unique to particular subjectivities. What is healing takes on flesh, translated into the body of our living, into the words of our speaking. The purely personal thing opens to shared existence with others in specific forms in which we dwell together, like going to a concert, a rally, a funeral. So what we might feel as essence translates into elements we share in common that we register as binding us to one another in communities in which we dwell. Subjectivity reveals itself as intersubjectivity, not fusion, not projection, but dwelling together, separate and among, with.

What is the essence then? Not a fixed static thing, but an epiphany that goes into livingness, not capturable except in interplay, playing forth like music we all hear. We see the whole and our place in it, even if just for this moment. The whole is made particular in this moment. For the epiphany is always embedded in our body, the body of our lives, and located in our particular cultural landscape, a language we recognize—of senses, smells, sounds of the familiar which are transformed by the revelatory into the strange, the new, the amazing, the miraculous. Thus the particular grounds us here and now as it also opens to the universal, the shared, the movement of psyche in all of us. We hear through the one note the all of music itself, see through the yellow announcing the end of winter in its daffodil presence, the miracle of color itself.

Such an experience can be extremely moving and positive, as if we love the particular, whatever it is, in everyone, love the anyone who receives the beauty given to all of us. Or the experience can be heart-stopping in its gratuitous meanness, its off-the-duck's-back imperviousness to the intimidation, the terror we inflict on each other. We see in the making nothing where before there was a particular something, the yawning abyss into which any of us can plunge at any moment.

Each of us acts as such a translator, in both directions: making the particular moment universal, and the shared into the singular. We experience origin and that we are original, creating out of what we find, finding what we create. In coming to understand something, to interpret it, to improvise it, we give our distinct stamp and pass it along to others. We draw upon accumulation of truth through many people's interpretations, reflections, which we again refigure. Thus a chain, the golden one (*catena aurea*) evoking the *Veni Creator*, the spirit coming each day, constructs links over the ages as it constructs us.

Knitting together manifestations of truth seen, reflected upon, articulated, seemingly contingent on particular circumstances, yet translated into essential moments and retranslated back into contingencies, builds a spiritual universe. Those particulars, like compost, nourish new growth, growth of the new. Originality becomes interdependence. We see truths exist and that we discover them, think them for a while, improvise upon them, give them back in our own particular forms that draw upon our peculiar complexes as well as our particular genius.[19]

Such reworking, knitting, stitching must include the bad too, the nothing places. For the particularity of love, and especially in analysis, reaches to those experiences where the person feels they have been annulled, not found. If the work goes well enough, the analysand links to what was lost, and translates its finding into psychic structure. What had not been there now is: I was dead, now I am alive. As one man said: I lost a precious part of myself for all of my seventy years and now I found it. Even recognizing that we missed a vital opportunity, or that we do not know love with a mate but do know this love as longing for a mate, fleshifies it, brings it into livingness where that unlived part mixes with all the lived parts and something happens.

With Orpheus, we hear the injunction don't look back, but he does, and what might have been fades into a shade beyond form, without blood. He tries to recapture what he lost in literal cast. He looks back, only to see he could not repeat the identical form of loving. He went, then, forward from shades to warm earth against his cheek and the translation of his longing into poetry.

Analysis includes looking back, revivifying what was lost, no longer reifying it into literal past. That moment of *kenosis*, of emptying, accepts the gaps in us, between us, both personal and international. We feel loss, know our ignorance, our helplessness. For example, one man bemoaned he had made all the wrong choices and now he is older, with less time left. That is time as Chronos eating his children, the tyranny of time disappearing into the past as if devoured forever, gone. Instead the stitching work of therapy gathers parts that we could not experience before and now we can afford to feel, even though they bring pain. Frozen places hurt as they thaw. What was irretrievably lost in *chronos* time, translates into time flowing into the *kairos* moment of an interpretation that clicks, an image that surprises, new figurings that reconfigure what was an issue in multiple patterns of meaning. Blood flows in, fleshing into particular instances of feeding life. We did not find a good relationship with an other, but now we decide to have a baby, or adopt a child, change our job, change to a new location to live, or stay exactly where we are in a deeper depth of reaching out to repair hurts, find joy.

Artists, scholars, painters, musicians do work for all of us in weaving around huge gaps of suffering gashed into human history by concentration camps, starvation marches, enslavements, genocides, terrorist bombings. They write into the silence, make poems over lost language, compose musical themes to witness haunting horror to throw a net of particular witnessing of gigantic suffering.[20]

Analysis is one of the few places in society where suffering is addressed, witnessed, translated into livingness, into surviving and thriving. What was irretrievably lost in *chronos* time appears again in *kairos* time with burst of unsuspected meanings to be lived forward as advent of meaning coming toward us.[21]

Because in analysis we reach to witness the bad too, we can afford in the present to link up to what was lost in the past mist of dissociation. We do not get pulled across into the death zone by multiple unclaimed losses; nor do we amputate traumatized parts of us by injunctions to "move on." Instead, analysis links the particularities of our narratives to what was gone, to what buried us or is buried in us. This translates death into life, again and again. That process feels like rebirth. Even the gaps in us become enlisted by the whole of us. Re-visiting, re-finding, leads to re-figuring, re-creating, making real in particular ways what we feared, where we were trapped. A man said, for example, in a burst of fury and liberation, "I have been serving the wrong mother! It is not my mother, but Earth Mother I belong to!" His insight climaxed long work to stay in his own experience and not give himself away, as he had for many years, as a small boy to make his emotionally fraught mother happy (because he loved her, and so she might then mother him), and as an adult in the grip of a need to please others to secure connection to them.

Translating into living then releases life in us from reification of literal trauma that wounded us, from rigid defenses against gaps where meaning disintegrates. All of it gets taken up into the process of seeing and seeing again, saying and saying again, because of new particularities, our ego tasks. These new translations get incarnated not reified, worked out in living, not concluded in intransigent positions.

Yet even our ego tasks translate back and forth into Self experiences. As Krishna says to Arjuna in the *Bhagavad Gita*, "I will destroy all this in time; it is your job right now to face fighting this battle."[22] The here and now thus partakes of the ultimate while not being the ultimate. Yet the question of what is ultimate lurks in the specific task—is it Krishna's reality and solution we believe in, or is it in another symbol of rebirth and meaning?

Self questions translate into particular ways of being an analyst, for example. The day's analytic work translates into the thrum, the beat, from which we work. Nothing is so small not be painted into the Still Life canvas; it is still life, full of aliveness. Nothing is too large not to be noticed lurking in one of the colors. No meaning so trivial not to be gathered up into the present discourse, and none too large not to be translated into our actual living, so that we can say with the great geniuses, such as the poet Marina Tsvetaeva, that her hand does not belong to herself but "to that which wants to exist through you."[23] A truth is ours that we belong to but do not invent, not coming from us but to us.

AMOR MUNDI

Such processes of translating the particular from a specific past moment at the same time we incarnate its present figuration in a future unfolding, imbues this meeting space with a loving. *Amor Fati* is to love our fate, to translate it into our own destiny. This takes effort not to be crushed by karma, by predestination that traps us in leaden limitations. Jung urges in *The Red Book* to make impersonal happenings that fall on us into personal events, woven into the body of the here and now of our particular lives.[24]

But we can be translated further, from *Amor Fati*, love of our fate, into *Amor Mundi*, love of the world. The world in particular, the particular bits of the world that generously pour out on us, meet us daily. We go beyond fate into active loving that is lucid, seeing what is there and not there, bad and good, that endures the stripping of projections and engages in imagining that bestows on the world perceptions that make it glow.

Such translating frees us from fixity, into instants of intensity that dissolve binary thinking. Inner and outer realities, times of then and now, of now and yet to come, spaces cosmic and particular partake of the meeting space between self and other, including the otherness of paintings, music, historical events, personages, and characters of novels, imaginary and real. Untamed realness finds its expression in nearness of immediate perception of the familiar. The gaps in us, and in human history, so painful and searing, keep the space always open, never foreclosed nor certain, no matter how dear the credited conventions among us. For we must participate in that space of meeting between us and others, bring our ability to respond, discern, reflect, say yes and no. For the whole is not a mystical fusion but a process of here and now simultaneously opening to the All and Vast. The unlimited, indeterminate infinite lodges in the wonder of the finite, visible, the precious particular.

Over the years working as an analyst, I have seen that the conclusion of analysis, if it has gone well enough, manifests as openness to the process of living one's ownmost life in the world, loving what is possible and wanting it. Even analysands who contracted terminal illness, poured their vitality into this particular nexus of life and death, so even there they made something out of what was happening to them. They made it their own, their particular pathway to death, thus edifying and instructing those of us who remained. We learned from what they made on and of this frontier.[25]

What can we say then of the particularity of love? We can speak of our own processes of loving, of loss and gap, of recreating, of loving the whole, in the particular joy of *Amor Mundi*.

NOTES

[1] Eric Partridge, *Origins: A Short Etymological Dictionary of Modern English* (New York: Macmillan Company, 1963), p. 472.

[2] Ann Ulanov and Barry Ulanov, *Transforming Sexuality: The Archetypal World of Anima and Animus* (Boston: Shambhala, 1994), p. 22.

[3] Vladimir Solovyev, *The Meaning of Love*, trans. Jane Marshall (London: Geoffrey Bless, 1945); see also Ann Belford Ulanov, *The Feminine in Jungian Psychology and in Christian Theology* (Evanston, IL: Northwestern University Press, 1971), pp. 295, 308-309.

[4] Richard Kearney, *Strangers, Gods and Monsters* (New York: Routledge, 2003), pp. 196-199; see also Charles P. Bigger, *Between Chora and the Good, Metaphor's Metaphysical Neighborhood* (New York: Fordham University Press, 2005).

[5] Melanie Klein, "The Importance of Symbol-Formation in Ego Development," in *Love, Guilt and Reparation & Other Works 1921-1945* (New York: Delacorte Press/Seymour Lawrence, 1975), pp. 219-233. Melanie Klein makes a distinction between symbolic equation, where the symbol is felt to be identical to the thing symbolized, and symbolic representation, where the symbol points to, but is not identical to, the thing symbolized.

[6] Ann Cannon, "Delusions That Will Not Be Denied," *Journal of Analytical Psychology* 25, no. 2, 1980, pp. 141-152. In this article she discusses Michael Fordham's article, "Defenses of the Self."

[7] Ann Belford Ulanov, *Finding Space: Winnicott, God, and Psychic Reality* (Louisville, KY: John Knox/Westminster Press, 2001), p. 55.

[8] Ann Belford Ulanov, *The Unshuttered Heart: Opening to Aliveness/Deadness in the Self* (Nashville, TN: Abingdon Press, 2007), chap. 9.

[9] *Ibid.*, chap. 6.

[10] Richard Kearney, *Anatheism* (New York: Columbia University Press, 2010), p. 48.

[11] *Concise Oxford Dictionary*, 5th ed., s.v. "winnow" (Oxford: Oxford University Press, 1864/1964); Ernest Weekley, *Concise Etymological Dictionary of Modern English*, s.v. "winnow" (New York: E.P. Dutton, 1952).

[12] Marion Milner, "D.W. Winnicott and the Two-Way Journey," in *Between Reality and Fantasy*, eds. Simon A. Grolnick and Leonard Barkin (New York: Jason Aronson, 1978), p. 42.

[13] Sigmund Freud, *Group Psychology and the Analysis of the Ego*, trans. James Strachey, in *Standard Edition XVIII* (London: Hogarth Press and the Institute of Psycho-Analysis 1921/1973), pp. 90-92; Jonathan Lear, *Love and Its Place in Nature* (New York: Farrar, Straus

& Giroux, 1990), pp. 140-141; Hans W. Loewald, "Psychoanalytic Theory and Psychoanalytic Process," in *Papers on Psychoanalysis* (New Haven: Yale University Press, 1970/1980), p. 297; Medard Boss, *Psychoanalysis and Daseinanalysis*, trans. L.B. Le Febre (New York: Basic Books, 1963), pp. 259-260; Thomas H. Ogden, *Interpretation and Reverie* (London: Karnac, 1999), pp. 43, 114, 159.

[14] Hilary Spurling, *The Unknown Matisse* (New York: Knopf: 1998), Vol. 1, p. 46.

[15] See Ann Belford Ulanov, "Follow-Up Treatment in Cases of Patient/Therapist Sex" and "Self-Service," in *The Functioning Transcendent* (Wilmette IL: Chiron, 1996), pp. 113-123 and pp. 143-159. See also Ann Belford Ulanov, "Countertransference and the Erotic," in *Journal of Religion and Health* 48 (2009), pp. 90-96.

[16] See George E. Atwood, *The Abyss of Madness* (New York: Routledge, 2011), chap. 5.

[17] C.G. Jung, "Psychology of the Transference," *Collected Works*, Vol. 16 (New York: Pantheon, 1946/1954), § 400, § 454.

[18] Ulanov, *The Unshuttered Heart,* pp. 192-196.

[19] See George E. Atwood and Robert Stolorow, *Faces in a Cloud* (New York: Jason Aronson, 1993), chap. 3.

[20] See Paul Celan, *Poems of Paul Celan,* trans. Michael Hamburger (New York: Persea Books, 1988). See also: Paul Celan, *Last Poems*, trans. Katherine Washburn and Margaret Guillemin (San Francisco: North Point Press, 1986); Ernestine Schlant, *The Language of Silence* (New York: Routledge, 1999); Krzysztof Penderecki, "Lamentations for the Children of Auschwitz," in *Dies Irae (Auschwitz Oratorium) / Polymorphia / De Natura Sonoris*, Audio Recording (Auschwitz Oratorio, 1986); Storm Swain, *Trauma and Transformation at Ground Zero* (Minneapolis: Fortress Press, 2012).

[21] Kearney, *Anatheism,* pp. 109-110.

[22] Barbara Stoler Miller, trans., *The Bhagavad-Gita* (New York: Bantam Classic, 1986), pp. 28f., 34-37.

[23] H. Muchnic, "Chosen and Used by Art," *The New York Times Book Review* (October 12, 1980), pp. 7, 32-33, cited in Donnel B. Stern, "Unformulated Experience: From Familiar Chaos to Creative Disorder," in *Relational Psychoanalysis: The Emergence of a Tradition,* eds. Stephen A. Mitchell and Lewis Aron (Hillsdale, NJ: The Analytic Press, 1983/1989), p. 96.

²⁴ C.G. Jung, *The Red Book, Liber Novus,* ed. Sonu Shamdasani, trans. Mark Kyburz, John Peck, Sonu Shamdasani (New York: Norton, 2009); see also Ann Belford Ulanov, "*The Red Book* and Unlived Life Both Here and Beyond" (Founders Day presentation, Chicago Jung Society and Loyola University Chicago's School of Continuing and Professional Studies, March 2011).

²⁵ See Ann Belford Ulanov, *The Wizards' Gate, Picturing Consciousness* (Einsiedeln, Switzerland: Daimon, 1994); and Ann Belford Ulanov, "Disguises of the Anima," in *The Functioning Transcendent,* chap. 9.

2

Opalescent Wings:
Butterflies *Ad Infinitum*

Mark Patrick Hederman

INTRODUCTION

C oming here to this very special place, to this very special group
of people, is more than fulfillment of an obligation to speak
at a conference. This invitation, this location, and this
community require of me to give voice to what the Holy Spirit is
prompting me to say: almost as toothpaste is squeezed from a tube.

I live in a monastery in Ireland, but there are groups like this one,
all over the world, who come together sporadically and who make up
a virtual community, a monastery without walls, who come like
migrating birds to holy places like this one, and who become in the
intensity of connection that they generate, pulsating hot-spots for the
Holy Spirit to land. None of us know who will be the chosen
mouthpiece for that Spirit but each of us must prepare to listen out
for, and to speak only those words that the Spirit inspires. Now that
it is my turn on the timetable to take the podium, I have to allow

myself to be pressurized by the fingers of circumstance and the *digitus Dei*, and not to interfere too much with the flow that is generated.

BUTTERFLIES *AD INFINITUM*

The last time I came here to Flüeli-Ranft in July 2006 for the first Jungian Odyssey Conference, I met Wallis Wilde-Menozzi the first day and she gave me an article she had written for the *Notre Dame Review* called "Seeing Butterflies." I read it that night before going to sleep:

> The butterfly was as small for a butterfly as I was tall for a woman. What I mean is that the orange-winged creature that zigzagged to my shoulder on a May day in Parma, Italy, where I was talking to the postman, was not much bigger than two of my unpainted fingernails. . . . What still brings sharp tears to my eyes, when I think about what happened next, is how life occasionally rustles, as if the every-day is caught and thrown back by a curtain's deep folds. The mind finds itself touching reality beyond ordinary dimensions. The butterfly, whose exact name I have never keyed out in a book, landed on my shoulder on the tenth anniversary of my son's birthday. My infant son, whom I found early on a California morning in his crib, cold, dead—I carried him wrapped within. I also carried that terrifying instant when life unveils its unconditional swiftness: the moment when I cradled him and knew there was no going back. He had been taken in his sleep, and I, as though an eagle had snatched me in its talons, had been dropped on a frozen mountaintop to face death. I had been left to find a path down, while all around me magnificent peaks and beautiful valleys murmured.
>
> The butterfly landed on my shoulder.
>
> The postman and I went on talking but all of my attention took the butterfly's stopping into my consciousness, my need, my anniversary. The postman knew nothing. He saw no candle burning on my shoulder. He felt no mystery or wind. We talked about a *sciopero*, a strike, the way Italian workers are treated with little regard.
>
> Then, ever so gently, I brushed the butterfly off.

I said good-bye to it. I did say good-bye and thank you in my heart, silently. Although I am married to a scientist, who would find it strange, silent inner speech flowed. I was talking to the butterfly. I loved the specificity of its coinciding touch on what would have been my son's tenth birthday. Warmed, I walked down the street to the house. Key in the lock, the phone started to ring, so I ran.

The door was open then. I left it open.

While I chatted on the phone, the butterfly, the orange fellow with a few dots and black parts (I'm sure it was the same one), came in. It went fast like a tiny toy plane, in little circles, passing my back and coming around to the front where my eyes noticed it circling as I talked. Then it fell to the floor. As if I were watching a trapeze artist who misses the swing, I gasped. I excused myself and hung up. In order to find the tiny insect on the marble tiles, I fell to my knees.

The butterfly flew or it leapt. The language is mine. I found it in my hand. The creature I had worried was injured settled in my hand and then it turned; moving away from the middle finger, it walked each one. I started to weep. My son's birthday, the butterfly's non-passive touching of my fingers opened my mind in pieces.

The butterfly stayed. It stayed until my tears were raining so hard on it, that for all I knew, it could have been thinking it was outside on a lilac bush in the rain. It didn't leave and for more than an hour I had what was an open door from inside me to its presence.

Finally I told the butterfly that it had to go. That thought went against the confused, intense, shockingly beautiful mystery I was in. The irrational impulse to pull back and break the spell was unbearable. As difficult, in a different way, as having been left on the mountain the first morning when I found my son in his crib. Outside in the garden, I held my hand high to the sky and waited for the butterfly to lift. By then the anniversary tears were a large flowing river. They were a peaceful river that Buddhist monks have written about. They were fountains that have been called "the still waters." The butterfly didn't budge. I told it so many things I can't tell you, readers, because they

were meant for him, and for the place he had reattached me to.
I didn't want him to go, but I knew he must. And eventually,
he flew, zigzagging up and up, leaving me—in a beautiful and
frightening way—to touch my empty palm.[1]

I read that story on my first night at the Jungian Odyssey at Flüeli-
Ranft. Next day we had a talk from Murray Stein:

> Magda was in her eighties when she died. For ten years prior
> to her death, she could not walk, so I visited her where she
> lived occasionally. Before that, for about five years, she had
> seen me in my office to discuss her dreams and emotional
> life. After she could no longer walk, she would say to me,
> quite seriously, but with a twinkle: "When I die and go to
> heaven, the first thing I want to do is kick up my heels and
> dance." She missed her legs which had previously been strong
> and able under her. When Magda died, my wife and I
> attended her funeral. Driving home, I noticed something
> fluttering around in the rear window of the car. My wife
> looked back and exclaimed, "It's a butterfly." I opened the
> windows to let the butterfly out, but of course it would not
> leave. When we got home, it was nearly dark, and my wife put
> her hand in the back of the car to get the butterfly to leave.
> Instead the small brown winged insect hopped to her hand
> and stayed there. We walked over to the street lamp to look
> at it more closely. (By this time we were calling the butterfly
> Magda, and were enjoying her mischievous company.)
> Suddenly the butterfly flew down to the sidewalk, and, as we
> watched, it began to dance energetically in circles, hopping
> occasionally to one or another of our feet. How could we not
> think that this was Magda, now with legs, in heaven, dancing
> freely and with abandon as she had hoped she would?

> About a year passed when, thanks to Magda's earlier request
> to Rome, I was able to get tickets for Edith Stein's canonization
> at the Vatican. The canonization ceremony took place in St.
> Peter's Square on October 11, 1998. We were standing
> upright in the warm sun for the benediction; the Pope was
> intoning his blessing in Latin. The text of this prayer was
> printed in four languages in the booklet prepared for the
> occasion, and I was following the Pope's slurred diction as
> best I could with the help of the text in my booklet. When
> he arrived at the line, *ex hoc nunc et usque in saeculum* ("now

and forever"), a brown butterfly with blue bits of color on its wings appeared out of nowhere from that crowd of thousands and alighted on the open page. It landed on the words "now and forever" and rested quietly there.

"It's the same butterfly!" my wife whispered.

Sure enough, the colors were the same as those of the one in Chicago.[2]

Later in Ireland two of my friends, one in Northern Ireland and one from the South, told me similar stories: Aideen McGinley wears butterflies and has butterflies as her logo. When her father died it was in December and still a butterfly managed to appear in the church to circle the coffin and land on the altar.

My friend Elizabeth who was chaplain at the time sent me this account today. Says Vera Magee:

> Two students from the Institute of Technology, Tallaght died in a fire in Belgium on January 6, 2008. The bodies of the two girls were brought home to Ireland for burial. Patricia was buried in her home place in Co. Monaghan where she had been brought up on a farm. She loved nature and particularly butterflies. During the Mass a butterfly flew around the church, and while the Gospel was being read the butterfly flew down and rested on the page. It then continued to fly around and eventually rested on the altar during the Consecration.

Kristina in Sydney, Australia:

> My mother passed away on September 30, 2008 from cancer at age sixty-five. Her favorite song to sing to her kids and grandkids was a song about a beautiful butterfly. The first November after she passed away, a particular brown and orange butterfly constantly hung around our front footpath, circling us, waiting for us when we would come home or exit the house. It hung around for months that first year. Every year in November the same type of butterfly has done the same thing— it has followed us down our driveway, run into our car, turned up when beloved friends have visited.

Mona Lester, New Bloomfield, Missouri, USA:

> My daughter Katey was killed by a drunk driver on February 14, 2006. She was only eighteen. On her Birthday last year, my

Mom was giving me a note that she had written for me. It said, "Butterflies are angels' way of letting us know they are watching over us." Right at that moment, as I was reading the note, a beautiful Monarch butterfly flew into my face and fluttered every so softly. Then the butterfly flew into my Mom's face. We looked at each other with tears in our eyes. For as suddenly as it had appeared, it was gone. Just like our Katey.

MIGRATING MONARCHS

The North American Monarch butterflies *Danaus plexippus* are unique in that they actually migrate to given overwintering sites every year. Monarchs west of the Rocky Mountains head for the Pacific coast, to groves of trees from north of San Francisco to near San Diego. Those who are east of the Rockies travel to the highlands of Central Mexico about sixty miles west of Mexico City. These Monarchs who go south do not succeed in returning to where they were born. Rather, their children or grandchildren do, without any elders to show them the way. One example: a female, who was tagged near Lake Michigan in the autumn, migrated some two thousand miles to Central Mexico and having over-wintered travelled northwards again and ended her life at Rocksprings, Texas, in a pumpkin garden. On her way she carried out substantial ovipositing to facilitate the continuation of the migratory chain for her great-grandchildren to return to Mexico at the end of the season.

These butterflies' choice of habitat is determined by food supply. Milkweed, of any variety, is the only plant that the monarch butterfly caterpillar can feed on. The familiar orange-and-black butterfly's entire lifecycle depends on milkweed. They will only lay their eggs on milkweed, which contains poison. Monarchs are able to store this poison within their own bodies, making themselves poisonous in turn. This helps to protect them from browsing animals and leaf-eating insects such grasshoppers. Monarchs are very brightly colored, both as a caterpillar and as an adult, which advertises that they are not good to eat and that they harbor a secret weapon.

According to people of certain areas of Mexico, Monarch butterflies carry the spirits of dead ancestors to visit. They arrive each year on (or near) the Day of the Dead (November 2), to visit and to take the souls of the newly-departed away with them. There may be as many interpretations of these apparitions as there are undoubtedly experiences of them. Murray Stein says that,

> at this moment the boundaries between this world and the next were breached. I could feel that in this sacred moment we were living both in time and eternity. Surely this was Magda dancing in the form of a butterfly.[3]

Whatever the explanation, I felt since my last visit to this place, that I was being forced to understand this reality and that I was a particularly obtuse student. I knew that I would be invited back to the Jungian Odyssey at some point and that when this happened I would be required to give an account of what I had been taught. So I have been studying it ever since. For Murray Stein these butterflies were sacraments or icons opening out to another world. They were the messengers revealing another dimension to the world of space and time in which we live: living windows in chronology giving glimpses of another kind of time and space, embodiments of *kairos* in the body of *chronos*. But, it seemed to me that they were also showing us in symbolic form the pattern and the purpose of our own lives: that we in our own way are destined to a life beyond this one as mirrored in the magic of the butterfly.

LARVA TO CHRYSALIS TO BUTTERFLY

When we are born into this world the possibility is that we have arrived into another womb, the womb of the world; that our development as human beings is threefold rather than twofold. That we go from larva to chrysalis to butterfly and that the natural world that we now inhabit, far from being the end of our journey is rather the crucible in which we are fashioned for eternity. The first womb was dark and we were passive. This second one is porous and we are hyperactive. The world we are about to enter is infinite and eternal. It can only suggest itself to us in our present intermediary condition by filtering hints into the cocoon of our incubator. If we are alive to such possibility we can pick up these hints and use them to prepare ourselves for the expansion and extension of our being that will be necessary to stretch us into the dimensions of eternity and infinity. The infinite and the eternal cannot fit themselves into a matchbox or an hourglass. They are by definition excluded from whatever is limited, enclosed, defined; whatever is temporal, momentary, time-serving. They surround the air bubble of geographical space and local time without being able to invade it. If they did, they would destroy its spatiotemporal identity causing it to flow out into unimpededness and extinction. We can only glimpse the reality that swirls outside our spaceship and beckons us as amphibians (the word "amphibious" comes from the Greek, meaning capable of life [*bios*] on both sides [*amphi*] of the divide) to flex our muscles and exercise our latent but dormant limbs that will allow us to fly heavenwards or swim oceanward, depending on whatever limited imagery we care to use, which will always be borrowed from our own spatio-temporal epistemology. There is nothing inside the time-space capsule that can even provide an inkling of what exists outside. And yet the outside itself can bruise or stain or pierce the paraphernalia of the inside sufficiently to leave a trail of clues for those with enough sensitivity, those with stereoscopic vision, to detect its presence. Such bruising, staining, piercing, echoing is what we call "revelation." The skin that is bruised, the wool that is stained, the ears that are pierced, the canyons or caves that are echoed into, are what we call symbols. The word comes from the Greek *ballein,* meaning "to throw," and *sym* or *syn,* meaning "with," "together," "at the same time." Symbols are whatever are thrown against eternity and forever afterwards bear the mark of that bruising encounter: Jacob's thigh or Veronica's veil.

Symbols are the things of this world that are drenched with some dew of endless night; impregnated with energy of eternal revolution; scarred with birthmarks of fingerless midwives; stamped with the imprint of verisimilitude; steeped in the aura of divine intervention. Incarnation of God in any or every leaf of the universe. Those who have eyes to see and ears to hear, noses to smell, fingers to touch, tongues to taste, get the message. It is stereoscopic vision: seeing the trees for the wood.[4]

LOVE: OUR MILKWEED

Love, for us, is as yet only in its infancy. The philosopher Vladimir Soloviev suggests that love in its present form is no more than a feeling. Just as reason in the animal kingdom before the evolution of rational consciousness was no more than a vague striving towards the organ of the brain, so love only exists as a rudimentary token of what it could be, if we were to live it in a way that forced us to make a similar breakthrough. The difference is that rational consciousness emerged in humankind, whereas the similar breakthrough in the realm of love would have to happen both in us and through us. It could not happen in spite of us.[5]

We, as a human species, are comparatively recent arrivals on earth in the form and shape we now enjoy. It took us, with a great deal of evolutionary effort, several thousand years to produce the first billion of our species; now, in this blessed twenty-first century, we are producing a billion every ten to fifteen years. We have reached the number of seven billion on the planet this year. Teilhard de Chardin hoped that the incremental increase of humanity, the tightening of the human mass, which necessarily throws us on top of one another, would force us to "enter the powerful, still unknown field of our basic affinities. In other words, that attraction will one day be born of enforced nearness." However, the fact that we are all going to be crushed together in the tube-train is not necessarily going to achieve intimacy of its own accord. Proximity does not mean closeness and never will, unless we transform the space between us into endearment. Teilhard believed in,

> the hidden existence and eventual release of forces of
> attraction between people who are as powerful in their own
> way as nuclear energy appears to be, at the other end of the
> spectrum of complexity.[6]

Teilhard continues,

> The entire complex of interhuman and intercosmic relations will
> become charged with an immediacy, an intimacy and a realism
> such as has long been dreamed of and apprehended by certain
> spirits particularly endowed with the "sense of the universal"
> but which has never yet been collectively applied. And it is in
> the depths and by the grace of this new inward sphere, the
> attribute of planetized life, that an event seems possible which
> has hitherto been incapable of realization: I mean the pervasion
> of the human mass by the power of sympathy. It may in part be
> passive sympathy, a communication of mind and spirit which

> will make the phenomenon of telepathy, still sporadic and
> haphazard, both general and normal. But above all it will be a
> state of active sympathy in which each separate human element,
> breaking out of its insulated state under the impulse of the high
> tensions generated in the Noosphere, will emerge into a field of
> prodigious affinities . . . For if the power of attraction between
> simple atoms is so great, what may we not expect if similar bonds
> are contracted between human molecules?[7]

The milkweed on which we feed in this world that gives us the
energy to reach our destiny, our final destination, is love. Love allows
us to make the great journey back to where we came from. Love enlarges
our hearts and allows us to burst through to infinity and eternity. And
love contains everything about what we are. So, poison is there also.
And this means that there are two ways to travel, as in the parable of
the elder brother and the prodigal son, or as Rainer Maria Rilke
differentiates his road to God from the way of his wife Clara:

> You are now going so straight toward the divine; no, you are
> flying toward it, over everything, in straightest flight which
> nothing opposes. And I have been there, always, even as a
> child, and am on my way walking thence and am sent out
> (not to proclaim), to be amidst the human, to see everything,
> to reject nothing, none of the thousand metamorphoses in
> which the extreme disguises and blackens itself and makes
> itself unrecognizable. I am like one who gathers mushrooms
> and medicinals among the herbs; one looks bent and busied
> with very small things then, while the tree trunks round about
> stand and worship. But the time will come when I shall prepare
> the potion. And that other time, when for its strength's sake I
> shall take it up, this potion in which all is condensed and
> combined, the most poisonous and most deadly; take it up to
> God, so that he may quench his thirst and feel his splendor
> streaming through his veins. . . .[8]

Bejeweled Cross

The mystery of the Eucharist in Christianity is the marvelous way
in which Jesus Christ, who came on earth as God in human form,
arranged for us to be able to eat his body and drink his blood in the
form of bread and wine, so that we might be filled with divine energy

and turn our hearts into centers of this divine love. Christianity becomes almost like a blood transfusion whereby the donor who died on the cross gives himself to us as in a heart transplant. We no longer move from our own energy, but having feasted on the milkweed, we now forge ahead from the alternative energy of divine love. We become extensions of the incarnation and our bodies become marked by the sign of the cross as though we were stigmatists.

The "sign of the cross" was the paramount symbol of God's love for us in early Christianity. The Middle Ages and the morose 19th Century turned it into a crucifix, with the dying body of Christ affixed. This aspect of the total mystery overshadowed all the rest and we were encouraged to revel in our own suffering and affliction, instead of recognizing the moment and the manifestation of the butterfly's release: the resurrection.

The projection of our own pathology swapped the glory for the gore. To concentrate upon the cross as an instrument of torture is to wrap ourselves in the cocoon when we should be in flight with the butterfly.

The sign of the cross should be the quintessence of the spiritual quest. The four spatial directions of the compass join together with the depth of the center. Just as we have five senses and five fingers with which to probe the world around us so this pentagram will be significant in probing the world of the spirit. Under this sign, blessing or benediction flows. Each of the wounds of Christ are effective against the five dark currents of human motivation: the desire to be great, the desire to take, the desire to keep, the desire to advance at the expense of others, the desire to hold on to, at the expense of others.[9]

The five wounds of Christ were a five-sense breakthrough into our world of the greedy senses and covetous limbs. His wounds are five boreholes that allow the five currents of the human will to be impregnated from above by the will of God. This is the "sign of the cross," the pentagram of the five wounds.

A wound is a door. The eye, for instance, is a wound covered by a mobile skin that we call an eyelid. Our eyes are open wounds. So are our other senses. They are wounds through which the world imposes itself on us. The five senses are organs of perception not of action. They are passive receptors. The five organs of action, on the other hand, are our two legs, our two arms, and our head. These must develop analogous wounds that will become the stigmata of our alignment to the cross of the divine will. The head, however, does not bear the fifth wound as we know from the paradigm of the Christian mystery. It bears the crown of thorns. These are the openings that allow for interdigitation between all three parts of our brain between themselves and with the promptings of the Holy Spirit.

The fifth wound is the wound of the heart, the wound of organic humility that replaces the natural current of the human will. The twentieth century made us more than ever aware of the currents of natural energy that normally motivate us and spur us to action. Three philosophers suggested one such instinct as the primary motivation for everything we do or say. Sigmund Freud nominated sex, Frederick Nietzsche the will to power, and Karl Marx thought money made the world go round.

In a corresponding assignation from the other side of the spectrum, generations of spiritual seekers stemmed the flow of these natural currents of selfishness by taking three corresponding vows: the vow of poverty attacks greed; the vow of chastity wounds lust; the vow of obedience attacks the will to power.

The only wound through which grace can flow is the freely opened human heart and will of an authentic lover of God. The bridge between them is created through open wounds on both sides. The pentagram of the five wounds is the victory sign of the Divine breakthrough. The secret wisdom hidden from the beginning of time is the mystery of God's love for us. And so powerful is this secret wisdom that the five gates of hell shall never prevail against the formula of the five wounds. There is an attitude we adopt, indeed a person we become, when we plumb the secret depths and decode the hidden knowledge of God. It requires a kind of attention or awareness essential for spiritual activity of any kind. Theologically speaking, in the Christian tradition, this is the mystery of *kenosis*, the Greek word for self-emptying. In the case of the Man-God, Jesus Christ, there was a double kenosis. He emptied Himself of His Godhead so that he could become a person in our world. His life on earth was a further self-emptying of that nature (ours) which he had assumed, right to the point zero, the draining of the last drop on the cross where the ultimate fusion occurred and the explosion of resurrection into a new kind of being, a new kind of loving occurred.

OPALESCENT WINGS

Our task is to strive in the direction of love as radiating outward energy, in such a way and to such an extent that this becomes the intentionality and the structure of our own being. We become embodied organisms of love. This, in turn, would radiate towards others making it easier for them to move into the space of otherness until, eventually, such specimens of humanity would become the exemplary forms towards which the evolutionary appetite would aspire until it would naturally take this shape and structure. Human beings would then be born to love. This would establish a very different kind of universe. One that did justice to that very word "uni-verse," meaning all of us turned towards each other, turned into one.

> Do you know what a pearl is and what an opal is? My soul when you came sauntering to me first through those sweet summer evenings was beautiful but with the pale passionless beauty of a pearl. Your love has passed through me and now I feel my mind something like an opal, that is, full of strange uncertain hues and colours, of warm lights and quick shadows and of broken music.[10]

This is James Joyce writing to his wife Nora on 21st August 1909.

The pearl and the opal are symbols of two different ways of achieving the beauty that human beings can radiate, if and when they become what they were intended to be. Such beauty is not something that we do, not something that we have, it is what we are, what we become, if the work of art rings true. Our bodies and our faces are icons of that inner equilibrium that life has accomplished in us by a wisdom kneaded through us to integrity. But we, in our spiritual traditions, have promoted one kind of love and despised the other. We have failed to see the possibility of the butterfly having opalescent wings.

The word opal comes from the Sanskrit *úpara*, meaning "lower," which is the comparative of *úpa*, meaning "under." At base it is a silica mineral, the principal constituent of most rocks, which is colorless. Disseminated impurities impart dull body colors to this undistinguished yet durable base. The so-called "milkiness" of texture is created by an abundance of tiny gas-filled cavities. However, colors flash and change when the stone is viewed from different directions.

This is caused by the interference of light along minute cracks and other internal inhomogeneities. In other words, because the stone is translucent and full of imperfections it becomes colorful and assumes its identity as a jewel.

Pearls, on the other hand, treasured throughout the world as jewelry, are the product of a fight against an invader. (Latin *pernulla*, unattested). Mollusks with double shells, such as clams, oysters, and mussels, lay down pearl as the inner layer of their shells. When some foreign matter, often parasitic larva, gets into the body, the mollusk forms a small sac around the foreign body, isolating it, and then builds layer upon layer of calcium carbonate around the sac, imprisoning the invader for ever and creating a pearl. Natural pearls are rare. Only one oyster in a thousand contains one.

An exaggerated emphasis on the "spiritual" and corresponding vilification of the carnal or physical, concentration upon self-contained identity (pearl) as contrasted with inescapable being-with-others as our inevitable situation in the world, has colored our relationship with ourselves and with others from our very earliest contacts. Such an option for the pearl as opposed to the opal dictates that our role models and preferred heroes will be solitary, celibate, rugged, and ascetic (usually) males. Those of us who cannot or will not embrace and realize these ideals will feel second-rate and frustrated. Such a program towards perfection produces in us a repressive reflex with regard to the physical. We cultivate an ingrained fear and guilt about all bodily, especially sexual, self-expression.

These orthodox ideals of virtue, however unrealistic and arbitrary they may be, can and do fashion certain exceptional individuals, do inspire exotic and awe-inspiring feats of asceticism, but these only promote in the ordinary lives of most people a despairing tension. Disregard for the emotional and sexual aspect of ourselves and the other-oriented structure of our bodies and personalities has two consequences: we develop defense mechanisms and outer armor, which allow us to survive in the desert without nourishment for our philanthropic appetites and we remain illiterate and undereducated in our relational faculties. Those who fail to become beautiful and impressive pearls or hermits have to stumble through the market-place of life guilty, insecure, awkward, and angry.

While not condemning the valid and valuable vocation of the few to the contemplative life and the life of the hermit, the beauty of the pearl, those promoting the equally valid formation of the opal suggest that a life of contact and intimacy with others has its own rigors, discipline, and demands, which we must be taught and we must learn to speak as a quite different and very specific language. The emotional and sexual sides of ourselves must be understood as an essential part of our human growth and development.

The most serious aspect of these divisions is the suggestion that Christian, especially Catholic orthodoxy is irrevocably aligned with the first of these attitudes. Christian teaching and principles, and therefore the belief structures of many of our people, defend and support the primacy and purity of the pearl.

If we are faced with a choice between supposedly "Christian" values and more contemporary "heretical" discoveries, we create once again oppositions that were never meant to be pitted against each other, certainly not by the founder of Christianity, whose salvation was sent to reach the ends of the earth, oppositions entirely of our own making. No one has the right or the mandate to deprive Christianity of any aspect of our humanity. Everything we discover about ourselves should be integrated into our Christian anthropology, so that "in the end," as Rilke says, "we shall have been marvelously prepared for divine relationship."

NOTES

[1] Wallis Wilde-Menozzi, first published as part of the longer essay, "Seeing Butterflies," in *Notre Dame Review, Signs and Surfaces*, Issue 22, Summer 2006 (Notre Dame, Indiana: Notre Dame Review, 2006), pp. 1-10. Reprinted by the kind permission of Wallis Wilde-Menozzi. For Wilde-Menozzi's other publications and creative activities see www.Wallis Wilde-Menozzi.com.

[2] Murray Stein, "When You Venture There, Uncertainties and Mysteries Abound," in *Intimacy: Venturing the Uncertainties of the Heart, Jungian Odyssey Series, Vol. 1* (New Orleans: Spring Journal Books, 2009), pp. 194-197.

[3] *Ibid.*

[4] After the first Jungian Odyssey at Flüeli-Ranft I went to le Chateau de Lavigny, where I wrote a book that contains some of these experiences: *Symbolism: The Glory of Escutcheoned Doors* (Dublin: Veritas, 2007).

[5] Vladimir Soloviev, *The Meaning of Love*, trans. Thomas R. Beyer (New York: Lindisfarne Books, 1985).

[6] Teilhard de Chardin, *The Future of Man*, trans. Norman Denny (Glasgow: Collins, Fount Paperbacks, 1977), p. 245.

[7] *Ibid.*, p. 184.

[8] Rainer Maria Rilke, "194, To Clara Rilke, 77 Rue de Varenne, Paris, September 4, 1908," in *Letters of Rainer Maria Rilke, 1892-1910*, trans. Jane Bannard Greene and M.D. Herter Norton, 1st Ed. (New York: W.W. Norton & Company, Inc., 1945), p. 336; cited from *Internet Archive* at digital copyright 2005/04/8, http://www.archive.org/details/lettersofrainerm030932mbp (accessed July 10, 2012).

[9] Anonymous, *Meditations on the Tarot: A Journey into Christian Hermeticism*, trans. Robert A. Powell (Boston: Element Books, 1973/1991), pp. 104-120. [This book has provided me with inspiration. Much of what I paraphrase in the last few lines was composed originally by the above-cited anonymous author, whose work was published after his death in 1973. He was born in Russia in 1900, and became a disciple of Rudolph Steiner before converting to Catholicism. His above-cited major work was originally written in French and completed in 1967. The translation is from the original French manuscript, and published in accordance with the author's intentions: anonymously and posthumously. I have written more about this in my book, *Tarot: Talisman or Taboo?* (Dublin: Currach Press, 2003).

[10] James Joyce, *The Selected Letters of James Joyce*, ed. Richard Ellmann (New York: The Viking Press, 1975), p. 161.

3

Tristan and Iseult: Song of the Soul or Sin of Adultery?

John Hill

I revisit the legend of Tristan and Iseult with trepidation.[1] This magnificent story was an inspiration of my youth, a challenge at midlife, and a consolation in maturity. Its haunting rhythm gives voice to the unutterable, form to the invisible, purpose to the heart's qualms. It throws a veil of enchantment over the world, as it re-awakens hymns to Eros, Dionysus, and the many figures of legend that have served the lores of love. As you listen to the story of Tristan and Iseult, your heart may hear its lyrical sounds tuning the strings of your soul.

THE STORY

The story opens with the battle between king Mark of Cornwall and the Morholt, a primitive giant from Ireland who has come to Cornwall to abduct its virgins as hostages. Mark is on the point of defeat, when Rivallin of Lohnois drives the Morholt back to Ireland.

In reward for his services Rivallin wins the king's sister, Blanchefleur. Soon tragedy intervenes: Rivallin is killed in battle; Blanchefleur dies in giving birth to Tristan.

Tristan is brought up by his maternal uncle, king Mark, and becomes the court's most celebrated knight. When the Morholt returns to Cornwall to take tribute, Tristan kills him, but is wounded by the Morholt's poisonous sword. Lesions putrefy his body; it blackens and gives off the foul stench of the dead. He is placed on a rudderless boat, which miraculously brings him to the shores of Ireland. A magic potion, brewed by the queen of the land, mother to Iseult, heals the wound.

Tristan returns to Cornwall and is made the king's heir. The barons of the land become jealous and urge Mark to find a wife in order to produce his own heir. At an auspicious moment a pair of swallows fly into Mark's chamber and drop a golden hair. Mark asks Tristan to find the woman of the golden hair. Tristan recognizes the hair of Iseult and sets sail for the shores of Ireland. There he defeats a dragon and wins the king's daughter, Iseult the Fair. Tristan is the true consort of Iseult, but deceives her by escorting her to Cornwall as the betrothed of Mark. Iseult's mother has brewed a love philter so that the aged king will love her daughter only: "They would share one death and one life, one sorrow and one joy."[2] But on the return voyage, Tristan and Iseult drink the magic potion by accident. Plunging into the realms of Eros, passion overcomes them, condemning them to a life of bliss and suffering.

> *Isot ma drue, Isot m'amie,*
> *En vos ma mort, en vos ma vie!*[3]

Once back in Cornwall, Tristan surrenders Iseult to his liege. The wedding between king Mark and Iseult is celebrated, but soon the good intentions of the lovers break down under the inebriating power of the potion. There follows a series of intrigues to protect the adulterous affair from the suspicions of Mark and his court. A dwarf betrays the lovers. Mark condemns Tristan to be burnt at the stake and banishes Iseult to a company of lepers. Both miraculously escape and flee to the forest of Morrois. There they partake of the fruits of love and are joined in mystical union. They enjoy passion's elixir until the intensive power of the potion wanes. One day Mark comes riding by and sees the lovers sleeping together with a separating sword between them. He replaces it with his own sword and blocks out the sun illuminating Iseult's face. The lovers, tired of the wilderness and longing to return to civilization, understand Mark's gesture as an offer of reconciliation. They return to court, but cannot refrain from entangling their glances. Once again they are caught; Tristan is banished and Iseult is forced to remain the unhappy wife of Mark.

Tristan undertakes many adventures and as a reward for his services wins Iseult of the White Hands. He marries her for her name only. He refrains from consummating the union because of a ring given to him by the first Iseult with whom he maintains secret contacts. As the story draws to an end, he rescues a damsel in distress, but receives a fatal wound in doing so. From the shores of Brittany a messenger is sent to fetch Iseult the Fair. Only she can heal him. He is to hoister a white sail if she consents and a black sail if she declines. Iseult of the White Hands sees the ship returning with a white sail, but, overcome by jealousy, reports a black sail. Tristan, on hearing the dark news, yields up his spirit; Iseult, once on shore, approaches her dead lover, holds him in her arms, kisses him, and takes her last breath, joining him in death.

On witnessing the death of his beloved wife and nephew, king Mark repents of his harsh judgments and has their bodies brought back to Cornwall. From their coffins a rose and a vine grow up entwined around each other. No matter who tries to cut them down, they grow again the next day. The earlier poets end the story by stating its purpose. It is a consolation for all the evils of love: jealousy, envy, possessiveness, violence, and injustice.

ORIGINS AND INTENT

It is well known that Europe's lost Celtic heritage re-surfaced in Arthurian legend. Irish and Welsh storytellers entertained the Norman courts of England and France with the myths and legends of their homelands. They were the source of inspiration for such writers as Chretian de Troyes, Thomas of Britain, Eilhart von Oberg, and Gottfried von Strassburg who fashioned them in the courtly literature of Medieval Europe. Arthurian legend signaled a re-emergence of Europe's lost Celtic heritage. Much of European literature has been inspired by these stories. They also spoke to the soul of C.G. Jung. In

Memories, Dreams, Reflections, Jung refers to himself as Perceval, the mute knight.[4] At one time he planned to write on the Grail, but he did not wish to interfere with his wife's field of studies.

The legend of Tristan and Iseult is one of the most popular, powerful, and beautiful stories of Arthurian Romance. Over eighty versions of the tale were extant up until the sixteenth century[5] of which there are innumerable later interpretations. The original prototype may be traced to the old Irish *Aithedas* (tales of elopement), the most prominent being *The Pursuit of Diarmuid and Grania.*[6]

In this paper I shall first examine the mythological sources that inspired the authors to create this tale of wonder. Welding together themes from Greek, Celtic, Christian, and alchemical sources, the story portrays the deeper structures of human passion. With focus on the historical context that gave birth to the narrative, one can begin to discern its secret intent. The tale presents an uncompromising challenge to the norms of medieval society by unveiling the dark shadows of human love. It is also a diagnosis of the soul's afflictions, particularly when confronting the maladies of love. Those afflictions remain with us today and still require treatment.

Tristan and Iseult is a tale of longing, primarily dedicated to the mysteries of Eros. I will attempt to elucidate the significance of Eros within the context of love's many faces. Several questions arise in attempting to make a psychological analysis of the legend. Is it simply a description of adultery, of an impossible love, of an ineffectual ghostly lover who is devoured by the Great Mother? Why does romantic love end tragically? How can one celebrate Eros, which in the name of love has destroyed kingdoms, honor, and marriage? Is Eros about relationship or the antithesis of relationship? Can Eros be cultivated and adapted to terrestrial life, or does its elixirs poison committed partnership? Does this tale contain a secret religious doctrine, signaling a re-emergence of the dualistic doctrines of Manichaeism, as advocated by Denis de Rougemont?[7] Perhaps its secret purpose is to open the heart to the soul's longing for transcendence within the context of today's secular society. But do we have the inner strength to contain that mystery?

This high tale of love may ravish the soul on different levels. It not only outlines the split between the marriage bond and passionate longing, but also provides a model of transformation for all who struggle with the strains of passion. Whatever approach we adopt, the legend constellates powerful emotions, activating a deep yearning for the ineffable. It bears within itself a rich cultural treasure, emanating from layers of human civilization. The authors have woven together an extraordinary syncretic composition of mythic, literary, and religious symbols. Its powerful message challenged the social, moral, and judicial traditions of the Middle Ages. Its roots, however, reach beyond medieval society. As a hymn to love, it transforms the heart in attempting to give expression to humanity's perennial yearning for wholeness.

RECOVERING THE MYTHIC HERITAGE

Tristan: A Medieval Dionysus

According to the legend, Tristan is born on the waters between Lohnois and Cornwall. His tragic epiphany is linked with the element of moisture. Shrouded by the winds and waves of the sea, love is turned to despair, joy to grief, life to death. Just as the lightning flash of Zeus destroyed Semele at the conception of Dionysus, so the seed of Rivallin annihilates Blanchefleur: "Of the child or tragic death within her she knew nothing."[8] She dies giving birth to Tristan; Rivallin is killed in battle. Tristan becomes the "Orphelin Solitaire," a hero without father or mother, and, like the god Eros, born of Wind and Night,[9] he represents the elemental forces of nature, free from the control of a patriarchal society.

Paradox, duality, and tragedy affirm the epiphany of this hero. Descriptions of the birth of Dionysus might equally be applied to that of Tristan:

> He who was born in this way is not only the exultant god, the god who brings man joy, he is the suffering and dying god, the god of tragic contrast, and the inner force of this duality is so great that he appears among men like a storm, he staggers them, and he tames their opposition with the whip of madness. All tradition, all order must be shattered. Life becomes suddenly an ecstasy—an ecstasy of blessedness, but an ecstasy no less of terror.[10]

One cannot but be impressed by the extraordinary similarity of key motifs that are indigenous to the Dionysian and Tristan legacy.

Dionysus, chased by the wrathful Lycurgus, finds refuge in the sea, realm of the goddess Thetis, his friend and protector.[11] The tides of the sea miraculously guide Tristan to the shores of Ireland and initiate healing through the fated encounter with Iseult. Both god and hero are associated with an intoxicating potion, both celebrate the mysteries of the vine, both possess the same totem animal, a wild boar, and both perform ecstatic rituals in the depth of the far-flung forests of times long ago. Dionysus and Tristan celebrate the rites of Spring, are the beloved of women, and herald a promise of freedom from the shackles of domestic conformity. These symmetries leave us no option but to pursue the anomalies surrounding the enigmatic epiphany of a pagan god in the Christian Middle Ages.

Hero and the Goddess

Before attempting such a quest, we must first explore an even more powerful source that has inspired the Tristan legend. Scholars have long recognized that the origins, structure, and motif of this legend can be traced to the stories of Celtic Ireland. Tristan is no ordinary hero of courtly society. Besides being skilled with sword, none can surpass him in jousting, hurling the lance, wrestling, leaping, playing the harp, or imitating the songs of birds. Most of these traits can be traced to attributes of ancient Celtic heroes. Gertrude Schoeperle[12] has suggested that Tristan is so accomplished in natural feats that he is hardly an ideal incarnation of a twelfth century courtly knight, but bears more resemblance to the Fianna warriors of ancient Ireland. The Fianna were a non-aristocratic band of men who, like Tristan, were lone warriors ready to perform many natural feats and were skilled in roaming through the wild forests and hills of Ireland.

The Morholt is certainly not the typical knight of Medieval Europe. His name is derived from the ancient Irish *Murgelt,* meaning "he who cleaves to the sea," implying a primeval monster, a sea lunatic or wanderer.[13] He is associated with the Fomors, a primitive, mythical race that ruled Ireland before the coming of the Tuath de Danaan, the gods of light and bringers of arts and crafts. In their intermarriage with the Tuath they guaranteed the fertility of the land. Like the Morholt, who was about to seize the virgins of Cornwall, they were notorious for levying tribute.[14]

Tristan's defeat of the Morholt symbolizes a victory over those forces that use women as mere spoils of warfare or as a means to gain power and wealth. The victory represents a heroic act of defiance against the practiced Christian code of marriage that had become a moral and legal acquiescence of brute instinct. When a king was converted, it was often the case that his subjects had to submit to the new faith for practical reasons. For the average person at that time, there was not much difference between God's will and the law of the prince, whether of church or state. Courtly love accentuated the opposition between "Amor" and "Roma." The oppression of woman as an instrument of pleasure or as a means to gain power continues throughout the legend. Even Tristan's betrothal to the second Iseult conveys a mockery of marriage and an abuse of woman. Having won her in battle, it is purely an outer deal. The authors of the legend are obviously implying that something is missing in the relationship between man and woman. In their search for that missing component, they had to resort to an older layer of civilization that was embodied in Celtic legends, which had survived on the peripheries of Western Europe. In Arthurian Romance Europe discovered its lost Celtic heritage, which re-awakened the yearnings of the suffering soul then imprisoned in courtly conventions and today fettered by the many distractions of a consumer society.

The love philter, so prominent in numerous Celtic stories, has always been associated with the choice of a new sovereign. It was an essential attribute of the goddess of the land. Without her approval, no warrior had the right to rule; without her consent the land would become barren and unfruitful. The following twelfth-century tale, which probably refers back to fourth century Celtic Ireland, reveals a hidden lineage between Irish myth and the Tristan legend:

> An old king is dying and sends out his five sons to find the water of life. The first son comes to a well guarded by an old hag. She will give him the water of life, if he will lie with her. He dismisses her and she refuses him the magic potion. The same happens with the next three sons. The fifth son, Niall, consents to lie with her, and the old hag becomes a beautiful young maiden. She calls herself Mise Flathius na h-Erinn (I am the Sovereignty of Ireland). She promises Niall the kingship of the land. Peace will prevail and the land will be fertile: the crops shall be manifold; the cows will give forth more milk; the rivers will be full of fish.[15]

Scholars have considered the tale and its many variations to be an offspring of the universal *hierosgamos* motif. It has been subject to innumerable interpretations—a joining of heaven and earth, a synchronizing of the energies of life with the norms of society, or, more specifically, as evidence of a tension and reciprocity between an earlier goddess-oriented culture and later Celtic patriarchal culture. The union of king and goddess is narrated in terms of the great cycle of life, death, and rebirth. When a king's reign is about to begin, he encounters a young maiden who offers him the waters of life. When it ends, he meets an old hag, and the rivers of the land run dry. "Sovereignty," as the old hag or young maiden, represents the earth goddess. As an old hag, she represents life's barrenness and infertility; as a young maiden, its springtime and abundance. The Celtic values of the tribe, represented in kingship, were subject to a continual process of transition. Everything, even the virtues, must live, die, and be reborn so that the clan's cultural institutions, norms, and beliefs retain their freshness and vitality. Expressed in contemporary language, the encounter with the old hag implies not only death and destruction—but also that a loving embrace of the repressed, unwanted, or excluded parts of one's personal psyche and one's cultural heritage bears the promise of a transformation that breathes new life into one that has become mere routine.

Alchemical Transformation

Before advancing further, we need to examine another powerful source that has molded our tale of enchantment. There is an effusion of alchemical motifs that affirm the tale's transformative intent, particularly in the text of Gottfried von Strassburg. The poisoned wound in the thigh not only associates Tristan with the Grail king. Poison in alchemy was one of the many definitions of the *prima materia*, the *nigredo*, or the *massa confusa*, all representing the raw materials of the soul to be transformed. This first stage of the alchemical process leads to the *putreficatio*, the decomposition of the blackened body, which takes place in the grave and gives off the foul stench of the dead. A process of suffering is necessary in order to gain consciousness of the *albedo*,[16] "the ash ... of the glorified body,"[17] or "the whiteness of Venus."[18] Through the poison, the blackened body of Tristan encounters the fair Iseult. In Gottfried's *Tristan and Isolde*,

Iseult is called the sun; her beauty competes with the brightness of
the sun. Such descriptions bear similarity to the visual impression of
an anima figure whose face shone like the sun in the dreams of physicist
Wolfgang Pauli. Jung amplifies this motif with the alchemical
solificatio.[19] When king Mark discovers the separating sword between
the lovers, he notices the sun illuminating Iseult's visage. He blocks
the windows, a symbolic act indicating an inability to understand the
sun's mysterious union with the womb of the earth. He is unable to
connect dreams of the spirit with desires of the flesh.

In Gottfried's version of the story, the lovers, having been banished
from Mark's court, find the fulfillment of their passion in love's grotto,
located in the wilderness of Morois. Gottfried describes the *Minnegrotto*
as being perfectly round. In the middle of this womb is a crystal bed:

> At the center, the bed of crystalline love was dedicated to her
> name. The man who had cut the crystal for her couch had
> divined her nature unerringly: love should be of crystal—
> transparent and translucent![20]

The cave calls to mind the function of the alchemical *Rotundum*
within which took place the transformation of the *prima materia*. The
physical fulfillment of the passion may be compared to the *unio
corporalis*, the fiery *Rubedo*, or reddening of the process. It is the
passion, arising from the *corruptio* and *putrefìcatio* of the Morholt's
poison, that transforms the lovers. The mandala structure of the
white cave and the visage of Iseult that competes with the sun's
radiance suggest the emergence of a new consciousness that reaches
down to the roots of our being, touching every cell in our body, and
transforms our physical existence.

Gottfried was highly educated, well versed in Latin texts, and had
knowledge of alchemy which "like a great wave broke on the shores of
France and Germany in the twelfth century."[21] He was also acquainted
with medieval mysticism and the revived Virgin cult, his *Tristan* being
a secular rendition of its erotic aspirations.[22] In Gottfried's text, the
vital energies, contained in the old fertility cults, were now transformed
into a celebration of Eros, liberated from the corrupting influence of
the Morholt. The crystalline bed of Gottfried's *Minnegrotto* becomes
the birthplace of a secularized, physical, yet spiritualized Eros, crystal
being one of the most rarified and subtilized of the minerals. In

Thomas' *Tristran*, the hero has a giant make a statue of Iseult trampling the dwarf who betrayed her, similar to the well-known images of Mary trampling a snake under her feet.[23] The image of an adulteress imitating Mary could only shock the medieval mind. If, however, we continue to uphold a medieval "mythic dissociation"[24] between spirit and flesh, we will find no place for Eros in the human heart. Wolfram von Eschenbach's "man's life is neither all black nor all white" in the opening lines of *Parzifal*,[25] or Jung's "Love is a force of destiny whose power reaches from heaven to hell,"[26] describes Eros as a transformative process, linking contraries, often beginning with physical attraction, but aspiring to the lofty realms of the spirit, bearing both "the colors of heaven and the colors of hell."[27] In Plato's *Symposium*, Diotima teaches those present that even sensually based Eros aspires to the non-corporeal, to the spiritual plane of existence.

A CHANGE OF ATTITUDE?

The authors of the Tristan story describe love as an unconscious process against which humanity is powerless. We must not forget that the potion was taken by accident. Tristan and Iseult become lovers against their will. If love were simply a fatal attraction, then surely this would cast doubt on love as a transformative process, enhancing consciousness and initiating a change of attitude. The accidental taking of the potion symbolizes a conflict between the conscious norms of the times and the unconscious desire to live a more fulfilled life. Mark and Tristan complement each other in that both together represent a split attitude toward Eros. The tale implies that for those who shun love's mysteries, the flame of Eros will assume archetypal characteristics, overcome the human will, and act in unconscious, destructive ways. When collective traditions allow no space for love's elixir, the transgressor will confuse love with power and the victim suffers the life of an outcast. Relationships become poisoned.

This is precisely what happens in the legend. When there is no place for Eros in the real world, all ends in tragedy. But death is not the final end. There is no end, for this tale lives on in the hearts and hopes of all who have not given up on love's aspirations. The true home of Eros lies in the imagination. Emerging from that abode, Eros lets fly his deadly arrows to incarnate in human relationships in unpredictable ways. Indeed the various authors unveil the secret intent of Eros. In heralding a victory of love over death, Eros transforms the soul. Despite death, the world should not become a wasteland. In Eilhart von Oberg's version, a rose and a vine arise from the coffins of the Iseult and Tristan and entwine around each other. No matter who cuts them down, they grow again the next day. In Wagner's opera, *Tristan and Isolde*, the lovers triumph in death. Tristan soars to the empyrean heights and Isolde finds fulfillment in the ecstasy of the *Liebestod*.

Eros may live forever in the imagination, but it would be a fatal mistake to think that humans can dwell in the abode of the gods. Such narcissistic longings would blind us to the contingencies of human relationships. Tied to the fetters of a ghostly lover or a Flying Dutchman, we risk running aground on the harsh rocks of betrayal, deception, and the innumerable delusions that we project on the fantasy lover. Having been impaled by the arrows of Eros, we are destined to become hierophants of love's mystery. We are to suffer its agony and its ecstasy, its raptures and its loss. We endure the glory of a god, and the devastation of an empty shell. If we can bear the poison in that liminal space between those extremes, we learn to become truly human. We are humbled, freed from delusions, perhaps to become loving servants to all that meets us on the path to redemption. Through love we transform the universe and heal the split between body and soul.

In the Tristan legend the death of the lovers represents a symbolic act which constellates change and resolution in all who witness this tragedy. It is not that the lovers change—their actions merely promote the tale's transformative intent—but their withdrawal from the stage of life evinces a remarkable change of attitude in king Mark, the sole survivor of the tragedy. On seeing the death of his beloved wife and nephew, his heart opens; he repents for not having understood the potion's mystery, and forgives. Repentance and forgiveness rescue Eros from oblivion. Mark recognizes the folly of possessiveness, his cruelty, rage, and jealousy. As king he represents the social and cultural values of the times. Hence the legend appeals to medieval humanity and to us all to reconsider our attitude to love. We cannot possess love; we cannot reduce love to the marriage contract; we cannot exclude Eros. Only in freedom will love blossom.

The Awakening of the Heart

The Tristan story describes Eros as a realm of light and darkness. Here we not only encounter the most primitive levels of the soul's longings: in the violence of the Morholt, the jealousy of the barons, the betrayal of the dwarf, or the cruelty of Mark. The legend also presents us with a more differentiated Eros. Tristan and Iseult represent a cultural refinement of Eros. When imprisoned by traditions supported by primitive power and sex drives, Eros will break the chains of convention, often through attachment to someone of the opposite gender. The human soul cannot stand a relationship that might outwardly be perfect but inwardly dead. Here we might encounter the complexities of a mid-life crisis that awaken us to the soul's longing for new horizons. Eros, however, frequently exposes our weakness and incites us to break boundaries. If the conscious ego does not maintain its presence, we can easily misinterpret its spiritual intention to connect body with soul. Eros can possess you, turn you into a demon lover,[28] activate your unlived life and undifferentiated narcissistic longings, condemning you to be ravished by a Don Juan, a Casanova, or a Venusian nymph, creating a delusional relationship, dissociated from the ego's perception and judgment of reality. This raises the question of whether Eros can be integrated into any human relationship? Is de Rougemont right in saying that Eros is ultimately a longing for death? Can Eros, the longing for life in all its fullness, ever be fulfilled in terrestrial existence?

In order to answer these questions I have resorted to the ancient Greek notion of love, a conception that had many faces: "Storge," "Philia," "Eros," "Agape," or "Xenia,"[29] which might be translated as love between parent and child, friendship, social communion, longing, and hospitality. In a similar fashion C. S. Lewis describes four kinds of human love: affection, friendship, Eros, and charity. Jung too enumerated the different forms of love: love of parents, of country, of one's neighbor, as well as the "pure flame of Eros."[30]

Whenever we taste the different fruits of love, we awaken ancient divinities. Caution is needed so as not to identify with nor exclude any one of them. Tristan and Iseult are semi-divine beings. If we identify with them, we risk losing our humanity. If we remain caught in projections, we burden a relationship with demands that are impossible to fulfill. If we exclude them, we become victims of an unlived life. I believe it would be misleading to assert that one can simply integrate Eros in a relationship. This force, rooted in the collective imagination, transcends personal relationships, even human institutions. Eros cannot be reduced to a relationship; rather it embodies the mystery of life in all its fullness, perhaps experienced in a moment of ecstasy in its fulfillment or despair over its loss. Through Eros we see the divine potentiality of the other, even if that particular person is not able to realize that potential. We can only attempt to contain its imaginative power, celebrate it, battle with it, and try to understand its intentions. In knowing that we cannot control archetypal forces, we need to look at them through the eyes of consciousness[31] and learn to live with them in non-destructive ways, wherever they dwell, in self or another.

In any relationship each partner needs to be free to pursue the meaning of his or her passion. It is crucial that the partner is at liberty to create friendships, interests, or activities outside of a committed relationship. This of course will bring tension, but tension brings dialogue, hopefully not just a love of self, but also a love of the other, and ultimately a strengthening of the committed relationship. If things go wrong and we discover that we are harming or abusing another, we must learn to contain our deficiencies, accept responsibility, repent for wrongdoing, and hope for forgiveness. Relationship is not a state but a process. Considering the ancient Greek understanding of love, one might encourage couples in an intimate relationship to avoid confusing love with passion. The task is to channel, cultivate, and contain the mystery of Eros within those other loves, known to the Greeks: love of family, friendship, profession, community, or hospitality. If we invite Eros to participate in our actual life situation, we may discover it offers a new life or renewal of the old. Marriages may have to die, but they may also be rebirthed.

In witnessing the tragedy of Tristan and Iseult, one can easily be swept away by the winds and tides of Eros, destroying those other loves that are perhaps more gentle, enduring, or committed. In whatever love you are anchored, be it in a family, friendship, or community, Eros will sooner or later appear. Like a wild Daimon he will challenge you, demanding to know if you are alive in whatever attachment you have established. One does not always have to break those relationships. But you do have to look within and ask yourself if your life has become an empty routine. Have you banished love from your heart and from your attachment to close ones? You might also need courage to feel what a new relationship is offering. Life is forever changing and Eros demands that we move with it. Remember you are not alone in the universe. You might need a sympathetic friend or empathic analyst, whose task will be to make sure you that you fathom the intentions of Eros in its poison and potion, in its destruction and creativity, and in its power to separate and its urge to unite, and that you do not surrender entirely your powers of discrimination. Eros is but one god among the many gods and goddesses that populate your universe.

NOTES

[1] There are many versions of Iseult's name: Yseut, Ysolt, Iseult, Isot, Iseut, Isolt, Isolde. I have chosen the one common in English usage. For one of the best English renditions of the tale see: *The Romance of Tristan and Iseult, retold by Joseph Bedier*, trans. Hilaire Belloc (New York: Dover, 2005 [1913]). Some passages in this paper have been taken from my unpublished thesis entitled, "The Tristan Legend," written in 1972 in fulfillment of the diploma requirements for the C.G. Jung Institute Zürich, Küsnacht.

[2] Gottfried von Strassburg, *Tristan*, trans. A.T. Hatto (Harmondsworth: Penguin, 1969), p. 192.

[3] Gottfried von Strassburg, "Epigraph," in Thomas Bedier, *Le Roman de Tristan et Iseut* (Paris: L'Edition d'Art, 1924), p. 59.

[4] C.G. Jung, *Memories, Dreams, Reflections,* ed. Aniela Jaffé (New York: Vintage, 1963), p. 215.

[5] Isabelle Ragnard, "Tristan and Yseut," text accompanying the recording, *Tristan et Yseut* by Alla Francesca (Paris: Production Alla Francesca, Realization Zig Zag, distribution Harmonia Mundi, 2004), p. 7.

[6] Tom Cross and Clark Slover, *Ancient Irish Tales* (Dublin: Allen Figgis, 1969 [1936]), pp. 370-421.

[7] Denis de Rougemont, *Passion and Society* (London: Faber & Faber, 1956).

[8] von Strassburg, *Tristan*, p. 58.

⁹ Carl Kerényi, *The Gods of the Greeks* (Harmondsworth: Penguin, 1958), p. 101.

¹⁰ Walter Otto, *Dionysus* (Bloomington: Indiana University Press, 1965), p. 78.

¹¹ *Ibid.*, p. 162.

¹² Gertrude Shoeperle, *Tristan and Isolt* (London: Nutt, 1913), p. 359.

¹³ Prionsias MacCana, "Aspects of the Theme of King and Goddess in Irish Literature," *Etudes Celtique*s, vol. 7 (Paris: 1955-56), p. 409.

¹⁴ Alwyn Rees and Brinley Rees, *Celtic Heritage* (London: Thames & Hudson, 1961), p. 33.

¹⁵ For an excellent description of this story see Cross and Slover, *Ancient Irish Tales*, pp. 508-513.

¹⁶ C.G. Jung, "The Personification of the Opposites," in *Mysterium Coniunctionis, The Collected Works of C. G. Jung,* Vol. 14, eds. Sir Herbert Read, Michael Fordham, Gerhard Adler, William McGuire, trans. R.F.C. Hull (Princeton, NJ: Princeton University Press, 1963), § 220. (Future references to Jung's *Collected Works* will be with chapter titles followed by volume and paragraph numbers.)

¹⁷ *Ibid.*, § 247.

¹⁸ *Ibid.*, § 139.

¹⁹ Jung, "Individual Dream Symbolism in Relation to Alchemy," CW 12, § 67-68.

²⁰ von Strassburg, *Tristan*, p. 264.

²¹ Peter C. Ober, "Alchemy and the 'Tristan' of Gottfried of Strassburg," *Monatsheft für deutschen Unterricht, deutsche Sprache und Literatur*, Vol. LVII, 1965, No. 7 (Madison: University of Wisconsin Press, 1965), p. 321.

²² A.T. Hatto, "Introduction" in von Strassburg, *Tristan*, p. 15.

²³ Thomas of Britain, *Tristran*, trans. A.T. Hatto (Harmondsworth: Penguin, 1969), p. 315.

²⁴ Joseph Campbell, *The Flight of the Wild Gander: Explorations in the Mythological Dimension* (New York: The Viking Press, 1969), p. 226.

²⁵ Wolfram von Eschenbach, *Parzival*, trans. Helen Mustard and Charles Passage (New York: Vintage, 1961), p. 3.

²⁶ Jung, "The Love Problem of a Student," CW 10, § 198.

²⁷ von Eschenbach, *Parzival*, p. 3.

[28] For an excellent description of the demon lover see: John R. Haule, *Pilgrimage of the Heart* (Boston and London: Shambhala, 1992), pp. 82-101.

[29] Pavel Florensky, *The Pillar and Ground of the Truth,* trans. Boris Jakim (Princeton and Oxford: Princeton University Press, 1997), pp. 286-293.

[30] Jung, "The Love Problem of a Student," CW 10, § 198-200.

[31] Robert Johnson, *We, Understanding the Psychology of Romantic Love* (New York: Harper & Row, 1983), p. 43.

4

The Eden Project *Redivivus*: Imagining Self and Other as Reappropriation of Being

James Hollis

What can one say about *love*, its perversions, animadversions, subversions, and necessary immersions after all these years? What can be proffered today that is not cliché, for is not cliché the re-cognition of the recognizable, over, and over, and over again? What can anyone old enough, mature enough to read this essay learn that we have not learned before? Perhaps this is the point, then, the paradox that humans are those animals capable of changing their behaviors, capable of reframing their realities, but seem nonetheless obliged to serve compelling archaic, archetypal realities over and over. None of us rise in the morning and, while brushing our teeth, look in the mirror and say, "Today you will do the same stupid, counter-productive things you have done for years and years." Yet, we do, and cannot, seemingly, help ourselves.

Creatures of desire, we forlornly yearn for what is infinite, yet live immersed in only finite possibilities. The tenebrous gap between is what always afflicts the heart, and often erodes the spirit. But the next day, it will be the same. After all, did not the ancients consider Eros a god, variously described as primordial, and thus at the fundament of all things, *and* an infant born ever anew in any given moment? Remember the gods coming to roar with laughter at the clever trap Haephaestus sprung on his adulterous wife Aphrodite during her tryst with promiscuous Ares? After all, were they not laughing at the oldest joke of all? And yet did not Hermes-Mercurius himself acknowledge that despite their ridicule, he would gladly enjoy their mockery for similar coition with Aphrodite? If even the gods suffer the pangs of insufficiency, the drives of desire, if even the gods cannot help themselves, what then of we lesser animal forms?

* * * *

We profess that we value relationships so highly, and yet so many lie about us, broken and bitter. Recalling that our lives begin and end with a radical, traumatic disconnect from the other, with severed relationships as our Alpha and Omega, we are forced to frame our desire for the other as a primal, archaic need for reunion, for re-membering, for reconnecting. Even the etymology of *religion* intimates estrangement, separation, and a desire for binding back to the primal other. The early psychoanalytic circles spoke much of birth trauma—especially Otto Rank in *The Trauma of Birth*—and its reverberations through our physiology and psychology, and rightly so. Radically separated as we are, we also long for return. Yet return is as forbidden for us as those first parents described by John Milton in *Paradise Lost* who were blocked from returning to Eden, the gates to the paradise of primal linkage guarded by forbidding angels with flaming swords.

Each of us carries the archaic imago of that connected state within our souls, just as all our ancestors had their tribal stories of a primal disconnect to account for the rigors of their obviously fallen or estranged condition. We watch the infant shriek with terror when it is pulled from the warm bosom; we see the elderly yearn for the home they left behind. We daily enact the primal forces tearing at us in every moment: the forces of regression to the source opposed by a reluctant progression to the *telos*. In his 1912 *Symbols of Transformation*, Jung pronounces the spirit of evil as the negation of the life force, with its developmental agenda of individuation, by fear of the magnitude of such a task. While historically, such regressive agendas were opposed by those "great psychotherapeutic systems called the religions,"[1] today the modern is generally stripped of meaningful rites of passage and symbolic channels for the progression of libido. Thus, as Robert Johnson observed in *We*, "romantic" love now embodies for great masses the numinous appeal once embodied by the great religions.[2]

* * * *

The Persian poet Rumi relates:

> The minute I heard my first love story,
> I started looking for you,
> Not knowing how blind that was.
> Lovers don't finally meet somewhere—
> They're in each other all along.[3]

How easily Rumi's verse can be conscripted into the romantic phantasy of a "soul-mate," that one special person ordained by the gods as our complement, our completion. But, from an analytic perspective we can also say that we carry an intra-psychic imago of that missing, primal other in our archaic psyches and project its contours onto various others until there seems a congruence, not unlike the projective process onto the Rorschach inkblot. As projections are unconscious by definition, we inevitably see the other through the distorting lens of our intra-psychic imago and immediately transfer the history of our relationships onto the other as well. As the other always remains "other," not the artifact of our agenda, this twin process—*projection* and *transference*—occupies five stages. First, the projection occurs, unbeknownst to us. Second, the other as "other" fails to line up perfectly with the contours of the projective expectations, and third, we fall into a power complex which seeks to maneuver the other into conformity again. Fourth, the projection collapses… to the dismay of the subject. And, fifth, occasionally, rarely, the subject realizes that he or she was the source of the energetic exchange, and that the charged psychodrama recently transpired was occasioned by one's own archaic imago projection along with its concomitant, transferential agenda. In most cases, the subject is confused, disoriented, and likely to blame the other for the failed project. After repeated experiences of this sort, one either ends the relational dance in bitterness or resignation, or, occasionally, in assimilated knowledge of oneself. While this latter outcome is highly prized, it is almost always experienced as a disappointment when compared to the archaic urge to merge.

One of the leading anodynes of popular Western culture for the mythic disconnection of our time is romantic love. Serving the agenda of fusion, such a state promises immersion in the estranged other. (Other compelling ideologies are *materialism*, the filling of one's emptiness with objects, *drugging*, to anaesthetize the gap between hope and possibility, and *distraction*). I am incomplete; you are incomplete; together we will become a whole person. Whatever love is will only be found after this phantasy has dissolved, and the projections collapsed. What survives may well be worthy of that appellation, and yet few relationships survive the erosion of projection, and the frustration of transferential agenda. Jung's famous four-sided diagram of projection and transference illustrates twelve different directions in which psychic energy may flow. No wonder relationships are so complex. And they are complexified even further by the various archaic values of trust/distrust; approach/avoidance; passive/aggressive; worth/deficit, *et al.* which spin like axes of an internal gyroscope and orient the person in a pre-conceived vector toward the unknown other. Add to that the history of relationships embodied in the intra-psychic imago, and acquired relational strategies of self and other, and we have an immense historic traffic imposed on any relationship at any given moment. It is a wonder that any relationship can function sufficiently to provide sustained caring and emotionally constructive exchanges. Underneath the panoply of relational engagements is the hidden hope that the other will complete us, nurture and protect us, and if we are really fortunate, spare us the rigors of the individuation project. Yet from the rubble of this agenda, doomed to inevitable frustration, a series of principles and aphorisms may yet emerge worthy of the name of "love" and the high calling to which we are summoned as individuals.

* * * *

A mature view of relationship, its dynamics and purpose suggest:

1. What we do not know about ourselves (the unconscious) or do not wish to know about ourselves (our shadow) will be projected onto the other.

2. We project our childhood wounds and their "messages" (pathology), our infantile longing (Eden project), and our narcissism (immensity of unmet need) onto the other.

3. Since, upon reflection, the other cannot (and should not) carry our wounds and deferred maturation, the projection wears through and most frequently deteriorates into the problem of power.

4. After the inevitable frustration, even collapse of the Eden project, one is summoned to responsibility both for one's own individuation task, and one's archaic needs.

The first three steps of these premises are inevitable, and the fourth is occasional at best, for it asks of us a strength, a personal accountability, and an insight attained only at the price of relinquishing the Edenic agenda. Of that third stage, where most relationships flounder, we recall Jung's observation that "where power prevails, love is not." The problem is not "power," for power is the energy to address needs, tasks, goals; the problem is when power is co-opted into those compelling but doomed archaic agendas. Thus, where consciousness and accountability are lacking, power replaces relatedness. When one is left to face the summons of the fourth stage, one is now obliged to say to oneself, "what am I asking of this other that I need to provide for myself?" This question is heroic in character, and opens the possibility of something called "love" which allows, even celebrates the otherness of the other.

* * * *

Of this process of unavoidable projection and transference, of inevitable erosion and disappointment, certain theses or propositions may emerge which call us to psychological maturity and accountability. They include:

> 1. We are led inexorably by the logic of fate and the inherent limit of things finite to the reluctant conclusion that, no matter how much we hope, expect, solicit from the other, we can never achieve a more evolved relationship with another than we have achieved with that "other" which lies within ourselves.

> 2. Since projections are unconscious, we do not know we are viewing the other through the lens of our own psychological history and its archaic agenda. When they "fail" the projective expectations, we are dismayed, disappointed, disoriented, and perhaps even angered. Sooner or later, we are obliged to recognize that we are the one with those expectations, that we are the one present in all the relational histories of our lives, and therefore it is more about us than about the other. At that moment, we may be able to say: what I put out on the other has now come back to me, what I expected of the other I now have to expect of myself, and what I have been asking of the other I now need to address myself. (In the abstract, this "logic" sounds obvious; in reality, we normally have to fail at this relationship business many times before that point is rammed home into our defensive consciousness).

> 3. Owning the expectations and agenda of our projections can actually free the other to remain what they are: *other*. One might even say that such a collapse of expectations can open the door for something called *love*, namely, the caring for the well-being of the other as *other*, not as accessory to our projective agenda. Then

we may be able to reach a point where we can say instead: this person, no person, can give me what I wish and desire fully (the agenda of our archaic history), but I can celebrate and invest in what this relationship can bring.

4. What, then, one enquires, can we reasonably expect of the other to bring to our common table? What the other may best bring, paradoxically, is their *otherness*, an otherness that generates dialectic rather than fusion. Dialectic, the meeting of opposites and their tension that spills over into a more evolved Gestalt embodying a bit of each of them, is the gift. Fusion is the dynamic that produces stasis, regression, even infantilization. Dialectic is the principle of growth and development, that which stretches the ego and obliges its enlargement.

5. The completion of the archaic project, the *telos* of the fusion phantasy, returns us ineluctably to earlier places in our history, to fixations that are the enemy of individuation. The ecstasies, the transports of the "in love" state always involve a secret imperialism, a desire to conquer, subdue, colonize the other in service to the shaky monarch who rules our conscious kingdom. Given that the other remaining "other" is their best service to us, an enormous amount of growth is asked of us, a maturation beyond our desire, a confrontation with our inherent narcissism, and a summons to enlargement in which the ego is repositioned in a more capacious frame of self and world. The by-product for us is enlargement; the reward for the other is that they are valued as they are.

6. If and when a person relinquishes the phantasy of the "magical other," the archaic urgency for fusion, then the immensity of our own journey opens before our timorous eyes. We are then invited to step into a larger sphere, to find our place in the universe itself

and not just the arms of the beloved. The immensity
of our own journey is the greatest agenda of all: the
summons to the dignity of our brief moment here
before it ends in death and dissolution; but, it is our
journey, our naked presence before the mystery of
being to which we are summoned, just as the other
has a comparable summons. In caring for another, we
may support them, but we cannot meet that
summons for them, nor they for us.

7. A mature apprehension of the other then brings
with it an ever-deepening engagement with
mystery. Jung wrote once that "life is a short pause
between two great mysteries." Relationship,
intimate relationship, is an even shorter pause, but
incarnates as a profound slice of those mysteries. If
we understand, and value, that we are a profound
mystery to ourselves, always swimming in another,
still larger mystery, then we can more fully bring the
mystery that we are to the mystery of that other and
deepen our wonder, and sometimes our terror also.
In engaging the other within ourselves, we are more
competent to engage the other within our partners.
This meeting of multiple mysteries is inherently
developmental, meaningful, and rewarding to the
degree that we can bear what is asked of us. When
Jung observed that, "we all walk in shoes too small for
us," we understand the necessity and role of our
psychological and behavioral adaptations, but we also
intuit that something larger still is asked of us. An
encounter with the mystery of the other summons
that dialectic which enlarges rather than infantilizes.

8. Rainer Maria Rilke's description of relationship as
sharing one's solitude with another is a profound
recognition that even when we are with another, we
are alone. We are alone not only in that sack of skin
we call our bodies, and those idiosyncratic memories,
cognitions, and histories which chart our course for

us, but in our appointments with destiny and with our own way of dying. Yet, when we have an evolved relationship with ourselves, when we achieve solitude, we are not alone—we are present to ourselves. And that relationship can produce a goodly dialogue, a developmental, inherently interesting conversation. I have often thought that the real goal of psychoanalysis is not the removal of pathology, though often desirable and sometimes possible, but the achievement of a more interesting conversation around the meaning of our own journeys. The flight from being alone depletes that dialogue, and in the end is a flight from being with ourselves, and therefore a flight from being ourselves. If we can bear, sustain, humbly listen to the dialogue with the various parts of ourselves, the "others" that exist in all of us, then we can not only bring more to the other whom we profess to love, but can free them of so much of our archaic neediness. Jung suggested that the quality of individuation is a continuing exploration of the ego's brief transit through the timeless starry archipelagos within. So the quality of our relationship to others—partner, children, society—is a function of what is either known, or unresolved within ourselves.

Jung addressed this paradox of relationship in his observation that, "the unrelated human being lacks wholeness, for he can achieve wholeness only through the soul, and the soul cannot exist without its other side which is always found in a "*You*.""[4] We need to remember that Jung was describing not only the dialectic with the other "out there," but the other "in here." There is a "you" within as well when we view our psychic congeries through the lens of an enlarged ego consciousness.

Jung goes on to add, "Wholeness is a combination of I and You, and these show themselves to be parts of a transcendent unity whose nature can only be grasped symbolically."[5] Not only is that more holistic perspective possible when we understand that the great conversation may be found within the disparate planets of our own psychic universe, but that we are also part of another from the beginning, the forgetting of which is the error of the narcissistic ego in its fall from grace. Just as the first parents are mythopoetically expelled from the garden of grace, so the ego necessarily must differentiate itself from its roots in order to meet the tasks of daily life, but in so doing also separates itself from what theologian Paul Tillich called "the ground of Being." This separation from Being, Tillich argued, was in fact our "original," but inevitable, sin.

In the nineteenth century, the English poet Percy Shelley and the German philosopher Arthur Schopenhauer asked how is it that we can sometimes escape our own narcissistic sack of identity to feel the suffering of the other, and sometimes even overcome our first, most primitive agenda of self-preservation. How is it that we can achieve "empathy" or "sympathy" (*pathos*: Gk. for "suffering") or "compassion" (*passio*: Lat. "suffering") or *Mitleid* (Ger. "suffering with")? Both concluded that these states are possible because of that particularly human quality called the imagination, the power of constructing a picture (Ger. *Einbildungskraft*) that lifts us out of solipsistic ego identification and can image the experience of another. Shelley goes so far as to say that it is the imagination, not normative standards, that is the secret of moral life, and I agree with him. It is not rules, not prescriptive laws or scriptures, but our capacity to imagine the "other" that has led to human rights progress, desultory as it has been through history. Those limited in imaginative powers can only image what they have been taught. Complexes have limited imaginations. They can only say what they have known, repeat whatever script they embody as programmed by history. This limitation is why we evolved education, and travel, and analysis, and dream work—so that we may be provided further, larger images than those to which our limited ego experience has hitherto attained. (Ger. *Fortbildung* is the strengthening, adding to of images of possibility equals "continuing education," and education is etymologically derived from *educe* which means to draw forth from within the possibilities of the soul, possibilities much larger than those of which the ego is capable).

The symbol for personal wholeness is the archetypal image of the mandala. The symbol for relational wholeness is accordingly the *mandorla*, each individual honored, but wholeness magnified and containing a part of each other in an enlarged third. This engagement of the mysteries of both parties thus transforms toward a still larger mystery. The mandorla is both this and that, me and you, and a symbol of the transcendent unity of all being. This transcendent unity is forgotten by the ego, and the fallen world, but it is re-membered by the archetypal imagination. Only the archetypal imagination can re-member the primal unity which lies beneath our separate lives. Only the archetypal imagination can re-member our participation in the ground of Being.

* * * *

The shadow side of individuation lies in our common confusion that independence from the other, while truly necessary, is the final goal, and not a way-station. In order to achieve a separation from the archaic, regressive tidal surge of parental and tribal imagoes, this differentiation is necessary; however, an identification of the ego with that separateness is also the forgetting of our archetypal unity with all Being. (As William Wordsworth put it in his "Ode: Intimations of Immortality Recollected from Scenes of Early Childhood," we arrive "trailing clouds of glory," but by adolescence this *coniunctio* has been forsaken, forgotten, eroded and "fades into the light of common day.") Put another way, the project of the first half of life is to overcome the archaic, regressive agenda of the Eden project, the desire to merge with the source, whether the parental surrogate or its external analogues. This obligatory process, nominally called "growing up," requires differentiating the ego from the ground of Being, with the Self as our local, personalized agency of primal being. One might then say that the project of the second half of life is the reconnection of the ego with the Self which, while maintaining the properties of conscious responsibility for enactments in the world, is finally to serve the intentions of the Self, namely, to submit the dilatory will of the ego to an ego-transcending vehicle of Being. Each ego is summoned before a question, then, not "what do I want," but "what wants to enter the world through me?"

As we suffer life's necessary separations, its attendant rhythm of attachment and loss, we frequently are stuck in the apparent conclusion that we are not enough in ourselves for ourselves. As Goethe plaintively inquired, "*Was dauert im Wechseln*"—"What abides amid change?" Thus we are compulsively driven to recover that lost connection by merging with the other, almost any other. We impose on that other what we have not been able to find within the ground of Being, namely, the

Self as both our personalized medium, *métier*, and means. Such narcissistic agendas spring from our estrangement from the Self, and therefore produce similar estrangements from the external objects to whom our urgent libido is directed: persons, positions, objects, substances, roles, *et al.*

Paradoxically, the *telos* of individuation is not the attainment of separation, though separation is necessary as a phase of the process, but the recovery of the essential energy, the archetypal movement of spirit whose constancy informs all passing forms. The triune stages of this archetypal process called "the quest myth" asks of all first *departure*, then *initiation* which brings regression or enlargement, and finally *return*, not return as recovery of the old ego place and position but return to a transformed "home." As Shelley and Schopenhauer suspected, the archetypal imagination alone—neither narcissistic isolation nor dependency upon the other—redeems the estrangements within our being. In those moments of encounter with the essential mystery of the other, and the mystery that we are, the ego is enlarged, illumined, and suffused with the numinosity that arises from the ground of Being itself. Only then are we released from our dependency on the other, as all the great religions and various Twelve Step programs have long averred. And what they call that archetypal imaginal source and access is sometimes *God*, sometimes *the gods*, sometimes the *Higher Power*. William Blake called it, in one of history's least elegant phrases, "reorganized innocence." Whatever the name, whatever the form, whatever the venue of summons that come to each person, the force which promotes that reunification of the sundered soul—if we may strip it long enough from all its personal complexes and cultural associations—is *love.*

NOTES

[1] C.G. Jung, "VII. The Dual Mother," *in Symbols of Transformation, The Collected Works of C. G. Jung,* Vol. 5, eds. Sir Herbert Read, Michael Fordham, Gerhard Adler, William McGuire, trans. R.F.C. Hull (Princeton, NJ: Princeton University Press, 1967), §§ 551-553. (Future references to Jung's *Collected Works* will be by chapter title followed by volume and paragraph numbers.)

[2] Robert A. Johnson, *We: Understanding the Psychology of Romantic Love* (New York: HarperCollins Publishers, 1983).

[3] Jalal al-Din Rumi, "The minute I heard my first love story . . .," *The Essential Rumi*, trans. Coleman Barks with John Moyne, New Expanded Edition (NY: HarperCollins Publishers, 2004), p. 106.

[4] C.G. Jung, "The Psychology of the Transference," CW 16, § 454.

[5] *Ibid.*

5

Eros and
Psyche Revisited

Bernard Sartorius

I t is rather obvious that the development of psychic life and eros—relatedness to oneself and others as well as to nature and civilization—are intimately related. Humanity did not wait for psychoanalysis and analytical psychology to acknowledge this connection. Love stories and poems have long celebrated love as the initiatory process into the life of the soul, as evidenced for instance in the oriental story, *One Thousand and One Nights,* in which the beautiful Scheherazade transforms the wounded, furious, and bloodthirsty King Shariar into a normal, loving human being. Closer to us, Freud, our spiritual great-grandfather, writes to Jung at the time of Jung's erotic entanglement with Sabina Spielrein, "love" is that "with which we operate" as psychoanalysts.[1] The French psychoanalyst Jacques Lacan echoes: "At the outset of the analytical experience … was love, …. a dense [French, *épais*] and confusing beginning."[2] And Jung says "the problem that love poses is an incredibly high mountain, which the more I experience, the higher and higher it becomes, especially when I thought I have reached its top…"[3]

It is not without intention that I include in this introduction literary love stories and poems along with some quotes by our analytical forefathers. This is to give you a foretaste of the different qualities of consciousness concerning the Eros-psyche connection: the literary expressions, as found in *One Thousand and One Nights*, are symbolical and evocative through stories, images, and surrealistic wordings, while the psychoanalytical viewpoint consists of rational, conceptual descriptions. What I say here is of course banal, obvious, but we will discover the deeper implications. Lacan writes that, for Freud, analysis need entail "work" with love, which means to strive towards increasing consciousness of love's "dense and confusing beginning." An important step has to take place from the living of erotic relatedness "just so," i.e. unconsciously, to becoming conscious of it. For nearly one century now, years on the couch or in a chair under a mandala have been the institutionalized aspect of this "becoming conscious" of Eros. But here comes a question, the one that I will try to deal with in this essay: Why did our much respected colleague James Hillman (sadly, recently deceased) feel compelled to publish with Michael Ventura, *We've Had a Hundred Years of Psychotherapy—And the World's Getting Worse?*[4] Could it be that Freud's strong scientific interest in Eros in the family, and Jung's interest in Eros within one's own depths, to a large extent compensated for a deteriorating erotic relatedness to life? We would here understand relatedness to oneself, to others, and to reality as such, of which nature is the basic dimension!

We will now have a closer look at this question by examining one of the most significant stories humanity has produced, to illustrate the close connection between erotic relatedness and psychic life as a whole: the tale of Eros and Psyche. We will follow the version as transcribed by the Roman author Apuleius (125-170 AD) in *The Golden Ass.*[5]

Re-visiting the tale of Eros and Psyche, we will omit a number of the various angles that can shape our view of relatedness. For instance we will not use a physiological angle, as in the neurosciences; nor will we enter the playground of psychoanalysis with its emotional point of view; nor shall we engage cognitive psychology and its view of structures that seem to appear in relatedness; nor shall we adopt a sociological angle, with its contribution to systemic family therapy. Such approaches all have in common the attempt to describe from the *outside* possible aspects of relatedness—but not what I am after, namely the *subjective experience itself.*

Our story, as told by Apuleius, begins with a scene of jealousy: Venus, goddess of love, notices that Psyche, a young human (not divine) girl is more beautiful than herself. To punish Psyche for this, Venus schemes for her son Eros to induce Psyche to fall in love with "the most ugly, miserable and disfigured man" who ever lived on earth. Psyche on the other hand, despite her beauty, is not happy. For, although she is much admired, her extreme beauty frightens every man who dares to draw near her. An oracle inspired by Venus tells Psyche's parents that her situation is so hopeless that she should best be abandoned on a mountaintop and left to be killed by "dangerous vipers."

The *prima materia*, the "primal substance" of relatedness, appears here right at the outset of the tale. As the tale proceeds, the substance will unfold gradually, containing jealousy as a mark of narcissistic need. It can be detected in signs of a hurtful, "not-having-been-enough-seen" by one's parents. In other words: being wounded seems to belong to the very basis of related, erotic psychic life. In the story we spot the classical attempt to exorcise the anxiety resulting from this wound—just as we sense such exorcism in the reductive tendencies of the above-mentioned objective sciences: A jealous Venus aims to reduce Psyche, in her seductive beauty, to an object fulfilling the desire of an "ugly old man." The notion of the old man's purely physical lust for the young girl is mirrored in the image of the "dangerous vipers," conjured up at Venus's hand to frighten Psyche's parents. The mountaintop location of this threat points to idealization as an additional element that belongs to relatedness. As we will see later with the intervention of Psyche's sisters, idealization is one of the trademarks of the family complex.

Psyche accepts her fate and proceeds to the mountaintop to "meet her noble husband, born to destroy all life on earth." In other words: Psyche implicitly accepts the anticipation of death. This mental acceptance, foreshadowing her death toward the end of the tale, indicates the necessity of "death" in relatedness—or at least the necessity of death to one's expectations of what relatedness or true Eros is supposed to be. Psyche's naïve acceptance of death implies positively a purity of mind—while a lucidity, a clear awareness, would at this point rather be a mark of resistance. We will later come fully to this tension between awareness and unconsciousness in relatedness.

Yet, once on the mountaintop, Psyche experiences a radical surprise: instead of being devoured by the vipers, she is abducted by a "soft zephyr," a warm wind. This wind drops her on the "soft lawn" of a magnificent castle, which "produces its own light, even when the sun is not shining." She then naïvely enjoys the gifts brought to her by invisible beings—good food, wine, perfumes, fine clothing. And then, a next surprise: a "soft sound" awakens her. She is afraid because "she fears more than anything the danger of the unknown." But "suddenly this unknown husband of hers appears, enters her bed, makes her his wife and then disappears before dawn."

Psyche "fears more than anything the unknown." Fear is the natural first reaction of the soul confronted by an unknown reality—even when, as here, it manifests itself as a "soft sound" and with the enticements of seduction. Fear is *natural* because any real existential novelty challenges the ruling, secure references and structures of consciousness. In this episode of the tale, the change of consciousness awaiting Psyche is symbolically anticipated in the mysterious castle that produces its own light independently of the sun. The sun itself is a more or less universal symbol of an extraverted awareness of the primary realities. That is, the sun symbolizes our conscious experience of outer facts and inner happenings (thoughts, emotions, sensations, etc.) So the meeting with Eros in this castle does not belong to the hermeneutical realm of solar consciousness that catches the *describable* forms of inner and outer reality. In other words, Eros's castle "producing its own light" points to the need to acknowledge that our psychological theories and observations *do not* express the mystery of erotic relatedness (to oneself, to God, to the world, to others). The only thing our science can do—and this is of course not nothing—is to describe the inert, dead traces that the passage of Eros leaves in the soul—be it in childhood or any other stage of life. So Psyche's "fear" is all the more natural, as she senses she will be taken into a realm that transcends ordinary perception—that is, the realm of love's *mystery*. Thus the very symbolical core of relatedness is expressed in the tale with this strict minimum of words, "Eros makes Psyche his wife." To say more would be to do nothing but to add excessive and hollow description.

The tale continues: Eros informs Psyche that her parents lament her loss, convinced she had been killed by the dangerous vipers. But her sisters, not quite believing she is dead, are trying to find her. Because Psyche is "in pain of this separation," Eros agrees to her meeting with her sisters, cautioning: "It's up to you to take this risk, for you must indeed follow the needs of you heart. But I warn you: do not be seduced by your sisters' deadly injunctions to reveal my shape [Latin: *forma*]. Sacrilegious curiosity might tempt you to do so."

Here we find ourselves in the core of the symbol of relatedness, a symbol that is developed in the tale as a whole: The family complex—personified by the sisters—cannot accept that Eros remains invisible, in the dark. A family complex results from the various imprints that each family history makes upon the individual. And whatever the more or less dramatic aspects of that history may be, for everyone the family complex has a common feature: it wants to be reassuring. It wants us to have a life with stable features—clear criteria and references, clearly perceivable emotional tones, etc. So it is natural that the sisters push Psyche to see the shape of Eros in clear light. Jacques Lacan, expressing his own ambivalent acceptance of the necessity for Eros to remain invisible, observes that,

> Freud's psychoanalysis makes of him the master of that frightening and formidable [French: *redoubtable*] god "Eros." Like Socrates, Freud chose to serve Eros in order to be served by Eros. But our problem begins with this desire to be served by Eros. To be served by Eros—for what purpose? For we know that the domain of Eros reaches *far beyond* our well-being.[6]

We are now rather far from the usual efforts of psychology and the neurosciences that want to define Eros's shapes on all levels—downward to the biological ones, and upward to the most intricately spiritual. Such sciences aim in one way or another, maybe unconsciously, to master Eros with their defining theories, with their supposed knowledge of his shapes.

The tale's next episode shows the objective fact of our normal psychic reality that the family complex ("the sisters") wants to "see clearly;" the complex wants to illuminate relatedness in order to describe its shapes. Psyche, who in the meantime has become pregnant, agrees to her sisters' visit in her husband's palace. Uttering terrifying conjectures—"your husband is probably a snake [Latin: *serpentem*, which could also mean "dragon"] and your child will devour you"— they prod Psyche to the fatal step: She should bring a "shaded light," they coax her, to illuminate Eros, and also a knife, "to cut the knot between the head and the neck of the monster."

We see here the depth of our need to clearly define our relationships, compelled by the family complex. The sisters' anticipatory anxiety of finding Psyche in the presence of a "monster" points to our own fear of the immeasurable depth of the mystery of life and death, and of the connection of the two. The fear that Eros might be dangerous is indeed not only a fear of the unfamiliar and unknown. It indicates also that Eros and Death are somehow connected—and this not always or only in a symbolic or purely psychological sense. Literature and reality abound with stories of those who have gone to their graves in the name of love. Under the spell of this fear, the equipment that Psyche carries is very "psychoanalytical:" her shaded lamp casting indirect light could be an image of Freud's "floating attention"—and her "sharp knife" an image of clear and incisive mind.

The tale even underlines the *unavoidable* necessity of this scenario: As Psyche is exhausted by the endless discussions with her sisters, "*Destiny*" herself [Latin: *fatum*] provides Psyche with the renewed energy to find the lamp and knife she will need to shed light upon Eros—despite his firm order not to do so. Being fostered by Destiny, the need constellated by the family complex to clearly perceive Eros leads to the experience of the *paradoxical* reality of relatedness: When she sheds light upon her sleeping husband, Psyche discovers his beauty. Fascinated, she plays with his arrows, only to wound herself with one of them. And with this Psyche falls totally in love. "Lovesick and drunken with happiness," she doesn't notice when a drop of hot lamp oil falls upon Eros's shoulder. He is awakened, and "seeing that his trust has been betrayed in a horrible way," he predicts a terrible punishment for the sisters and declares that Psyche has lost him forever. Thus he departs, leaving Psyche "so unhappy that she wants to die."

Eros must remain hidden in the dark and at the same time, the family complex demands Eros's illumination. This paradoxical quality of relatedness reaches its peak when Psyche—having perceived Eros's beauty—injures herself with one of his arrows, falls fully and consciously in love—and, *at that very moment* loses him. In other words, the family complex induces us to see clearly those whom we love— and thus pushes us into the paroxysms of love in which the greatest proximity coincides with the greatest distance. Later in this essay I will venture a hypothesis about the finality of the paradox "when I have it, I lose it." We experience the same paradox, by the way, not only in relationship to others but also in relationship to ourselves— for instance, in the dead-end of introspection, and in relationship to any essential goal we might pursue. In artistic creativity this paradox is experienced intensely: The clearer the goal in the artist's mind—be that goal a piece of writing, a painting, a musical composition—the lesser is the chance to produce an important piece of art. And yet, without a goal, nothing will be produced.

At this point we might ask, could this unavoidable paradox— found in the very core of relatedness—contain *in itself finality*, that is, meaning for the so-called individuation process? I repeat: the most intense consciousness of relatedness presents the greatest risk of losing it. To illustrate this riddle, Lacan refers to the painting *Cupid and Psyche* by the Italian Renaissance artist, Jacopo Zucchi.[7]

This painting, depicted in Figure 1 on the next page, and Lacan's commentary might give us a lead concerning the inherent meaning of the Erotic paradox. Lacan sees what he calls a "castration complex" symbolized in Psyche's knife conjoined with an image of the flowers that seem to hide … nothing! "If the myth of Eros and Psyche has meaning," Lacan writes,

> … it is because Psyche begins to live as Psyche not simply by her extraordinary beauty equal to that of Venus and by having been given the invisible and mysterious gift of an infinite and fathomless happiness in "the love of Eros," no: she becomes fully Psyche by suffering pain, the pain specific to the soul and consisting in the fact that, in the very moment her desire fulfills her, it vanishes and leaves her. It is from that very moment on that Psyche's adventures and real life begin, from that abutment [French: *point-butée*], the castration complex.[8]

What does Lacan mean here? "Castration" of what? The answer seems to appear in Zucchi's painting. As Lacan sees it, the castration

Fig. 1: *Amor and Psyche* (1589) by Jacopo Zucchi (1541-1589), oil on canvas, 173x130 cm, in the Galleria Borghese, Rome.[9]

of the phallus here means the castration of "masculine intentionality"—with this understood to be a quality of consciousness existing in both genders at the very outset of relatedness: "I *want* this love, I *want* to save that marriage," etc. Lacan goes on: "The 'phallus,' as image of desire, is experienced only in as much as it obtains meaning and for that, 'the phallus' has to be cut."[10]

In other words: without castration of the phallic intention to possess the person we love, our desire would not be experienced as meaningful. Instead, as is probably the case with animals, we might be either satisfied or frustrated. But our desire would not result in meaningfulness in the sense of a psychic space through which we love this particular person beyond the satisfaction or frustration of desires. Thus we more clearly discern why love flourishes under the very light that also lets love vanish (see the flowers in the painting and their location). The impossibility in any relationship to penetrate the reality of the Other and the suffering linked with it creates a *new psychic space* in which, as Lacan writes, "begin Psyche's adventures." Implied here is a *history* of relatedness with its ups and downs, its crises and reconciliations, proximities and distances—in a word: a life of relatedness not in fantasy, but in real time and space. It is a life of love not reduced to the satisfaction of emotional, sensuous, and affective needs. To quote Lacan again: "From the conjunction of desire with an *inadequate* object will arise that meaningful experience we call *love*."[11] Thus the archetypal finality of the unavoidable paradox inherent in erotic relatedness means, practically speaking: The more clearly we are convinced about whom we desire, the lesser is the possibility of fulfillment. And this paradoxical situation creates a soul-space in which love—now irreducible to satisfied or frustrated desire—can be experienced as a "space" in which the meaning of love relates to *this* particular person, to *this* particular relationship.

The tale's succeeding episodes illustrate that the soul-space opened by the erotic paradox is, symbolically speaking, THE space of psychic evolution, of individuation. Apuleius tells us: after suffering the wound from the oil-lamp, Eros discloses his love for Psyche to his mother, Venus. As mother, the goddess is scandalized, and here we detect resonances of the Oedipal triangulation. But we notice that Eros's suffering, resulting from the erotic paradox, has indeed a maturing effect. For now Eros is able to confront his mother with his own story— a story that is no longer entangled in a mother-son symbiosis. His symbolical castration through the wounding (recall the "castrated" Eros of Zucchi's painting) accompanies his coming to adulthood.

Psyche, on her side, must flee the pursuing Venus, who is infuriated not only by Psyche's beauty but now also by the betrayal of her motherly love for Eros. This psychic situation points again, now in connection with the image of mother, to the basic reason why any truly new experience arouses fear: When we conceive "mother" as the matrix of everything that exists in our lives, then through infantile attachments we cling to this matrix. Anything *new*—remember, Psyche is pregnant—transgresses "mother." In this sense, guilt feelings always accompany erotic "adventures"—from the extraverted and "real" to the introverted and inner ones.

When Psyche tries to resist Venus she is subjected to mistreatment by Venus's employees, who bear the undisguised names, "Worry" and "Sorrow." Psyche is then obliged to undergo four tests, whose sole aim, in Venus's mind, is to insure Psyche's failure. Each test—which we shall presently examine—describes an aspect of the individuation process unfolding through the unsolvable erotic paradox. To enter into paradox—such as that in relatedness (when I have it, I lose it)—is to enter a conscious way of experiencing the psyche's underlying *dialectical* ongoings. And, at depth, Psyche's failure of Venus's tests proves to be another symbolic expression of the castration of masculine intentionality (as we have marked it Zucchi's painting, thanks to Lacan).

First, Psyche is given one single night to sort a huge quantity of seeds. As it evolves, not Psyche herself, but a group of ants perform this job for her. This test suggests that the ego alone is unable to sort or to structure the psychic potential—itself symbolized by the seeds. The ants—as insects and impossible to "relate to"—suggest self-structuring possibilities that lie far from the ego in Jung's "psychoid" dimension, where soul is embedded in the neurological body. Structuring impulses coming from the outside, for instance in our relations with parents, would be ineffectual without this archetypal and probably chromosomal self-structuring potential.

Unsatisfied with the successfully sorted seeds, Venus requires Psyche to bring her the golden wool that can be obtained only from the backs of the dangerous rams belonging to the sun god Apollo. Psyche hopes this deadly exposure to the rams will put an end to her suffering. A reed growing nearby, "in his simple sympathy for human beings," advises her to search for the wool "at the beginning of the evening when the sun has lost its heat" and the rams are settling down. Following the advice, Psyche is safe from attack by the rams, and manages to collect the wool that is caught in the low branches of some trees.

This test could illustrate the inner dynamics of the symbolic castration resulting from the erotic paradox. At first, the phallic drive of Desire has a stubborn and dangerous "sun ram" quality—"I *want* to see clearly if she/he loves me or not." The same drive is perceptible in Psyche's death wish: "Either I am re-united with Eros, or I succumb to death." To pass the test, Psyche needs advice from the reed, a plant having its roots in the water, in Yin, the feminine force. Aptly, the reed's advice is to take the wool at a moment "when the sun goes down," that is, when the strength of solar conscious— phallic intentionality—has weakened. *The Green Ray [Le Rayon vert]*, a movie by the French filmmaker Éric Rohmer, illustrates rather well the necessary and unavoidable dimming of intentional consciousness in relatedness. In this movie a young woman has spent the whole summer fruitlessly in search of a boyfriend. On her way back to Paris she waits for the train, sad and depressed. A man also waits for the train, sad and depressed for about the same reason. They meet on the platform, and now begins their love story. Taking the woman to watch an ocean sunset, the man tells her: "Look, at the very moment when the sun disappears behind the horizon, it emits a green ray." With the green ray recalling the green reed, it is as if the film, too, highlights a state in which consciousness loses its "sun-ram" intense, aggressive, and compulsive intentionality.

Of course, Venus is unhappy with Psyche's second success and submits her to a third test. Now she must collect water that flows from a mountain peak, but not just any water. It must be the water that springs from the River Styx, which flows through the Underworld. Psyche, still suicidal, climbs the mountain, where she is threatened by "those horrible waters" that are guarded by dangerous dragons who roar: "What are you doing here? Go away! Go away!" When Psyche wants to give up, "Fate sees the depression affecting this innocent soul [*anima*]," and the eagle of Jupiter, the supreme god, fetches the water that Venus wants.

This episode provides another view of the paradoxical quality of relatedness, symbolizing here more specifically the way we often experience it: Our important relationships are often highly idealized, containing lofty notions about our partners, our relationships as such, and how to live them. This would include the relationship to ourselves when we are, for instance, in analysis or in some other initiatory process or spiritual endeavor. As you know, the ideal is often symbolized by high mountains inhabited by gods, spirits, or other sources of divine revelation—Sinai, Arafat, Everest, and the Jungfrau in Switzerland. In our tale, the shadow side of the elevated ideal appears in the "horrible" infernal waters guarded by dragons, whose repellent roar—"go away, go away!"—points to the danger of idealization: To be too far "up" is to be remote from reality, and this has to be compensated by a counter-weight, the "infernal waters." Only the "eagle of Jupiter" can help, that is: The way out of this kind of relational muddle is not by resort to what we imagine should be achieved or avoided—but to rely upon an unexpected insight, a powerful, striking inspiration or intuition.

Of course Venus makes a fourth attempt to foil Psyche—and this time she will succeed. Now Psyche must use Venus's special box to collect a portion of the beauty that belongs Proserpine, the queen of the Underworld. Psyche, still wanting to end her suffering, climbs a tower, meaning to throw herself from its top. But the tower speaks, preventing her jump and providing advice. Above all, Psyche should not open the box after she receives Proserpine's beauty. Psyche manages to avoid all the traps except the last one: "Under the spell of a foolish curiosity, she opens the box. Instead of beauty, a deadly sleep overpowers her and she becomes at once a sleeping corpse [Latin: *cadaver dormiens*]."

The striking element in this episode is the tower giving good advice. This is a man-made construction that links the heights and the depths, the spiritual realm to the concrete. The "good advice" thus emerges from the integration of meaning with concrete reality, fact. But unlike a tree that might span the same dimensions in a natural spontaneous way, the constructed tower could refer to the indispensable role of culture, of human civilization, when Eros vanishes. We could speak of the moments or phases in relational life when Eros disappears behind pragmatic functioning and other extraverted "lights." To continue without great damage in an Eros-less period, a relationship would appear to require cultural references—values such those as we find in ethics, religion, and even analysis—for analysis itself is a cultural construct. Notice that Psyche could also have used the "tower" to kill herself: Cultural constructs, when misused—for instance to devalue one's self or others—can be deadly.

The purpose of Psyche's expedition into the Underworld—to obtain the box of beauty—could indicate the finality of the individuation process, in the sense of a direction but not of a goal to be reached through one's erotic life: each individual learns to accept the beauty of his or her soul and the mystery of his or her individuality. Thus we find ourselves again in the realm of the *not*-illuminated Eros— a realm not reducible to anything that conditions its shape—be that geography, culture, family, history, biology, etc. That's why this "beauty" must remain hidden in the "box." In Islamic spirituality, Allah and Beauty (*djamilah*) are symbolically connected, and this connection becomes visible for instance in the abstract, geometrical, mathematical features of the ornamentation and architecture of the mosques, and in craftsmanship and music. But in this case, we encounter a Beauty that points radically beyond itself to the Absolute Mystery. In other words, Allah is the totally non-describable "door" to life and death, which are united in Him. Similarly, Psyche's natural curiosity for beauty and death conjoin: opening the box, she hopes to obtain the beauty that belongs to the life of the young woman she is, and her death inevitably comes along with this encounter.

The *objective* impossibility of escaping the dilemma of "unconscious erotic relatedness or losing it"—and the impossibility for Psyche alone to master the four tests—parallel the impossibility for our egos to master our really important relationships. This is the case, despite various psychological recipes and techniques—analysis included. The situation as such pushes Psyche to surrender to what *is*—to a condition already visible in Zucchi's painting—namely the objective limit of phallic intentionality, which ultimately takes form in Psyche's sleeping corpse. And this is when, *synchronistically* the *miracle*—yes, the miracle—happens: In radical contradiction to Eros's promise that Psyche would never see him again, he returns to her sleeping corpse and awakens her. Thus she can complete the last task imposed upon her by Venus, to bring a portion of Proserpine's beauty.

The central quality of relatedness we have met throughout the tale is now illustrated in yet another way, namely in the image of Eros reappearing to revive Psyche even after he had vowed never to meet her again—and in his return despite her illusory hope to regain him by her own efforts. Ontologically Eros is, in its very essence, *unpredictable* and not makeable, whatever the technique, be it a psychological or a spiritual one. Eros appears synchronistically ("at the same time") at the moment of Psyche's deathly sleep, and this does not result from Psyche's failure or success—if she had had any to speak of. There is *no causal* connection between Eros's presence or absence and any kind of ego achievement. Eros's return occurs autonomously, we could say as an impulse from the unconscious (had this notion not in the last decades become increasingly a clinical concept in the service of ego-psychotherapy). It is the insolvable riddle—Eros wanting to stay in the dark juxtaposed with ego-consciousness wanting to see Eros clearly—that fosters the necessary castration of phallic intentionality. Thus this whole tale illustrates the psychology of living relatedness. Eros's unexpected re-appearance, conjoined with the motif of his intrinsic hiddenness, indicates that psychology does not and cannot explain relatedness. The best it can do is to point *toward* the reality of relatedness as it manifests itself visibly in neurological and emotional forms. In its very essence, it is miraculous.

The tale's very last episode takes place in heaven, where Eros introduces Psyche to the assembly of gods and goddesses. They bestow upon Psyche the status of an immortal, whereupon the marriage of Eros and Psyche is celebrated among all the deities. This marriage in heaven points toward the fact that our desire to connect with other people, with ourselves, and with reality as such does not belong to our ordinary desire to concretize everything. We can only agree with Hamlet: "To be [as one is], or not to be [by imagining that one should be different], that is the question." As the Q'uran says over and over again when referring to Eros—to the relatedness between man and God: *Allahou ouahdou iahlamou alhaqiqati*—"God alone knows the truth."[12] Or to follow Lacan: "To the egocentric question, 'who am I?,' there is from the perspective of the Other no other answer than: 'Let yourself be as you are.'"[13]

Let us now conclude:

As Apuleius' tale relays Psyche's search for Eros, every step of the way he illuminates our own psyche's experience of Eros. Thus we meet symbolically the paradoxical, essentially dialectical quality of living relatedness: Eros meets Psyche in darkness because he belongs to the divine mystery of life. The darkness that surrounds Eros is necessarily in tension with the normal, family complex-induced need to "see clearly," to define our relatedness. This often painful paradox results in the greater or smaller loss of that which we consciously seek, thus "castrating" the "phallic" intentionality inherent in our need to be related. There is no way out of this paradox; it is *the* place of Eros, a place that Lacan describes as *atopique*—a "no-place"—which is the no-place of the meaning of any specific relatedness.[14]

The four tests inflicted upon Psyche by Venus cannot be seen, in my view, as a set of tasks to be accomplished with the aim of retrieving lost love (although this is certainly Psyche's motivation). This is because with every success Venus presents Psyche with a new test until she fails. These tests are *as such* illustrations of the paradoxical and hence dialectical quality of relatedness: the dialectical interaction between our consciousness (Psyche) and our basic, psychoid, neuro-psychic structures (the ants); between our clear and active intention (solar rams) and our non-active expectancy (the reed's advice). Such dialectics result in the dimming or the "castration" (wool collected at sunset) of our too wild intentionality. We have also the dialectical interactions between our ideals of relatedness (mountaintop) and in close proximity, the unconscious, destructive impulses (waters from the Styx). This constitutes a relational dead-lock that can only be unlocked by a fresh, non-fabricated, genuine inspiration (eagle of Jupiter). Last, but not least, the dialectical quality of relatedness exists in the tension between being erotically alive (Psyche's urge to possess beauty) and the inherently accompanying abyss of nothingness, which can mean psychic or even physical death (the deathly sleep). This psychic tension can be held, disrupted, or destroyed with the help of cultural structures (the tower).

The dialectical quality of erotic relatedness implies the need for a specific hermeneutical approach particularly in our trade, psychoanalysis: we must come to accept the objective impossibility to adequately conceptualize what happens in relatedness and relationships. From the very moment we use such concepts we do of course carry Psyche's lamp and with its help, we glimpse Eros's outer shapes. But as analysts we are equally obliged to be aware of the consequences of our identification with this lamp. Moreover our analytic "light" does not illuminate Eros's waking life—but only his sleep. At any rate, attempts to conceptualize a dialectical, paradoxical reality such as relatedness, are, hermeneutically speaking, an illusory undertaking because *all* the elements of living relatedness need each other and thus cannot be isolated from one another by a collection of concepts.

This helps us to distinguish the diverging *intentions* of psychoanalysis and psychotherapy. On the basis of their own analyses (among other things) analysts realize that true relatedness to oneself, to others, to one's destiny, to reality, cannot be fabricated but is always again a miracle. Through repeated experience of this fact, we might, *Deo concedente* (as Jung put it), follow our clients' destinies—and together traverse the pathway toward individuation. In the process, psychic and even physical symptoms might decrease, and might even sometimes disappear. But this is not the intention of analysis. In analysis Eros and his abysmal depths—including morbidity and death—can be gradually accepted as unmanageable realities. Contrarily in psychotherapy we follow our patients' conscious aims to be relieved from problems and suffering, a goal that is largely carried by today's collective hopes for a "healthy" life. In service to this collective goal, we will try to use all possible "lamps"—be they scientific, rational knowledge or insights—to discover the causes of pathologies. And we will use the "knife" of adequate technique to relieve our patients' sufferings. Psychotherapy can of course deploy (and misuse?) Jungian analytical concepts (e.g. "shadow," "anima," "Self") and techniques (symbolic painting, active imagination). But this kind of practice ought not be allowed to blur the different *aims* of analysis and psychotherapy.

At the outset of this essay I asked if—starting with Freud and continuing with Jung—the analytical attempt to shed light upon the "night of Eros" might have attempted to compensate a creeping deterioration of human relatedness in modern civilization. My look at the archetypal story of Eros and Psyche could, in my view, confirm the hypothesis that indeed our post-industrial civilization witnesses the diminishment of living relatedness. After all, Freud and Jung were aware that "love is the substance of their work,"[15] and their re-discovery of the darkness of Eros—the "unconscious"—transpired slowly but surely within the 20th century. Yet their insights have been increasingly used by an ego-oriented psychotherapy and its utilitarian-minded "sisters-of-Psyche." Today's collective norms demand clarity and nothing but clarity. Psychiatry and psychotherapy often seem to serve not relatedness but the rupture of the dialectical life that would hold together the life-giving mystery and the regressive but reassuring light. Legislators ruling on the applications of psychotherapy want only academic, rational certainties. They are much surprised when Eros shows his dark, unpredictable quality, for instance in the growing public opposition against technical management of relational issues in education and health policies, or when those collective efforts meet unexpected failures.

Conclusion to these conclusions: A Tunisian colleague with an academic degree from the Sorbonne shared with me some of his own thoughts on the erotic paradox. He told me that for him, as a Muslim, it is self-evident that Eros wants to remain in the dark, because Eros is one of the manifestations of the Ultimate Reality, of the radically unknowable mystery of God. I thus conclude that the potential to live with Eros's mystery is indeed a religious one.

Al-hamdul'Illah

NOTES

[1] Sigmund Freud to C.G. Jung, Letter "134F," March 9, 1909, in Sigmund Freud and C.G. Jung, *The Freud/Jung Letters*, ed. William McGuire, trans. R.F.C. Hull and Rolf Mannheim, Abridged Edition (New Jersey: Princeton University Press, 1979), p. 100. For the original German, see Sigmund Freud, C.G. Jung, *Briefwechsel* (Frankfurt: S. Fischer-Verlag, 1974), p. 233.

[2] Jacques Lacan, *Le Séminaire, Livre VIII, le Transfert* (Paris: le Seuil, 1991), p. 12, my translation of Lacan here and throughout. [Eds.' note: In English, see Jacques Lacan, *The Seminar of Jacques Lacan: The Psychoses* (*Vol. Book III*), ed. Jacques Alain-Miller, trans. Russell Grigg (New York: W.W. Norton & Co., 1997).]

[3] C.G. Jung, Letter to Theodor Bovet, 25 November, 1922 in *C.G. Jung, Briefe I* (Olten: Walter-Verlag: 1973), p. 60, my translation. [Eds.' note: in English, see C.G. Jung, *Letters*, Vol. 1, 1906-1950, eds. Erhard

Adler and Aniela Jaffé, trans. R.F.C. Hull (Princeton, NJ: Princeton University Press, 1973).]

⁴ James Hillman and Michael Ventura, *We've Had a Hundred Years of Psychotherapy—And the World's Getting Worse* (New York: San Francisco, 1992).

⁵ Apulée, *Les Metamorphoses ou l'Âne d'or*, ed. and trans. Olivier Sers (Paris: Belles-Lettres, 2007). I follow this version because it contains the original Latin text. My translation and/or paraphrase throughout. [Eds.' note: In English, see Apuleius, *The Golden Ass, Or Metamorphosis*, ed. and trans. E.J. Kennedy (London: Penguin Books, 1998/2004)].

⁶ Lacan, *Le Seminar*, p. 18.

⁷ *Ibid.*, p. 268.

⁸ *Ibid*, p. 272.

⁹ Jacopo Zucchi's *Amor and Psyche* is in the public domain.

¹⁰ *Ibid.*

¹¹ *Ibid.*, Lacan's emphases.

¹² See for instance the Koran, Surah 27/6.

¹³ Lacan, *Le Seminar*, p. 284.

¹⁴ *Ibid.*, p.117.

¹⁵ Freud, in *Briefwechsel*, my translation, p. 233.

6

The Importance of Kissing: The Embrace in the Crayon Drawings of Aloïse

Lucienne Marguerat

Kisses can be given out of awe, respect, admiration, affection, or love and on different parts of the body—the forehead, the cheeks, the hands, the feet, the head, etc. Kisses are most sublime when they express love. Only when lovers kiss one another on the mouth, often with tongues touching, is a kiss not a one-way gift but an exchange, a mutual giving and receiving at the same time. All her life Aloïse Corbaz (1886-1964) dreamed of such a delight of the senses, of heart and soul. Her longing for love, passionate and idealistic, was never to be fulfilled. Locked up in an asylum from age thirty-two, diagnosed with paranoïd schizophrenia, she found in her art a way of surviving and even healing her wounds. We shall see that during nearly forty years of unrelenting creative work, her repeatedly drawn couples gradually come to life and turn toward each other, finally with arms and lips touching. Aloïse was in her seventies when her pictures finally expressed sensuous joy and tenderness. We can only guess that she herself finally found through her figures some kind of inner acceptance and love.

A BRIEF HISTORY OF KISSING

Before proceeding with Aloïse Corbaz, let us glimpse a short history of kissing. To put it very briefly, the *Kamasutra* (6th and 7th centuries) bears witness to the age-old art of sexual love and kissing. Sadly, of the sophisticated distinction the Romans made between three different sorts of kisses, little has survived in Western culture. The *basium* was the kiss of affection within the family. An *osculum* was exchanged as a sign of belonging and respect among peers, whereas the *suavium* was the sensuous love kiss. Only *basium* remained as a root in the Indo-European languages, to designate them all.

The early Christians practice the *basium*—a kiss of peace on the mouth—as a strong sign of belonging to the "family" of Christians. As the church establishes itself and the Christian community expands, kisses are exchanged among a growing number of men and women. So much so that Pope Innocent III finally decides that this type of kissing is going too far. In the early 13th century he generally prohibits the Christian kiss, permitting it only to a restricted group of priests on certain religious occasions.

At the same time, the *Minnesang* (12th and 13th century) is blossoming, poems and songs are extolling profane love and the delights of kissing. Love kisses reappear at the time of Renaissance (15th and 16th century). In 1534 the erudite young Dutch Johannes Secundus re-introduces the kiss into educated circles with his collection of nineteen poems on the ways of kissing.[1] He dies two years later, at the young age of twenty-four. In 2011 the Swiss journalist Christoph Bauer calls Secundus the "King of Kissers," thus attributing his important cultural contribution.[2]

Inspired by Secundus, in 1560 the Italian philosopher Francesco Patrizi wonders about the unique sweetness of love kisses.[3] He explains that by kissing on the mouth, lovers exchange vital fluids that nourish and rejuvenate their hearts. Other poets of that time are equally convinced that kisses have the power of prolonging life and bringing health and happiness. But only love will invoke the miracle: "*Un baiser n'est rien quand le coeur est muet*"—"a kiss is nothing if the heart keeps silent." French poets such as Louise Labé (1524-1566) and Pierre de Ronsard (1524-1585) give free rein to their delight:

Kiss me once more, kiss me again and kiss:
Give me one of your most savory ones,
Give me one of your most loving ones:
I will return you four, hotter than embers.
What do you complain? Oh, that I may appease this ache
By giving you ten more sweet ones.
Thus exchanging our kisses so blissful
Let us enjoy each other at our will.
Then double as long a life will follow.[4]

Thousand and thousand kisses give me, I beg you,
Love wants all unnumbered, love knows no law.[5]

Nevertheless a number of poems do not fail to note the ambivalent quality of kisses and the potential ferocity of passion. If kisses are truly a "key to paradise," their "burning sweetness" can grow into cruel bites.

In the name of modernity in 1764, the seventy-year-old Voltaire launches a campaign against kissing with his *Dictionnaire philosophique*.[6] Kissing, he criticizes, practiced among the aristocracy and the clergy and supposedly a sign of piety, is hypocritical and by common sense ought to be rejected. But Voltaire's fulminating rhetoric has no chance against the sweeping success of the love story published only a few years earlier by his young arch enemy Jean-Jacques Rousseau. Rousseau's novel, *Julie, or the New Heloise* (*La Nouvelle Héloïse*)—where the kiss is presented as a meeting of souls—wins the hearts of a whole generation, especially the scene in which the teacher St. Preux and his pupil Julie discover their impossible love in the exchange of a kiss.

Thirty years later Marquis de Sade's libertine novels also lay great emphasis on kissing—now however as a formidable asset in the game of seduction and abuse.[7] While Rousseau's idealistic view fades away, undeterred exponents of love's kiss remain. Heinrich Heine (1797-1856) for example evokes its ephemeral bliss:

Secrecy and silence should rest over love kisses, as over all else that regards the soul of love, so that the butterfly's wings may not lose their delicate down.[8]

In 1859 Francesco Hayez's light-hearted painting, *The Kiss* (*Il bacio*), makes its appearance and opens a short era of visually represented kisses. Toulouse Lautrec exhibits in 1892 the daring drawing, *In Bed, The Kiss* (*Dans le lit, le baiser*), which depicts two women lovers kissing. Auguste Rodin's 1898 sculpture *The Kiss* (*Le baiser*), showing a couple in a sensuous embrace, becomes immediately a public magnet. Francesco Brancusi's archaic sculpture, *The Kiss* (1907), consisting of a stone block divided by one single vertical groove, shows a couple kissing in a tight, inseparable embrace. Gustav Klimt's melancholic painting, *The Kiss* (1908), seems on the contrary to express the improbable meeting of man and woman. In 1928 René Magritte's *The Lovers* (*Les amants*) depicts a pair of lovers kissing blindly and without touching, for each of their heads are wrapped with veils. Ten years after the horrors of World War I, the belief in romantic love has dimmed. The question arises, is the communion of souls nothing more than pretense or illusion?

The young American film industry, with its puritanical stance against eroticism, permits only, as the lesser of evils, the strictly regulated kiss, which lasts at most three seconds. For twenty years (1934-1954), the Hays Code rules over "excessive or lustful kissing" in movies. Ironically, such restrictions make of kisses the epitome of love—no happy ending without a kiss. The film industry makes the Western custom of the kiss on the mouth known to the rest of the world.

Early psychoanalysts such as Sandor Ferenczi see in the love kiss a reconnection to mother's breast, which calls forth early memories of sweet sensations connected to a feeling of total dependency.[9] For a great number of men, Ferenczi posits, this might make of kissing an uneasy experience marked with a diffuse threat to their manhood. A later Freudian, Adam Phillips,[10] reflects also on a connection to early experience but in a lighter, more optimistic tone. As he sees it, the "apprenticeship of kissing in adolescence" is a second chance, or "oral education resumed." Hermann Schmitz,[11] an incisive phenomenologist, sees the mouth, within the context of the infant's early bodily experiences, as a first conveyer of subjectivity. The cavern of the mouth acts like a microcosm in which the baby probes the contacts of its soft tongue with hard obstacles (palate, jaws, later teeth) and thus obtains a first sense of "me" and "not-me"—or of "subject and object." To support his hypothesis, Schmitz mentions the delight taken by babies at playing with their lips and tongue, smacking their lips and producing sounds with their mouth. The sociologist and philosopher Edgar Morin looks back to the Renaissance spirit and age-old beliefs to reaffirm the numinous power of kisses, capable of bridging sensuality and spirituality:

> The kiss revives unconscious myths that identify the breath coming out of the mouth with the soul. It symbolizes a communion, a fusion of souls. It brings eros to the soul and mystery to the body.[12]

In 2011 two French authors simultaneously publish books that take a strong stand in favor of kissing, which they maintain has gone out of fashion: For Belinda Cannone,[13] a love kiss may truly be at odds with the world and the spirit of our time, but precisely this gives the kiss its unique charm. It means a surrender, a consent to the inner world of desire, and breaks with the usual pace of existence and flow of time. "In long moments of kissing," she writes, "we are coiled inside the world, with no questions and no needs, in perfect bliss."[14] Cannone emphasizes as well the numinous character of this exchange. When you kiss, she says, you enter the other's world—its smells, tastes, and memories. A kiss is a magical gesture opening the way to a whole cosmos unfolding beyond the body of the person kissed. A kiss is a mediation connecting two worlds, here and beyond; it is an experience at once physical and spiritual.[15]

Cannone's contemporary, Alexandre Lacroix,[16] observes a higher quality, a special nimbus that marks the difference between the sexual act and kissing. While intercourse might be a simple, instinctual act requiring no relationship, kissing is more intimate, springing from a need for a deeper union with the other:

> You can make love to someone when you have no feelings left for the person, and still enjoy it. But to kiss this person slowly, sensuously every day would be a torture.[17]

Lacroix speaks out of his own experience when he states that many men are no good at kissing, that they feel embarrassed and tend to "go straight to the body" rather than sharing a long kiss. Lacroix himself "[has] the feeling, excuse me, that kissing is 'something for girls.'"[18] Many men cope with it as they do with their own feminine side: Just as they generally want to restrain the feminine within themselves, so they also try to hold their kisses within certain limits. As Lacroix puts it,

> Whereas [men] feel strengthened in their manhood in the sexual
> act, especially in penetration, a long kiss feels to them like getting
> stuck in something slimy, some kind of surrender they had better
> not give in to.[19]

Thus for men, to be good at kissing would mean to lay down their
arms, that is, to give up the cynicism of the conqueror and to draw
on the tenderness of their "inner woman." Yet kissing is not just
pretty and sweet, but involves necessarily both inner parts of the
lover, the feminine and the masculine. In other words, kissing needs
time, slowness, and tenderness, but it wants also playfulness,
audacity, and roughness.

In epilogue to this section, let me summon the Austrian-born poet
of our time, Erich Fried (1921-1988). I shall kiss "not only your navel,"
he muses, "but also your questions . . ."[20]

CORBAZ IN THE TRADITION OF ART BRUT

The French artist Jean Dubuffet discovered the drawings of Aloïse
Corbaz in 1948. This discovery led Dubuffet to coin the term, "Art
Brut"—"raw art"—and to become the first collector of *Art Brut* works.
His interest was in the works of artists who were untrained and
"uncooked" by collective culture. In English-language realms the term
has sometimes been translated to the more widely inclusive "Outsider
Art." However in Europe *Art Brut* tends to retain Dubuffet's original
association to the purity and authenticity of the art of the mentally
ill, the subject of my interest.

Already in 1921, the highly prolific Adolf Wölfli (1864-1930), a
psychotic patient, had become known, thanks to the Swiss psychiatrist
Walter Morgentaler and his book on Wölfli's works.[21] In 1922 the
German psychiatrist and art historian Hans Prinzhorn published the
first comprehensive study of art produced in European mental
asylums.[22] Prinzhorn's study came to appeal very much to avant-garde
artists such as Paul Klee and Max Ernst as well as to Dubuffet himself.
Dubuffet's personal collection, begun officially in 1948, included
works by both Adolf Wölfli and Aloïse Corbaz, and it formed the basis
of what is now the *Collection de l'art brut*, housed permanently in
Lausanne, Switzerland.

Today Aloïse Corbaz is considered to be the most outstanding *Art
Brut* artist next to Adolf Wölfli. In the pages to come, I refer to her

colorful crayon drawings in a rather general way. Outstanding examples are held in the Lausanne *Collection de l'art brut*, which can be followed by online viewing.[23]

A Hidden Artist

For nearly her whole life Aloïse kept her passionate heart and mystical soul well hidden from most people. It seems that, like others with mental illness, as a young woman she failed to bring her idealistic yearnings down into the reality of *physis* and society. Instead, she suffered the constraints of a life locked up and cast away from the world. Not until after her death did it become obvious that her mind had been strong enough to construct an elaborate, grandiose, sacred world of her own. This was thanks to the discovery of her written opus about a universe immersed in light and love—a universe in which her suffering was elevated to a sacrifice comparable with Christ's.[24] But Aloïse nevertheless did open up during her lifetime. By revealing to her psychiatrist the drawings she had been creating in secrecy for almost twenty years, she allowed him some insight into the richness of her inner life. He and the woman doctor (general practitioner) who succeeded him were the ones who not only noticed Aloïse's natural talent, but were also deeply moved by the earnestness and depth of her quest for love.

For more than forty years of her artistic activity, Aloïse Corbaz struggles with portraying the couple, revealing a deep ambivalence in relationship to a masculine Other. During these years she creates innumerable portraits of an imposing, voluptuous woman of royal composure. The woman—whom Aloïse often names after famous historical or mythical female figures—generally faces the viewer, her bright red dress exposing her naked breasts. The man typically appears as a minute, barely noticeable figure. He either stands in a corner of the richly ornamented surroundings, or lies in the woman's lap, his gaze often turned toward her.

This striking imbalance changes very gradually in the course of the years. As the man's size increases and the woman becomes smaller, they come to meet eye-to-eye, and both figures lose some of their stiffness. They touch, sometimes even embrace each other, and kiss. Aloïse is over sixty years old when the man and woman finally come to life in her pictures and their mutual attraction becomes palpable.

According to Jacqueline Porret-Forel, the doctor who remained close to her to the end, by this time Aloïse herself has changed. In the last fifteen years of her life, as sensuousness and joy begin to spill into her drawings, she calms down and becomes more open to others.

PSYCHOSIS AND THE KISS OF INDIVIDUATION

Aloïse's is the rough story of an individuation process, pursued completely on its own, aided solely by artistic creativity, and supported at a respectful distance by a few individuals within her narrow circle. Becoming better acquainted with Aloïse, observing her more closely in her daily life and work, we may be able to understand what she was doing as she obstinately re-drew the couple's scene, and what might have been happening to her as the man and woman of her pictures were gradually transforming.

Aloïse Corbaz grows up as the seventh of eight children in Lausanne in the French part of Switzerland. Her father, an alcoholic, works for the post office. Her mother has a severe heart condition and dies when Aloïse is thirteen. Aloïse is intelligent. When she graduates from high school at eighteen, she speaks German as well as French. While she longs to become an opera singer, she starts to work as a teacher and then goes on to work as a supervisor in boarding schools. When she is twenty-five her family ends her passionate love affair with a former priest. With this, she leaves for Germany to work as a tutor for an aristocratic family in Leipzig.

Shortly afterward she moves to Potsdam, to work for the family of the emperor's minister. Life at the court of Emperor William II is pompous, strictly regimented and quite puritanical. Aloïse, having taken singing lessons, performs several times for the emperor. In 1913 or 1914, as World War I is about to break out, she returns to Switzerland. By this time, she has fallen deeply, obsessively, and delusionally in love with William II. Three years later she has her first psychotic breakdown. She becomes increasingly agitated. In 1918, when she is thirty-two, her family takes her to the psychiatric clinic where she is diagnosed with paranoïd schizophrenia. Two years later she is transferred to La Rosière, the clinic where she will be retained until her death at the age of seventy-eight.

In the clinic, Aloïse is sometimes totally apathetic, practically autistic. At other times she behaves obscenely, and can have sudden fits of jealousy or of rage. She falls passionately in love with a well-known minister, Pasteur Chamorel, whom she has never met. Again her longing goes to a prestigious man beyond her reach, a nearly divine figure. She writes imaginative, fiery letters, sometimes expressing her complaints against him. But she is a fiercely private person and keeps her writings to herself. She mumbles incomprehensible things in a language of her own, but does not communicate with others. She likes to sing at her open window, adding her own lyrics to melodies from operas. The appearance of this tall, redheaded woman with the strong voice is impressive. Neighbors call her "the opera singer." She loves to dress formally and go to the annual dances organized by the clinic. Her exquisite manners and elegance are unusual, and some nurses find her to be haughty.

Soon Aloïse starts to write in hiding, using a tiny, neat script to transcribe the vision of her own fantastic universe. She completes her first body of writing during her first three years at the clinic. She then begins to draw in secret, at first with pencils, on small pieces of paper. As time goes by, she starts to work with dark mixed colors. She gradually adopts an unwavering routine. In the mornings she irons laundry for the clinic, enjoying this neat, meticulous task. Her afternoons are devoted to drawing.

She is fifty-one, and has spent nearly twenty years in the clinic when she finally shows her drawings to her psychiatrist, Hans Steck. He supports her and begins to collect her drawings. In 1941 Steck encourages the general practioner, Dr. Jacqueline Porret-Forel, to meet Aloïse. Porret-Forel arranges an appointment, and appears for it wearing a green dress. Aloïse refuses to talk to her. "Go away," she commands, "you have no color!" Porret-Forel nevertheless sustains interest. She provides Aloïse with paper and crayons, and in the course of time, begins to collect her drawings. Over the years, the drawings become larger and the colors lighten up. When Aloïse is short of materials, she takes whatever paper she can find, smoothes it carefully and sews pieces together to obtain larger surfaces. If need be, she uses flowers or tooth paste for color.

With the passage of time Aloïse's isolation starts to give way. She allows Porret-Forel to approach and watch her at work. She offers her drawings to the medical staff or to interested visitors (among them Jean Dubuffet). Porret-Forel describes how Aloïse creates rolls of drawings by stitching together large sheets of wrapping paper.[25] By 1946, around the age of sixty, Aloïse is assembling monumental images measuring up to fourteen feet (fourteen meters) high. Bright red is her favorite color, applied to gowns, lips, and breasts. Her second favorite is blue, used for some clothing and for her figures' eyes, which she draws without pupils. Finally, she is also fond of green and yellow. She usually draws without a plan, seemingly talking to someone as she works. Porret-Forel understands that Aloïse is negotiating with her inner figures—who know how they want to be presented on paper, and whose will determines what Aloïse draws. Once finished, the drawings lose all interest for her. She does not find them beautiful or even worth saving. In her last years however she grows vaguely aware that they might be of interest to other people, and so she agrees to save them for Dr. Porret-Forel. At age seventy-seven, viewing the 1963 exhibition of her work at the Museum of Fine Arts in Lausanne, Aloïse is at first shocked and ashamed, refusing to recognize these "ugly" pictures as her own. On second sight, she is able to accept the public recognition. Unlike Adolf Wölfli, however, she remains doubtful and does not consider herself to be an artist.

Aloïse is well over sixty when she begins to have normal conversations with the few people she cares about, namely Dr. Porret-Forel and a nurse, Mrs. Berney, whom she particularly likes. With others she sustains her incoherent, "crazy" language. Aloïse eventually confides her regrets for having been afraid of love and for having "not dared to kiss" because of her religious upbringing:

> I have remained a bit candle, a bit Catholic, that's why I would like the other ladies to do the contrary, to have a good time. [I did not have children because I] never knew too well how to kiss. [I was] too little, did not dare kiss . . . at twenty you are shy, fearful, you don't dare, you run away.[26]

What a contrast to the gorgeous, self-confident heroines in her pictures! On paper, Aloïse seems to bring an ideal self-image, which we might understand as a compensation to the far too belittled self she identifies with consciously. The feminine figures she pictures are majestic, dressed in sumptuous, ornate garments, with streams of gems on their ample bosoms, and sometimes a tiara on their abundant hair. The ornate, formal surroundings evoke a theater or a royal court, a setting for role play and a show of splendor verging on the sacred.

For about twenty-five years, the radiant inner figure keeps wanting to come out on paper, dressed in and surrounded by much red. Yet again and again, Aloïse sets the stage for the appearance of an *unequal* couple, consisting of a sovereign "She" and a minor "Other." While the man gravitates like a satellite around the woman, either turned toward her or lying in her lap, the woman herself usually stares straight forward, indifferent to his presence. Apparently without Aloïse's awareness, the regal main figure seems to assert her deep, unflinching desire to be seen and loved. It is remarkable that, given her miserable inner state, Aloïse does not indulge in a narcissistic, grandiose self-representation. Instead, from early on and as if by necessity, most of her pictures include "the other," the man.

CONCLUSION

If we transpose Aloïse's archetypal search for a soul mate to the intra-psychic realm, we initially see an ego, a "She," nearly filling the whole psychic space, seeming to be only vaguely aware of a foreign, barely conscious "He" as "Other," and incapable of or unwilling to respond to his presence. Like a male persecutor in a repetitive dream, this neglected, denied psychic content persists and repeatedly demands to enter the picture. Gradually, with advances and retreats, the dominant "She" or ego grants "Him" more space. The self-ideal surrenders its splendid isolation, lets go of its absolute control, and recognizes the existence of another psychic force. While their sizes adjust to each other, She becoming smaller and He growing larger, their hips, arms, and faces lose their stiff appearance.

Trying for decades to bring these unequal and armored figures into closer proximity to one another, Aloïse finally allows them to become a couple joined in bodily trust, loving kisses, vibrant embrace. We can guess that Aloïse's late representations of the couple result from an individuation process where the trust and love that she had been circumambulating, at the same time reaching for and fearing them, have finally gained space within her psyche. The joyful union of opposites that has come out of her relentless creative work bears witness to an expansion of her psychic space, and her acceptance of an inner soul mate. At this time Jacqueline Porret-Forel notes that Aloïse has found some relief and is shyly opening up.

In her late years, Aloïse draws with more ease. Dr. Porret-Forel is convinced that she has found the way back to our world, to humanity and mortality. By means of her powerful creativity, under unconscious guidance and supported by few people, she has seemingly found a way to self acceptance and self love, enabling her to open up to others.

NOTES

[1] Joannes Secundus, *The Basia of Johannes Secundus*, ed. Wallace Rice, [translator uncited], Kessinger Publishing's Rare Reprints (Whitefish, MT: Kessinger Publishing, 2005; originally published by F.M. Morris, 1901).

[2] Christoph Bauer, "König der Küsser," *Neue Zürcher Zeitung*, December 16, 2011, my translation.

[3] Francesco Patrizi, cited in Alexandre Lacroix, *Contribution à la théorie du baiser* (Paris: Autrement, 2011), p. 36. Patrizi's dialogue about kissing, *Il Delfino, overo del bacio, dialogo*, was written in 1560.

[4] Louise Labé, 1555, *Sonnet XVIII*, quoted in Belinda Cannone, *Le baiser peut-être* (Paris: Alam, 2011), p. 23, my translation.

[5] Pierre de Ronsard, 1578, *Sonnets pour Hélène,* quoted in *ibid.*, p. 40, my translation.

[6] Voltaire, "Kissing," in *Philosophical Dictionary*, ed. and trans. H.I. Woolf, Hanover Historical Texts Project, Scanned by the Hanover College Department of History, 1995 (New York: Knopf, 1924), viewable at http://history.hanover.edu/texts/voltaire/volindex.html (accessed November 25, 2012).

[7] See for instance Marquis de Sade, "Justine or the Misfortunes of Virtue," in *The Complete Marquis de Sade*, Vol. I, trans. Dr. Paul J. Gillette (Los Angeles, CA: Holloway Publishing Company, 2005).

[8] Heinrich Heine, quoted in Christopher Nyrop, *The Kiss and Its History* (General Books LLC, 2009), p. 28.

[9] Sandor Ferenczi, *Thalassa: Psychanalyse des origines de la vie sexuelle* (1924), cited in Alexandre Lacroix, *Contribution à la théorie du baiser* (Paris: Autrement, 2011), p. 88.

[10] Adam Phillips, "Plotting for Kisses," in *On Kissing, Tickling and Being Bored* (London: Faber and Faber, 1991), pp. 99-107.

[11] Hermann Schmitz, "Der Mund," in *Der Leib* (Bonn: Bouvier: 1965), pp. 305-316.

[12] Edgar Morin, 1957, *Les stars*, quoted in Jean-Luc Tournier, *Petite encyclopédie du baiser* (Lausanne: Favre SA, 1984), p. 57, my translation.

[13] Belinda Cannone, *Le baiser peut-être* (Paris: Alma, 2011)

[14] *Ibid.*, p. 15, my translation.

[15] *Ibid.*, p. 103.

[16] Alexandre Lacroix, *Contribution à la théorie du baiser* (Paris: Autrement, 2011).

[17] *Ibid.*, p. 62, my translation.

[18] *Ibid.*, p. 86, my translation.

[19] *Ibid.*, p. 86, my translation.

[20] Erich Fried, "As You Should be Kissed," from "Wie Du solltest geküsst werden," translator unknown, viewable at http://articulosparapensar.wordpress.com/2012/10/31/erich-fried-como-debes-ser-besado/ (accessed May 4, 2013). Many of Fried's poems in English are collected in *Love Poems: Erich Fried*, trans. Stuart Hood (London: Alma Classics, 2012).

[21] Walter Morgentaler, *Ein Geisteskranker als Künstler: Adolf Wölfli*, Reprint (Berlin: Medusa Verlag, 1985); to my best knowledge, this work is not available in English.

[22] Hans Prinzhorn, *Artistry of the Mentally Ill: A Contribution to the Psychology and Psychopathology of Configuration* (1st publication in German, 1922), trans. Eric von Brockdorff, 2nd German edition, introduction by James L. Foy (Wien, New York: Springer-Verlag, 1995).

[23] Aloïse Corbaz, in *Collection de l'art brut Lausanne*, http://www.artbrut.ch/en/21004/1000/aloise (accessed May 4 2013).

[24] Jacqueline Porret-Forel, *La voleuse de mappemonde* (Carouge-Genève: Zoé, 2004).

[25] Jacqueline Porret-Forel, "Aloïse," in *L'Art Brut*, Compagnie de L'Art Brut (Paris: Fascicule 7, 1966).

[26] *Ibid.*, p. 89, my translation.

7

Girumeta dalla Montagna: The Divine Girl in Two Traditional Italian Folksongs

Regine Schweizer-Vüllers

Fig. 1: *Val di Campo* (Photo by Samuel Langmeier, 2008).

THE DIVINE GIRL

Following the topic of the Jungian Odyssey 2012, *Love: Traversing its Peaks and Valleys*, I will begin my essay with a song from the mountains of Ticino, the southern and Italian-speaking part of Switzerland. The song is very old, at least five hundred years and—if you are fortunate—you can still hear it live today. It is one of the very rare songs that originates from Ticino rather than from Italy, and it is of the type that arose in landscapes such as the one in Figure 1 above. The song is called "Girumeta dalla montagna," and it is quite short:

> *Girumeta dalla montagna*
> *vieni giù al pian*
> *veni un po' giù al pian, Girumeta bella*
> *suonarem la piva, balarem un po'.*

My translation:

> Girumeta, girl from the mountains,
> come down to the valley.
> Come down a little to the plain, beautiful Girumeta.
> Let us play the *piva* (bagpipe). Let us dance a little.

(I invite you to listen to two interpretations of this song—one by the music and acting trio *Tinta Blu*;[1] and one by the singers Roberto and Dimitri.[2] These and the other songs mentioned in this essay can be heard at: www.regineschweizer-vuellers.com).

I would like to ask you, what comes to your mind after having heard this song? What kind of feelings and emotions? What kind of images—inner images—are present while listening to it? Maybe you felt nothing special, because you were concerned about other things. But maybe this song touched something in your soul, a feeling that you know from your own experience. A sentiment you have had, a very personal experience suddenly comes up and into your consciousness. The song makes something become audible. A psychic string is touched in you. And thus this song becomes *your* song, although it is in a foreign language and it comes from a culture and country that you do not know. In other words, the song expresses a psychic experience that we may share with other human beings. It emerges from the collective layers of the soul. It is like a collective dream accompanied by a melody. Both the text and the melody may activate something in the depth of your psyche, make it alive, and in this way bring it closer to your heart.

In the following I will circumambulate (which literally means "walking around") this song with my own thoughts and ideas. And through this circumambulation or amplification, I hope I can make it clear that the main figure of the song, Girumeta, is a divine girl.

The text is very simple. There are just four lines. It is only one image or, better, it is just a wish. Someone—this can be a man or a woman, maybe a whole community, many individuals—wish that a girl comes down from the mountains to the valley, to the plain, maybe also into the village, where people live, in order to play music and to dance *un po'*—just a little bit. Who is that girl?

We do not know much about her. We know that she comes from the mountains. We know that she has a name. We know that she is beautiful. And we know that one human being or many human beings are longing for her. This girl can be an image for a new love, for a new enlivening experience of love. She may also represent an image for a new way of understanding the experience of love. For if we say she is an "image" (of something), then we mean that through her a new understanding occurs, a new meaning, for instance, of what love can be, of what love really means. In any case, it seems that the girl represents something of highest psychic value. She represents something divine or numinous, even as, in the song, she is clearly a human being. And this divine is not only expressed through the text, but more through the music that accompanies the text. Psychologically, she is an image of the archetype of the feminine. But she is a manifestation (or an aspect) of that archetype which is quite young, quite new, even eternal. She is a divine girl or a Kore. When she occurs in dreams she represents a certain aspect of the anima, the unconscious image of the feminine in a man and of the Self—Jung calls it the "inner, greater personality"—in a woman.[3]

Let me show you this with two dreams. One comes from a man, fifty-five years old, who had several dreams in which a young girl appeared. One of them goes like this:

> Someone wishes that a girl should stay with us. But
> the girl runs away as if she were in a panic. I call her
> and she comes back. I take her into my arms and talk

> to her as to a friend. I ask her whether she is afraid of
> lightning, and tell her that I am not afraid of lightning
> or of thunder. Then I suggest that she could stay with
> us. My wife joins us. She sees that we have a good time
> together and leaves again. Then the girl starts to play
> the lyre on the balcony. I become more and more
> friendly with her.

Dealing with such a dream, it is important whether the dreamer is
emotionally touched by the dream or not. The girl symbolizes a young
and new feeling value in this man, something that wants to develop
in him. We can call this "something" psyche or soul or anima. In the
dream she plays the lyre. She plays music. Music means expression of
feelings or emotions. This man later experienced a deep love with a
woman in quite a new way. It is as if the unconscious anticipated this
later numinous experience.

The dreamer of the following dream is a woman, forty-seven years
old. It is the initial dream of her analysis. She is a musician. But for
many years she could not play music.

> I see a child. It must be a girl, for she wears a little
> skirt. She stands in a room. I come into this room and
> see her. I look at her. But, looking at her, I can hear
> music. It is a wonderful music, music of Bach—the
> Italian symphony. The music sounds loud and clear,
> *forte*, but still very, very musical. It is the girl who
> plays this music. But there is no piano in the room.
> The girl is just standing there. The music must come
> from her. She is the source and the origin of it.
> Looking at her I can hear this wonderful music.

The girl, the source and origin of the music in the dream, stands for
the dreamer's overwhelming experience of finding a new approach to
her psyche, to the world of dreams and inner images in the process of
her analysis. But the girl represents also her love for music, the
experience of being a musician that she could not have for such a long
time. I think the girl in this dream is really a divine girl, magic and
numinous, an image for the Self, for the greater personality that wants
to be recognized in the dreamer.

THE MANDALA DANCE OR THE CIRCLE

I think we can compare the girl in our song with the girl of such dreams. She represents a young anima in a man or the Self in a woman. Now, the girl in the song has a name. Her name, "Girumeta," is a strange one. It is not ordinarily used as a first name in the Italian language. In order to find out more about this name (and thus more about the girl), we have to look at the hidden meaning of it. "Girumeta" contains two aspects: the word *méta*, that is, the "aim" (*arrivare alla méta* means "to reach the goal"), and the word *girare*. *Giro* is the circle, the round one. *Girare* can mean "to turn something around"—but also "to turn around one's own bodily axis." *Girasole* is Italian for sunflower, because this flower turns itself around to always face the sun. *Girasoline* is the small sunflower. In German, we call it the *Sonnenauge*—literally translated, the "suneye."

This means that Girumeta is a female being who circles around her own axis, thus creating roundness or wholeness. High up in the mountains, Girumeta enacts or dances a mandala—"mandala" being Sanskrit for "circle" (*giro*), or she herself embodies a mandala. It is very strange that the longing for love or the longing for an encounter with the beloved in this song is expressed by a girl, a human being, but, at the same time, by a circle or a mandala. This is a paradox. It could mean that this love (or the encounter with the divine girl), besides the concrete experience, secretly has an inner aim (*méta*), namely, to lead a man or a woman to his or her inner wholeness. This would be the circle or the mandala.

In his article, "Concerning Mandala Symbolism," Jung writes:

> There are innumerable variants of the motif . . . . Their basic motive is the premonition of a centre of personality, a kind of central point within the psyche, to which everything is related, by which everything is arranged, and which is itself a source of energy. The energy of the central point is manifested in the almost irresistible compulsion and urge *to become what one is*, just as every organism is driven to assume the form that is characteristic of its nature, no matter what the circumstances. This centre is not felt or thought of as the ego but, if one may so express it, as the *self*. [4]

And in another place Jung says, "the mandala, that is . . . the innermost divine essence of man, is characterized by symbols which can just as well express a God-image, namely the image of a Deity unfolding in the world, in nature, and in man."[5]

Mandalas are not only painted or drawn or made out of colored sand on the floor as the monks in Tibet and the Navajo Indians do. Mandalas can also be danced. In India such a dance is called *mandala nrithya*, mandala dance.[6] When people paint a mandala or make mandalas out of stones or dance the mandala dance, they try instinctively to be related with a "center of personality" or a "central point within the psyche," as Jung puts it. But in the song it is not a human being in the valley; it is the girl in the mountains, it is Girumeta who is—far away and high up—turning around or dancing the mandala dance. She does not represent a human ego, but rather an inner image or a psychic value. She or this image is turning around. "Moving or circling around" normally means psychic development. It means creation or the dawning of a new consciousness in the psyche. Something new wants to develop or has been created already. This new idea or consciousness or value does not come from the ego. It comes from the mountains, that is, from the Beyond. This new value wants to incarnate in a man's or a woman's psyche. It wants to come to earth, so to speak. Thus it arouses longing in a man's or a woman's heart. If accepted it can help us to become what we are or to find "our innermost core," as Jung describes it.

Anadyomene is the Greek word for a goddess, who arises all of sudden and thus appears as a new-born divine being. Aphrodite was called an *anadyomene* because she appeared suddenly out of the sea. We might also call Girumeta dalla montagna an *anadyomene* and thus compare her with Aphrodite Kore (Aphrodite as a young girl or as a young goddess), who arises in the mountains, in the Beyond, and now should come down and descend to the valley and into human reality. I wonder whether this coming down to earth can be connected with the fact that the song originates from the era of the Renaissance.

Now we may ask ourselves: "Can we compare the highly revered Greek goddess Aphrodite with Girumeta, the girl in this humble song from the mountains of Ticino? Isn't it a little bit overdone?" The question brought me to the music and to a consideration of whether something could be found in the music or in the musical structures of the song that corresponds with my interpretation of the text. Does the music express the same psychic value as the words? Might we even find aspects of the archetypal image in the music that cannot be seen in the text alone? The problem is, how are we to understand musical structures or the language of music in terms of Jungian psychology? I pondered this question for several years and cannot go into all the details. But I would like to show you two or three aspects.[7]

MUSICAL STRUCTURES: THE MELODY THAT FORMS A CIRCLE

Traditionally the text of the song is sung four times, two times in a minor key and two times in a major key.[8] The song starts in D minor, changes to D major, then goes back to D minor and finally returns to D major. For me this is a circle. (See Figure 2 below) It is a fourfold structured circle or a fourfold structured mandala, spread out in time. Major and minor are opposites. They give expression to opposites in the domain of feelings and emotions. When we listen to the song—first in minor, then in major, then in minor, then in major again, we "know" through our feelings that longing and desire, sadness and happiness, despair and fulfillment, resignation and hope all belong necessarily to the experience of love or to the encounter with the divine girl.

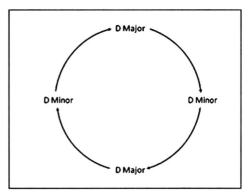

Fig. 2: D Major and D Minor—A Circle or a Mandala.

D minor and D major are opposites, expressed musically.[9] When you try to accompany the song with a guitar or a piano you will realize this immediately. The only thing that both keys have in common is the keynote or the basic sound "D." But still, despite their being—musically—opposites, they belong together. Through their opposition they form a whole or a circle.

Musical Structures: The Sixth and its Symbolic Meaning

Let us come to the melody. A melody is a sequence of single sounds. These sounds are related to each other. And the relationship between them is expressed through numbers.[10] We have the fourth, the fifth, the octave, and so on. There is a long tradition, throughout the Middle Ages, going back to Pythagoras and even further back in history, according to which musical intervals are numbers that resound—"ringing numbers," so to say. In Jungian psychology we consider numbers as symbols. Thus we understand numbers not only in their quantitative aspect but in their qualitative aspect as well. Marie-Louise von Franz tried to describe this empirically in her book, *Number and Time*.[11] Each number—let us say from 1 to 10—expresses a symbol referring to something alive. It has or expresses a psychic quality. In other words, each number represents an archetypal image. To each one belongs a specific deity. To the number three belongs a deity, to the number two, to four, and so on. If we, therefore, understand musical intervals as numbers that resound, then we can also understand them as symbols or as archetypal images. Thus to each interval belongs a particular deity as well. Now, in our song, there is one interval that dominates from the beginning to the end. And that is the sixth.

The melody starts with a triad in minor (D-F-A) and leads from the basic sound D to the fifth. But it does not stop here. (See Figure 3 below) It goes one step higher, namely, to the sixth (to the minor sixth) in order to go down from this point or return in some smaller

Fig. 3: Musical Score to "Girumeta" (Trad.).

movements to the basic sound D and the word *pian*. The sixth is—
melodically seen—the aim (*méta*) that is hidden in the name of the
girl, Gi-ru-me-ta. It is the goal or the highest value in the song. The
melody leads to the sixth also in the second sequence, but this time
in a kind of scale. It climbs up to the top as on a staircase (*scala* means
staircase in Italian) in order to return again in some smaller movements
to the basic sound (D).

The whole musical space in which the melody unfolds is not more
than a sixth, whether in minor or in major. That is, the whole song
and what should be expressed through it takes place in the frame of
this interval. Therefore we have to look now to the symbolic meaning
of the number six. Which deity is associated with this number?

Six is considered the "perfect number"—*arithmos teleios*.[12] "*Teleios*"
means "complete," "bringing fulfillment," "effective." Six is the number
of harmony and the number of a harmonic relation of the opposites.
The opposites are mathematically seen as two and three, but
symbolically seen as female and male. Six is the number of Eros. In
nature it appears for instance in the hexagonal cells of the honeycomb.
Within these cells is created the honey, which according to many
religions, is the "sweetness of the earth." In Greek the number six was
called *gamos*,[13] which means wedding or *coniunctio*. It symbolizes the
union between a man and a woman, male and female, heaven and
earth, spirit and body. In alchemy the number six is the link between
spirit and body, namely the soul. The sixth is called the number "most
suited to generation" (*numerus generationi aptissimus*) or the number
of "creation and evolution."[14] Finally six is the number of Aphrodite
or Venus, who appears in heaven as the six-pointed morning star. In
an old treatise from the 4th century the relationship between the
number six and the goddess Aphrodite or the morning star is described,
and there it is said:

> ... the number six is soul-producing . . ., because it multiplies
> itself into the world-sphere . . ., and because in it the opposites
> are mingled. It leads to like-mindedness (*homonoia*) and
> friendship, giving health to the body, harmony to songs and
> music, virtue to the soul, prosperity to the state, and forethought
> (*pronoia*) to the universe.[15]

Some musicians call the sixth "the interval of longing." For instance,
in Mozart's opera, *The Magic Flute*, there is an aria which starts with

the words: "This picture is enchanting fair." Prince Tamino holds a picture of Pamina for the first time in his hands. He sees the image. It is the moment when he becomes conscious of his love. The first interval in this aria on the words "this picture" is the major sixth. In the last part of the opera, Tamino and Pamina, the man and the woman, have to go through water and fire. Before they undergo this initiation they meet and see each other after a long period of troubles, misunderstandings, and pains. It is a moment of great relief and fulfillment. Pamina sings: "My Tamino, oh what happiness." The first interval, the interval on the name of her beloved, Tamino, is the major sixth. He answers her and begins with the fourth.

Girumeta and the Animals

Let us now return to the song to explore two further aspects, namely the relationship between Girumeta and the animals, and the symbolic meaning of the mountains. Regarding her relationship with the animals, *girare* has a second meaning. It not only means "to turn around oneself," but also to "wander around" or "stroll around." And *giro* is not only a "circle." It also means "walking tour" as well. Therefore, "Girumeta dalla montagna" is not only the one who is turning around and becoming herself through this movement. She is also the one who strolls around in the mountains, who walks around, namely, with and among the animals. In the translations of the song she is always called "shepherdess." Thus, she can be seen as the young girl who lives in the mountains with a flock of animals. She keeps these animals together. She protects them. She leads them to the pastures with good grass. *Pecore*, "small cattle," as are they called in the Ticino. They could be sheep, but mostly they were goats, or both. And indeed, in former times mainly the women and the young girls or the children took care of them and had to provide for them.

Actually life in the mountains and with the cattle was or is like a circle. It is a huge circle, the circle of nature through the whole year, always according to the position of the sun. In spring, when the cows left the stables for the new grass, men and the older boys did that work. They left the valleys and went up to the mountains, always following the growing grass, from one alp to the other higher one until they came down in autumn, slowly, step by step and always in the same annual rhythm. At the latest at Christmas they had to be back in the villages. But apart from the meadows for the cows—that is, in the forests, or in places where it was much too steep and too dangerous for them, and up on the highest slopes and in small places where there was grass between stones and rocks—the young women, the young girls, or the children cared for the *pecore*, the sheep and the goats, during the summer. That was their world. Thus, Girumeta is also the shepherdess, who lives with her flock of animals high up in the mountains and strolls around with them.

Considering the concrete reality of these children who had to tend to the goats or sheep during the summer, we have to imagine what it meant to live alone or in pairs with the animals high up in the mountains, with the hot sun, with wind, storm, and rain, with very primitive shelters, sometimes only a rock or a cave or a little hut. And these children were eight or ten, twelve or sixteen years old. However, when you have the chance to speak with old people in the Ticino and when they start telling you about these things, then it seems that it was the best time of their whole life. They were young. They were children. They were free, standing on their own feet, responsible only for themselves and for the animals. There was no control through mother and father, and the neighbors and the teachers or the church. Sure enough, it was a hard life. But it was also an intensive life. And we have to assume that inner images, archetypal images like Girumeta, the shepherd girl in the song, are rooted in the daily life of men and women and cannot be seen as separated from their concrete experiences. The experiences of generations of men and women are connected with these images. They come from the depth of their soul.

But apart from this concrete historical reality, the shepherdess, who walks around with her animals from one place to another, is an archetypal image as well. Symbolically speaking, she is a mistress of the animals, not of wild animals like Artemis or other goddesses, but of domesticated animals that give people nourishment, meat, cheese, milk or protection and warmth, wool and leather. So Girumeta, the divine girl, is connected with this animal side in women and in men, with the supportive drives and instincts. She knows how to deal with them. She holds them together. She takes care of them and looks after them, so that they are nourished and get their daily food.

I cannot avoid mentioning the "Song of Songs" in the Bible, where the beloved woman is also a shepherdess. She says: "Tell me, you whom my soul loves, where you pasture your flock, where you make it lie down at noon?"[16] And her beloved replies, "If you do not know, o most beautiful among women, follow in the tracks of the flock, and pasture your young goats beside the shepherd's tent."[17] He continues,

> Behold, you are beautiful, my love, behold, you are beautiful! Your eyes are doves behind your veil. Your hair is like a flock of goats, leaping down the slopes of Gilead, your teeth are like a flock of shorn ewes that have come up from the washing all of which bear twins, and not one among them has lost its young.[18]

And then he says to her:

> Come with me from Lebanon, my bride; come with me from Lebanon. Depart from the peak of Amana, from the peak of Senir and Hermon, from the dens of the lions, from the mountains of leopards.[19]

COMING DOWN FROM THE MOUNTAINS

This brings us to the motif of the mountains. "Girumeta" is called *dalla montagna*—"of or belonging to the mountains." Maybe the mountains even belong to her. What is the symbolic meaning of the mountains? What do they represent and why does Girumeta come from there? Imagine you are in the mountains or in a mountain valley (*al pian'*), and it is evening and you look up to the mountains. Then on the summits of the mountains everything is full of sun and full of light, while down in the valley it has already become shady and cool. And when the sun has disappeared, when the last light is gone, then it is dark and it is night and it is cold. And imagine, you awake early enough the next morning and you go outside. Then again the valley is still lying in the shadow or in darkness. But on the summits of the mountains you can see the first light. This light becomes bigger. Suddenly the sun appears. It or its rays come down slowly, slowly. They bring the light. They bring the day. They bring the warmth. For people living in the mountains, it is a primeval, archetypal experience that the sun, and with it the light, comes from the mountains. That's where Girumeta comes from. She comes out of a world full of light and full of sun.

Yes, we can say, she is the light. She is the new light and the new sun, which—according to the song—should come down to the people who live in the valley, on the plain.

There is a marvelous myth told by the Navajo Indians, which Jung quotes in his lecture about the visions of Zosimos.[20] The myth tells that a young goddess revealed herself on the top of a mountain. When the ancestors found her, she was a stone, a turquoise. Then she turned into, or gave birth to "the woman who rejuvenates or transforms herself"—that was the meaning of her name, *Estsanatlehi*. She was called "the mother or the grandmother of all gods." And she was so sacred that it was forbidden to make an image of her. Even the other gods were not allowed look on her face. Jung called her "a true *Dea Natura*." She is the whole of nature. As nature she grows old and rejuvenates herself as a young girl again and again. Of course Girumeta is not quite the same. She does not represent the whole of nature. She represents a certain aspect of nature. But, like the "turquoise goddess" of the Navajo, she also reveals herself on the top of the mountains or in the mountains.

The mountain, or the mountains in general, are a symbol of the Self. The mountains are the domain of the Gods or the demons. Or the mountain is the Godhead itself. There is the cosmic mountain, the center of the whole world, which as the *axis mundi*, connects heaven and earth. In India it is Mount Meru, the mountain from which all waters of the earth come down. So, in fact, not only the new light, the new sun, comes from the mountains. All the waters, brooks, rivers, and streams come from there too. That means that all psychic life comes from there as well, because water is life. In the *I Ching*, Hexagram 52, "Keeping Still" or "The Mountain," it is said: The mountain "is the mysterious place where all things begin and end, where death and birth pass one into the other."[21] Thus mountains are not only the place where a development begins. They are also where it comes to an end. And they are where things can change.

The mountains are the domain of the Beyond, which is the world of the archetypes. People have always projected the unconscious onto (and also experienced them as) such a realm. That is, a realm in which the human region, the cultivated land and the built up area have come to an end. In this sense the sea can be the collective unconscious. Or today very often it is the universe. But also mountains can symbolize the world of the unknown unconscious. Therefore "Girumeta dalla montagna" would be the divine girl, the Kore, who arises and should come down out of the unconscious or out of the eternal world to the valley, that is, to the human world. That is the essence of the song.

Toward an Inner Meaning of the Divine Girl

Now I will consider the meaning or the aim (*méta*) of an encounter with the divine girl. The song "Girumeta dalla montagna" mirrors the longing of many people. It is the deep longing for an experience of true love. But it is also the longing for an understanding of such an encounter. Maybe we can say it is the longing for a new God image, a new feminine God image. As I wondered what an encounter with the divine girl might mean and what could belong to this new God image, four aspects came to my mind. And to a fifth aspect we will come when we look at the second song.

In the last chapter of *Memories, Dreams, Reflections*, Jung quotes St. Paul, in I Corinthians 13. You may be familiar with St. Paul's words:

> If I speak in the tongues of men and of angels, but have not love, I am a noisy gong or a clanging cymbal. And if I have prophetic powers, and understand all mysteries and all knowledge, and if I have all faith, so as to remove mountains, but have not love, I am nothing. If I give away all I have, and if I deliver my body to be burned, but have not love, I gain nothing. Love is patient and kind; love is not jealous or boastful; it is not arrogant or rude. Love does not insist on its own way; it is not irritable or resentful; it does not rejoice at wrong, but rejoices in the right. Love bears all things, believes all things, hopes all things, endures all things. Love never ends.

This means Eros or love has strong religious overtones. Jung comments on this passage as follows:

> Love "bears all things" and "endures all things" (I Cor. 13:7). These words say all there is to be said; nothing can be added to them. For we are in the deepest sense the victims and the instruments of cosmogonic "love." I put the word in quotation marks to indicate that I do not use it in its connotations of desiring, preferring, favoring, wishing, and similar feelings, but as something superior to the individual, a unified and undivided whole. Being a part, man [or the human being] cannot grasp the whole. He is at its mercy. He may assent to it or rebel against

it; but he [or she] is always caught up by it and enclosed within
it. He [or she] is dependent upon it and is sustained by it. Love
is his [or her] light and his [or her] darkness, whose end he [or
she] one cannot see.[22]

Jung speaks about "cosmogonic love" and this is the second aspect.
"Cosmogonic" literally means "creating the world." You can think of
what we have said in connection with the number six, which is also
called "creating the world." And the creation of the world means the
beginning of consciousness. Without the human being, without
human consciousness no one exists to see this world. "Eros is a
kosmogonos, a creator and father-mother of all higher consciousness,"
says Jung.[23] Eros as the *kosmogonos* was worshipped in Greece at several
places. He was also called *protogonos*, "the one who was born first."
That means that Eros was looked at as the first living being in the
whole cosmos, out of whom everything came to existence. But there
was *one* place in Greece, a village in Attica called Phlya, where the
people worshipped the goddess Kore, "the girl." This young goddess,
this divine girl was also called *protogone*. She was the *protogone koura*,
the "first born Kore," out of whom everything came into existence and
everything was created, the whole cosmos and the whole human world.
That means that the experience of love represented by the divine girl,
the Kore, can be an image for a love that is "cosmogonic" as well. She
can also be a source of consciousness. She can also be "father-mother
of all higher consciousness."

The third aspect is what I would call "the love of Sophia." The
experience of love wants to lead to her. Sophia means wisdom. Wisdom
is something completely different than knowledge or intelligence.
According to von Franz, it is "an attitude of love towards mankind."
In her book, *Puer Aeternus*, she wrote:

Sophia means wisdom. . . . As you know, the Sophia is called
"philanthropos" (in the Old Testament), the one who loves man.
She is an attitude of love towards mankind, which naturally
means being human, being a human being among human beings
and loving other human beings. That is the highest form of Eros.[24]

The fourth aspect—and you see, we come down slowly, slowly
back to the song—the fourth aspect would be beauty. Girumeta is
beautiful, *Girumeta bella*. "Come down to the valley, beautiful

Girumeta." Love is beautiful. In the eyes of love the beloved person appears as a beautiful being. Inner images can be overwhelmingly beautiful as well. Beauty is a completely subjective feeling value. But it is a symbol too. Beauty always means or indicates a highest value. What we experience as beautiful is the highest psychic value, the goal, *meta* in Italian. In folksongs, fairytales, poetry, and in our dreams as well, the highest inner value is—not always but often—beautiful.

To the beauty of the divine girl in the song belongs music and dancing. "Let us play the *piva*, let us play the bagpipe. Let us dance a little." Dancing means psychic movement. To dance with each other means to be moved emotionally in the same way. I have told you a lot about the girl and about love. But what is the music? "Music expresses, in some way, the movement of the feelings (or emotional values) that cling to the unconscious processes," Jung writes in a letter, and continues: "Music expresses in sounds what fantasies and visions express in visual images."[25]

"Let us play the *piva*," the bagpipe. The bagpipe is the old, very old, instrument of the farmers and shepherds, the herdsmen, of people who live for centuries in nature and with the animals. Maybe we have

Fig 4: *Stable in the Mountains* (Photo by Andreas Schweizer, 2011).

to imagine such music, if we want to understand on a feeling level what it means: "being a human being among human beings and loving other human beings." Or in other words, the humble music of the *piva* could be the music that expresses in the best way the love of Sophia, "the highest form of Eros." The main essence of this song is: The highest of forms is, at the same time, the most humble of forms. Or, the divine girl, the feminine *numen*, the Goddess if you like, wants to incarnate in the humbleness of human reality or in the humbleness of a human soul.

LA FIGLIA D' UN PASTOR: THE DARK ASPECTS OF LOVE

The song "Girumeta dalla montagna" is unique among the songs of Ticino. I don't know any other song like it. The feminine appears as a highest numinous value. The shepherd girl coming down from the mountains represents a value that many people seem to expect. It talks about the arrival of or longing for a new kind of love, a love through which the Self reveals itself.[26] But when we look at other old songs from the canton Ticino dealing with the topic of love or the fate of a woman, then we will see how they can completely differ. Love can appear in an entirely dark aspect, as for instance in the song "La figlia d' un pastor." Therefore, I first of all want to remind you what Jung writes about love—he calls it "Eros"—in *Memories, Dreams, Reflections*:

> In classical times, when such things were properly understood, Eros was considered a god whose divinity transcended our human limits, and who therefore could neither be comprehended nor represented in any way. I might, as many before me have attempted to do, venture an approach to *this daimon, whose range or activity extends from the endless space of the heavens to the dark abysses of hell;* but I falter before the task of finding the language which might adequately express the incalculable paradoxes of love. Eros is a *kosmogonos*, a creator and father-mother of all higher consciousness . . .[27]

Therefore, we have to ask ourselves, in which way can the experience of the dark side of love also be the "father-mother of all higher consciousness"? Does this song show additional aspects of love that also want to become conscious and which want to be integrated in the collective image of the feminine? Or, to put it another way, can

this song also be considered compensatory to the ruling collective—
let us say—masculine or Christian attitude towards love?

"La figlia d'un pastor"—"The Shepherd's Daughter"—is a very
old ballad, certainly around five hundred years old, and it probably
does not come from the valleys of the southern Alps or from the Ticino.
In the 16th century its different versions were spread all over Italy. In
terms of type it belongs to the pastoral epic, which might have
originated in the Italian courts and later was adopted by the common
people. In the valleys of Ticino, even today, people sing the song. I
know three versions and will now share with you the simplest one (See
Figure 5 with the musical score of the song):

> *Era figlia d' un pastor. / Tutti i disan, che l' è bella.*
> *L' era bella come un fior. / I tre soldà l' han menà via.*
> *L' han menada da luntan, / cencinquanta miglia via.*
> *L' han metüda in un castel, / in una torre di lei sola.*
> *L' han tegnuda la sett an, / senza vede ne sol ne luna.*
> *"O papà, caro papà! / Cosa i dis da mi là in Francia?"*
> *"Tutti dicono di te, / che tu sei una figlia rubada."*
> *"L' anelin che porti al did, / a le da quel che ma spusada."*

My translation:

> She was a shepherd's daughter. / Everyone says she is beautiful.
> She was as beautiful as a flower. / And three soldiers took
> her away.
> They took her far away, / one hundred and fifty miles away.
> They brought her into a castle, / into a tower, which was
> for her alone.
> For seven years they kept her there, / And she could see
> neither the sun nor the moon.
> "O father, dear father! / What do they say there, about
> me, in France?"

Fig 5: Musical Score to "Era figlia d'un pastor" (Trad.).

"Everyone says of you, / you're a daughter who was stolen [or abducted and ravished]."
"The little ring that I wear on my finger / is from him who married me."

(At my above-mentioned website, www.regineschweitzer-vuellers.com, there is an interpretation by Roberto Maggini and Pietro Bianchi.[28])

A longer version of the song stems from Gresso, a village in the valley of Onsernone. It is called "Cattivo custode," "The Frightful Guardian." I will also focus on this song, mainly because of its end:

> L'è la figlia di un bacan. / Tütt i disan che l'è bèla.
> Se l'è bèla come i dis, / la faremo rimirare.
> La faremo rimirar, / ma da tre soldati armati.
> Il più bello di quei tre / l'è sctai quell che l'ha robada.
> L'ann menada in un castel, / 'na prigion profonda e oscura.
> L'ann tenüda là sètt an, / senza mai vede la luna.
> Alla fine di sètt an / gh'ann verdüü la finestròla.
> Finestròla gh'ann verdüü, / che guardava verso il mare.
> E la vide il suo papà, / che tornava dalla Francia.
> "Oh papà caro papà, / cos' i dis la gent in Francia?"
> "Tütt i disan mal di te, / che tu sei 'na fija robada."
> "Fija robada più non son, / ma son donna maridada."
> Ed è nato un fanciullin, / che portava già la spada.
> E la punta l'è de or / e la maneta l'è d'argento.

My translation:

> She was the daughter of a peasant [or a shepherd][29]. / Everyone says she is beautiful.
> If she is as beautiful as they say / we will look at her in awe.
> We will look at her in awe. / But three armed soldiers came.
> The most beautiful of the three soldiers / was the one who ravished her.
> They brought her into a castle, / into a deep and dark prison.
> For seven years they kept her there / and she could never see the moon.
> When the seven years had passed / they opened a little window.
> They opened a little window / so that she could gaze on the sea.
> And she saw her father, / who'd just returned from France.
> "Oh father, dear father, / what do the people in France say?"
> "They all speak ill of you / that you are a daughter who was ravished."

"A ravished daughter I am no more. / But I am a
married woman."
And she had given birth to a little child / who already
carried a sword.
And the tip is of gold / and its handle is of silver.

THE SHEPHERD'S DAUGHTER

The girl of this song—the *figlia d'un pastor*—is also a shepherdess.
But, unlike Girumeta, she does not come from the mountains, from
the Beyond or from eternity. She is also not eternally young. The girl
in this song is a daughter, with a human father. She is born in and
attached to the human world. And in this world she has a certain
destination or a fate. To this fate belongs, according to the song, the
experience of the male as a dark, overwhelming power. And this fate
makes her, among other things, a *figlia rubata*—a "ravished, dishonored
and humiliated daughter." That is what the song tells us. But before
coming to the song itself, we must try to find out how we can
understand its heroine psychologically. Is she merely a human woman
who has suffered a terrible fate, expelled from a paradisiacal world
totally unexpectedly, raped and imprisoned—only to finally tell her
father in a strange dialogue that she is no longer dishonored—but now
married and has even give birth to a son, who already carries a sword?

Over the centuries uncountable numbers of women have suffered
a similar fate. They were raped, impregnated, carried off, imprisoned.
However, I believe that this song, sung for some five hundred years,
does not make sense if understood in this concrete, historical way. We
might also understand the story as an inner fate that occurs to many
women. Then the song can be understood as addressing a certain kind
of possession that the daughter experienced, a terrible animus
possession—this may have been a love possession—breaking into her
life completely unexpectedly and taking her far away, imprisoning her
for seven years, and isolating her completely from other human
relationships in the darkness of a tower. She cannot see the sun or the
moon, which means that she is mentally in the shadow, maybe
deranged. For a long time she is disconnected from the eternal world
and from the life-giving lights of heaven, from the sun and moon.

One can interpret the song this way. I think it makes sense. But
then the end of the song is still difficult to understand. What is the

meaning of the strange question to the father at the end: "*Cosa i dis da mi la in Francia?*" "What do the people in France say about me?" Why is it so important what the people in France say about her—which corresponds obviously with her father's opinion? This collective voice tells the daughter something she already knows. "You have been ravished. You are a *rubada*." In Jungian language that would mean: "You have been ravished and possessed by the animus. You are an animus-possessed daughter—*una figlia rubada*." And to this judgment the daughter replies, "No, I am no longer possessed. I am a married woman now." This means psychologically: "During the time of complete darkness I found a man"—I think we should conclude that this is an inner man, an animus—"to whom I belong and who can accept me as a woman." This man might be one of the soldiers—"the most beautiful one"—or any other man, but certainly a positive animus, a clear spiritual attitude of the woman, a male figure within her that loves her and accepts her as she is. That is the symbolic meaning of being a *donna maridada*, a married woman. It is a woman with an animus who acknowledges her as a woman, in her feminine value. Then she is no longer possessed.

Thus we can conclude that the dialogue between the daughter and her father is not telling us something about any outward thing but instead dealing with something very important, i.e., the inner meaning of the whole story. In this way the Onsernone valley version of the song is much more differentiated. It says not only that the *figlia* found a man during her long imprisonment, but also that she has given birth to a son—a son of darkness and not of light—an infant and a little warrior already carrying a sword. This son is not an ordinary soldier, but rather a hero, a divine son, a *puer aeternus*. The weapon he carries is quite special: ". . . the tip is of gold and its handle is of silver." Psychologically speaking, this sword is a spiritual instrument, an instrument of understanding in which the eternal world appears, connecting the opposites of gold and silver, i.e., the sun and moon. "*E la punta l'è de or è la maneta l'è d'argento.*" In alchemy this son would represent the *filius philosophorum*, Mercurius, who also is a son of darkness, several times depicted with a sword.

We could understand the song in this way. It seems to be meaningful. But I am still not completely satisfied with this, especially if I consider the deep empathy with which particularly old men in the Ticino sing this song. Obviously the fate of the *figlia d'un pastor* moved these men and touched their feelings deeply, and normally an animus-possessed woman does not touch the heart of men. Thus she must also have a meaning in terms of the anima of men. In other words, she is also a Kore, a divine girl, and does not just represent the ego of a woman. Therefore, we have to interpret her in a similar way as we would interpret the heroine of a fairy tale. The song tells us not only what can happen to one woman or to many women on a personal level. Rather it tells us what may happen to the female in general or to the human soul. Yes, I believe that this song tells us what may happen to love itself, love as it is embodied in this girl, very young, totally pure, innocent, and as beautiful as a blooming flower (*l'era bella come un fior*). "We will look at her in awe," says the song from Onsernone valley. "If she"—namely love—"is as beautiful as they say, we will look at her with awe." This young, new, and emerging love has a certain fate. And this fate and its meaning is what the song talks about.

Here the story of the rape of Persephone by Hades comes to mind. Indeed, the song could be related to the old myth and the initiation rite of Eleusis, not in an historical sense, of course, but in an archetypal sense. It seems like a rebirth of the pagan myth in a Christian realm. It was not without reason that our second song spread throughout Italy during the sixteenth century. Then the song would tell us the experience of love as it is represented in the divine girl entails a journey to Hades and the underworld. It is a collective human experience. It is part of the feminine God image. It is not a journey to the underworld by a male god like Osiris or Christ. It is an underworld journey of the feminine, the girl or the daughter— in fact, of love itself Here, in the underworld, in "the dark abysses of hell," to which, according to Jung, Eros also belongs, in this place she gives birth to a son. And I think this son can be compared with the divine child of the mysteries of Eleusis.

THE FATHER AS THE SHEPHERD

But there is a big difference between our song and the ancient myth. The girl, the innocent child of the song, does not appear as a daughter of a mother, who in the antique myth would be the goddess Demeter, but as a daughter of a father. Now, I would like to have a look at the symbolic meaning of this father.

On a personal level, but also understood as a collective symbol, the father represents traditional values and ideas. He "knows" what is good and what is bad, what is right and what is wrong. He incorporates a collective attitude, rooted in the values of the past, or as Jung writes, "the sum of conventional opinions."[30] In a positive sense the father transmits what I would call a spiritual attitude, the fact that life must have a spiritual dimension, too. In the life of a woman—still according to Jung—this requires "the capacity for reflection, deliberation, and self-knowledge,"[31] that is, the ability to reflect, to think about something and to recognize it. Therefore the father is also the representative of the traditional ruling *Weltanschauung*. And of course, to this collective view belongs also the traditional god-image.

The father in our song is a *pastore*, a shepherd, or a peasant who lives or is moving around with his animals. He knows them, protects them, and takes care of them. That is quite a peaceful image. It is a completely archaic, even archetypal image, and goes back to primeval times. For thousands of years men have moved from place to place with their animals. Which instinct is it that the father herds? A herd means a group or community. To be connected with a community is a deep instinctual need in humans. Therefore, the father in the song is someone who takes care of this instinctual need.

But the word *pastore* has a religious meaning, being the Italian also for "preacher." Christ himself is the good shepherd. Therefore we may also see the father in the song, although he is a quite normal and humble man, as a representation of the Christian God. This man, who lives in nature with his animals, is, so to say, a living image of the son of God. He is a representative of a good God, who takes care of men just as a good shepherd takes care of his herd. And also in this context we can say that the instinct, which belongs to this image of God, is a collective urge, an instinctual urge of being a member of a community. It is a form of Eros. Maybe we can say it is the Christian way of love.

THE RITE IN ELEUSIS AND THE MYSTERY OF TRANSFORMATION

Let us now come back to the daughter. She is also an image, an image of the archetypal experience of the feminine in the shape of Kore or the divine girl. This image is much older than the Christian god image, maybe even as old as the archetypal image of the shepherd. It has its roots in the pagan understanding of nature, in the antique cultures and religions, in a psychic layer that values the feminine and also the experience of love far higher than the later Christian religion. To this pagan world belongs the myth of Hades and Persephone. It tells us about Kore's journey to the underworld, her rape and being overwhelmed by a dark male power, but also about her return to the world of humankind. This rebirth after a long time of infertility and stagnation brings about a renewal of the whole of nature. With the reappearance of Kore the corn starts to grow, the green grass begins to sprout, the flowers to bloom, the animals, men, and women are nourished again. Even the gods are nourished again, since people can make ritual sacrifices as before.

Now according to the myth, this reappearance is not a mere return to the beginning. When she comes back to the human world, the divine girl is not just Kore anymore. Since she comes from the underworld, she is now contaminated with its dark powers. She is Kore and she is not Kore. In the mysteries of Eleusis she is called "Brimo," "the terrible one," or "the one who arouses fear."[32] Kore, the divine girl—and she still is the divine girl: innocent, pure, and eternally young—and Brimo, the terrible one, who arises from the world of the dead: they both belong together in a mysterious way. They are one. They are opposites that normally cannot be connected, neither rationally nor emotionally. When they are one, nevertheless, this unity, this light-dark Kore, this Kore-Brimo, is experienced by the initiated as a redeeming and healing symbol, a unifying or reconciling symbol.[33] And it is this Kore-Brimo who has given birth to the divine son in Eleusis. She gave birth to him not only once. In each initiate, in each initiated man or woman, she gives birth to the divine son. This son is called "Brimos." Thus the threatening aspect is also part of him.

What people have experienced in the mysteries in former times can be compared with psychic processes that people experience today, for instance, in the process of individuation. But what did the initiates in Eleusis experience? The mysteries of Eleusis deal with the experience of death and the immortality of the human soul. Going through the mysteries, the initiates became immortal. According to the rite, these men and women were, or experienced themselves as, both human and divine. He or she was human when looking and longing for the divine girl who had disappeared into the underworld, calling her and trying to find her with torches, running around in the darkness, finally celebrating a dance with the torches.[34] But the initiate was also Kore, which means divine. In that moment, when the initiate had to face a terrible and deeply moving experience—we do not know exactly what it was—in this moment, he or she became Kore. In this moment he or she became divine. There exists a relief that shows that the initiate had to kiss a snake. Jung suspects that this could be the deeply terrifying experience during the mysteries. But it is not certain. The mysteries of Eleusis remain a secret. In the moment of the terrible, overwhelming experience—the *tremendum*—the initiates became Kore-like, being emotionally raped and ravished into the dark abyss. But the initiates also experienced something like a resurrection. And in the same moment, when the priest announced, "Today, the Brimo has given birth to the Brimos," he or she became a human being again. Brimos is the divine son. I think we can compare him with the *filius* in alchemy and with the alchemical *Lapis*.

In Eleusis, the deep and mysterious inner experience of the initiate was connected with the whole of nature, and with the experience that nature dies and resurrects each year. But it was also connected with an inner psychic process, a psychic transformation, in which a divine value, the Kore, is ravished by a dark power in order to reappear in the human world after a long period of searching and waiting.

THE SOLDIERS

The young feminine being in the song, "La figlia d' un pastor," is also ravished by a dark male power—not by Hades, the god of the underworld (since she is not a goddess like Persephone), but by three soldiers. Archetypally speaking, these soldiers belong to Mars, the god of war. Mars means aggression, power, brutality. He is a god of violence. He represents a dynamic male power and also emotion. It must have been a tremendous emotion that overwhelmed the girl and took her far away (*luntan*), a hundred and fifty miles away, into a castle and into darkness, into total isolation from human relationship. This is also a journey into the underworld. The divine girl, the Kore, is carried away by a dark, underlying male trinity. What kind of power takes the girl away? We said that the three soldiers belong to Mars. The instinctual base of this god, of this archetypal image, is aggression. Aggression belongs to the survival instinct, to the instinct of self-preservation. This instinct separates the single being from other beings. And of course, this is just the opposite of what we call the urge or the instinct to be a member of a community. It seems that the soldiers represent a psychic reality, namely that the father of the girl is totally missing. Here the peaceful world of a herd with its shepherd, and there the world of war and violence. But aggression, like other instincts, also belongs to nature. It is a part of the human totality. It belongs to the Self.

For seven years the girl or the young woman has to stay in the power of the soldiers. That is a long time. But it is also a time of psychic development and transformation. Thus after the seven years something happens. The soldiers open a small window in the tower to let the prisoner look outside. The impulse to change comes from the dark side, from below and from within. It does not come from the outside or from above. It seems that during the long time of imprisonment by the dark power, this power itself has changed. The song tells about an underyling, *coniunctio* (death-wedding). But in this *coniunctio* both sides become transformed—the prisoner, the daughter, and the aggressive male power, the soldiers. The prisoner can now look through a little window. She sees the light. She sees the ocean, the whole infinite world of the unconscious. And she sees her father who is just now returning from France.

DIALOGUE WITH THE FATHER

And now a kind of dialogue between the daughter and her father begins. This dialogue contains the essential meaning of the song. We have already spoken about it. The father represents and delivers to the daughter a traditional, maybe a traditional Christian, understanding. But he also tells her "what the people in France say." Both belong together in this song. "France" represents the land of Eros. Think of the songs of the troubadours from the south of France, of all the love poetry and the so-called courtly love during the Middle Ages. "What the people in France say" refers to a particular conception of Eros, a specific idea about the feminine and love. According to this conventional Christian comprehension, the girl's journey to the underworld—her confrontation with and suffering from darkness and aggression, her encounter with "the dark abysses of hell," as Jung says—is only possession. Love itself has been *rubada*, or has fallen into the hands of the devil—to use this Christian term. Thus she is psychically dead.

According to our interpretation, love or the feminine itself turns against this position. In other words, against this light and idealistic Christian understanding stands the experience of darkness. The woman—and now she is woman—says: "No, I am no longer ravished, no more in the hands of the devil, no more a *rubada,* and above all no longer a daughter. I am a *donna maridada*, a married woman." And from the second song of the valley of Onsernone we know that the man she has married is the most beautiful of the three soldiers, *"il piu bello di quei tre."* Thus we can say a male attitude, a kind of firmness and strength, a part of male aggression in its positive aspects, is now connected with love. It is united with the too young, too beautiful, and too innocent feminine. Through this union or *coniunctio*, the son, the *puer aeternus*, has been born. It seems that this *filius*, this divine son, has received the sword from his father, but from his mother he has inherited the principle of Eros; thus the union of gold and silver, or of the sun and moon.

What does that mean in terms of psychology? We have seen that in this song the father represents, so to speak, the traditional perception of love: what love is, what it should be and what it should not be, what belongs to love and what doesn't. As long as this traditional idea of love is connected and contaminated with the Christian God image, which considers God only as good, no psychological understanding of the dark side of love is possible. It may be experienced, but it cannot be understood. In this sense it seems that the song with its pagan background really has a healing effect. If Eros is a creator and "father-mother of all higher consciousness," then these dark experiences themselves are also "father-mother of all higher consciousness."

The song deals with a new understanding of love. In other words, the feminine God image, which should come down from the mountains as "Girumeta," is new only when such human experiences as darkness and aggression are contained within it.

I can tell you this with some sincerity, since in my work as a Jungian analyst and in my personal surroundings I have met a number of people who have fallen into complete despair because of their experience of the dark side of love. And when someone has fallen into complete despair, it is terrible, because he or she then is only bitter, only hard or resentful against him- or herself and against others. It is as if something has been extinguished. Not infrequently a latent psychic illness can in such moments become manifest. Even if one cannot judge an individual case, today I think that if these people had had an understanding of love that included the dark side, if they had been able to understand that hatred, aggression, and despair may belong to their experience of love too, then they would have found meaning in their suffering, and that—maybe—would have helped them.

I now come to the end. These dark sides of love are not human. They belong to the realm of the gods and the demons. They are "superhuman" or "subhuman." They are archetypal. The individual has to separate him- or herself from them. This separation is the indispensable precondition through which the experience of love, even in its dark aspects, can become "father-mother of all higher consciousness."

To close, I invite you to listen to the song again, now a version from the Valley of Onsernone interpreted by the group, *Vent Negru*.[35]

NOTES

[1] "Girumeta dalla montagna," interpreted by Cornelia Montani, Joe Sebastian Fenner, Philipp Galizia on *Cod Bai Frends: Tandem Tinta Blu, Lieder und Musik aus dem Tessin und Norditalien* [*Goodbye Friends by Tandem Tinta Blu, Songs and Music form the Ticino and Northern Italy*], Audio CD, released by Klaus Grimmer, Kyburg, Switzerland 2000.

[2] "Girumeta dalla montagna," interpreted by Roberto and Dimitri on *Roberto e Dimitri: Canti popolari nel Ticino* [*Roberto and Dimitri: Traditional Folksongs from Ticino*], Audio CD, released by Claves Records, Thun, Switzerland 1993.

[3] "The 'Kore' has her psychological counterpart in those archetypes which I have called the self or supraordinate personality on the one hand, and the anima on the other." C.G. Jung, "The Psychological Aspects of the Kore," *The Archetypes of the Collective Unconscious, Collected Works of C.G. Jung*, Vol. 9i, eds. Sir Herbert Read, Michael Fordham, Gerhard Adler, William McGuire, trans.

R.F.C. Hull, Bollingen series XX, 2nd ed. (Princeton: Princeton University Press, 1968), § 306. Further references to Jung's *Collected Works*, abbreviated to CW, will be by chapter title, followed by the volume and paragraph numbers.

[4] Jung, "Concerning Mandala Symbolism," CW 9i, § 634, Jung's italics.

[5] Jung, "Appendix," CW 9i, § 717.

[6] Jung, "Commentary on *The Secret of the Golden Flower*," CW 13, § 32.

[7] In a letter to Serge Moreux, the French editor of a musical journal, Jung demonstrated his psychological understanding of music:

> Music certainly has to do with the collective unconscious—as the drama does too. . . . Music expresses, in some way, the movement of the feelings (or emotional values) that cling to the unconscious processes. The nature of what happens in the collective unconscious is archetypal, and archetypes always have a numinous quality that expresses itself in emotional stress. Music expresses in sounds what fantasies and visions express in visual images. I am not a musician and would not be able to develop these ideas for you in detail. I can only draw your attention to the fact that music represents the movement, development and transformation of motifs of the collective unconscious. (C.G. Jung, "Letter to Serge Moreux, 20 January 1950," in *Letters, Vol. 1: 1906-1950*, eds. Gerhard Adler and Aniela Jaffe, trans. R.F.C. Hull, Bollingen Series XCV:1 [Princeton: Princeton University Press, 1973], p. 542.)

[8] In the interpretation of the song by *Tandem Tinta Blu*, the text occurs only three times. One time the group whistles the melody instead of using the words. But this is an exception.

[9] The parallel key of D minor would F major. The parallel key of D major would be B minor.

[10] The main relationship is their distance from a central root or "home" tone.

[11] Marie-Louise von Franz, *Number and Time: Reflections Leading Toward a Unification of Psychology and Physics,* trans. Andrea Dykes (Evanston: Northwestern University Press, 1974).

[12] *Der Kleine Pauly: Lexikon der Antike in fünf Bänden*, ed. Konrad Ziegler, *et al.*, Vol. 5 (Munich: Verlag GmbH & Co. KG, DTV, 1979), column 1449.

[13] *Ibid.*

[14] Jung, "Concerning Mandala Symbolism," CW 9i, § 679.

[15] Johannes Lydus (Laurentius), *De mensibus,* ed. von Richard Wuensch, Vol. II (Leipzig 1898), p. 11. See also Jung, "Psychology of the Transference," CW 16, § 451, footnote 8.

[16] Song of Solomon 1:7, in *The Holy Bible,* English Standard Version (ESV).

[17] *Ibid.*, 1:8.

[18] *Ibid.*, 4:1-2.

[19] *Ibid.*, 4:8. The lions and the leopards may represent the enormous emotions, the desire which belong to each deep experience of love.

[20] Jung, "The Visions of Zosimos," CW 13, §§ 130 ff. See also Margaret Schevill, *Beautiful on the Earth* (Santa Fe, N.M.: Hazel Dreis Editions, 1945), p. 24 ff. and p. 38 ff.

[21] Richard Wilhelm, trans., *The I Ching or Book of Changes,* Bollingen Series XIX, English by Cary Baynes (Princeton: Princeton University Press, 1977), p. 652.

[22] C.G. Jung, *Memories, Dreams, Reflections,* Revised Edition, ed. Aniela Jaffe, trans. Richard and Clara Winston (New York: Random House, 1989), p. 354. See also Marie-Louise von Franz, *Corpus Alchemicum Arabicum, Vol. IA* [*Book of the Explanation of the Symbols Kitab Hall ar-Rumuz by Muhammad ibn Umail*], eds. Theo Abt and Wilferd Madelung (Zürich: Living Human Heritage Publications, 2006), p. 39ff.

[23] Jung, *Memories, Dreams, Reflections,* p. 354.

[24] Marie-Louise von Franz, *Puer Aeternus,* 2nd Edition (Boston: Sigo Press, 1977), p. 229 ff.

[25] Jung, *Letters,* Vol. 1, p. 542.

[26] Jung, "Psychology of the Transference," CW 16, § 449.

[27] Jung, *Memories, Dreams, Reflections,* p. 353, my italics.

[28] "Il cattivo custode," interpreted by Pietro Bianchi and Roberto Maggini on *Cantà pai sass* [*Songs for the Stones*], Audio CD, released by Emilia Pennella and Paolo Rimoldi, Studio 2 della RSI 2002.

[29] "Bacan" is difficult to translate. It means "a man from the countryside, a farmer, a peasant or shepherd, but also a simple man."

[30] Jung, CW 9ii, § 29.

[31] *Ibid.*, § 33.

[32] In one picture Kore is even depicted with horns. Quotation from Carl Kerenyi, "Kore," in C.G. Jung and Carl Kerenyi, *Essays on a Science of Mythology: The Myth of the Divine Child and the Mysteries of Eleusis*, trans. R.F.C. Hull, Bollingen Series XXII (Princeton: Princeton University Press, 1993), p. 142 ff.

[33] For Jung's concept of the unifying symbol, see Jung, "The Significance of the Uniting Symbol," CW 6, §§ 318-374. See also "Definitions: 51. Symbol," CW 6, §§ 814-829.

[34] For this dance, see Carl Kerenyi, "Kore," p. 149.

[35] "Il cattivo custode," interpreted by Gabriele Martini, Esther Rietschin, Mauro Garbani on *Vent Negru* [*Strong Wind*], Audio CD, released by Jürgen Fischer, Losone Switzerland 1999.

8

A Doll's House: Henrik Ibsen's Play as a Masquerade and Love Story

Doris Lier

INTRODUCTION

A Doll's House is a three-act play, written in 1879 by the Norwegian author Henrik Ibsen.[1] The author's intention was to write a socio-critical play against the legal suppression of women's rights of his time. In this intent Ibsen depicts Nora, the main character, and how she surmounts the social order by leaving her husband at the end of the play. The present interpretation proceeds on the assumption that the play, in addition to the author's expressed intent, also illustrates a topic which exceeds 19th century problems and issues of women's rights: I suggest that the play also demonstrates a kind of love which can be called the love for truthfulness. In following Nora's development throughout the play, I will attempt to clarify in what sense this love differs for example from charity, from desire, and from the love of another person. I will also try to show why Nora's wish for truthfulness at first appears in a masked form, i.e. staying initially hidden behind a masquerade.

My essay is divided into four parts: The first part gives a short synopsis of the play. The second part explores Ibsen's intention in writing the play. The third part discusses how the play was received initially and how it is received today. And finally, the fourth part interprets the play as a masquerade and love story.

SYNOPSIS

For this synopsis I am especially indebted to Frances Gray, who authored the "Notes" to a recent edition of *A Doll's House.*[2]

The entire play takes place in the living room of main characters Nora and Torvald Helmer, who have been married for eight years and have three children. The setting displays modest prosperity, being "furnished inexpensively, but with taste."[3] The other main characters are: Dr. Rank, a family friend; Mrs. Kristina Linde, Nora's old friend; Nils Krogstad, a barrister, money-lender, and Nora's blackmailer; Anna Maria, the nurse; a housemaid and a porter.

Before going any further, I would like to orient you about my use of names for the cast of characters, which follows Ibsen and/or the social convention of the European 19th century: Nora usually goes by her first name. In general the other characters go by their last names. In the context of intimate conversation Nora's husband is sometimes called by his first name, "Torvald"—and Mrs. Linde, Nora's friend, is sometimes called "Kristina." Also, following Frances Gray—whose notes follow Ibsen's own dramatic device—I let stand many ambiguities, puzzles, and paradoxes, which gain meaning only in the course of the narrative.

Act 1: The play begins on Christmas Eve. Nora, a beautiful woman, arrives home with a Christmas tree and many presents for her family and household staff. She gives the porter a generous tip and, finding herself alone, nibbles some macaroons until her husband, Torvald, comes out of his study to see what she has bought. Torvald calls Nora his "songbird" and "sweet little squirrel," while chiding her about her extravagant spending. She protests that his promotion to manager of the local bank will come with a high salary. When Torvald asks Nora what she wants for Christmas, her answer is money. He is reluctant, calls her a spendthrift, and asks if she has been frivolously spending money on sweets, which she denies. Their conversation is interrupted by the announcement of two visitors. One of them is Dr. Rank, a family friend. He and Helmer withdraw into the study.

The other visitor is Mrs. Kristina Linde, an old friend of Nora's who has fallen on hard times and is looking for employment. She hopes Nora may influence Helmer to help her obtain a job at the bank. Kristina Linde discloses to Nora the struggles she had during her marriage to a man she did not love, and the struggles she continues to have after his death. By comparison, she perceives Nora's life to be secure and easy. Nora feels offended and counters that she too has struggled: Helmer nearly died from overwork during the first year of their marriage. The only prospect for his recovery was a full year's rest in Italy. Because Helmer was unwilling to pay for the trip, Nora herself raised the money for it. This she did by forging her father's signature to acquire a loan and pretending to her husband that the money for the trip was a gift from her father. She then reveals to Mrs. Linde that she has been secretly working to pay off this loan for the last seven years.

Soon another visitor arrives: Nils Krogstad, who is a clerk at Helmer's bank. Krogstad's presence obviously troubles Nora, although he comes not to visit her, but her husband. Dr. Rank emerges from the study, allowing Krogstad to talk privately with Helmer. Nora, Dr. Rank, and Kristina Linde are now in the living room together. Rank begins a conversation about "moral invalids" and how they should be dealt with. Becoming agitated by the realization that, in his new position as bank manager, her husband will have power over Krogstad, Nora passes round the macaroons, pretending they are a present from Mrs. Linde. Helmer joins the group in the living room, and immediately agrees to give Mrs. Linde a job at the bank. Helmer soon departs with Mrs. Linde and Dr. Rank, leaving Nora at home to play with her children. She is interrupted by Krogstad, who returns after the others have gone. Alarmed at the danger of being dismissed from his job at the bank, he has come to blackmail Nora into using her influence to help him keep it. It emerges that Krogstad was the source of the loan Nora had acquired to fund her and Torvald's trip to Italy, and he knows that Nora forged her father's signature in order to guarantee it. Krogstad threatens to reveal everything to Helmer if Nora does not secure his job.

Helmer returns home in time to see Krogstad leaving. Assuming Krogstad had come to play on Nora's goodwill, and becoming angered by Nora's denial, Helmer pronounces that liars like Krogstad—and, even worse, "lying mothers"—damage their children. Alone again, Nora is deeply troubled. She instructs their nursemaid that she does not want to see her children during the next hours.

Act 2 begins on Christmas Day. Nora is still upset and wants to be alone. The nurse enters with Nora's outfit for the fancy dress party she and Helmer will attend that night. The dress is designed for the Tarantella, a dance that Nora learned while staying in Italy, and that she will perform at the party.[4]

Mrs. Linde arrives to mend Nora's costume, and with the ulterior motive of discovering if Krogstad has mentioned her to Nora. As Helmer arrives, Mrs. Linde bundles the dress up and leaves because Helmer cannot bear to watch ordinary mending. When Nora tries to intercede with her husband on Krogstad's behalf, Helmer becomes angry. Finally, overcome with emotion, he sends Krogstad a letter of dismissal. Nora panics and pleads with him to change his mind; however, before retiring into his study, Torvald patronizingly declares that he is "man enough" to deal with any trouble.

Dr. Rank arrives. He has come to tell Nora that he is going to die. He and Nora discuss his illness, syphilis, and start to flirt. Asking Dr. Rank to help her decide which silk stockings she should wear to the party, Nora employs a coquettish strategy in the hope of gaining his help with the threatened blackmail. Just as she has begun to sound him out, Dr. Rank declares his love for her. She reproves him, and now refusing to continue with her request for a favor, sends him out to visit Helmer. Krogstad arrives once more. He is furious about his dismissal from the bank and informs Nora that now he wants an even higher position than the one he has lost. Panicking, Nora thinks of suicide while Krogstad leaves a note in a locked letterbox, revealing everything to Helmer.

Mrs. Linde arrives and Nora confides in her. Mrs. Linde enjoins that the truth should come out, but offers to speak with Krogstad, who once loved her. Mrs. Linde leaves, and Nora begins, confusingly, to anticipate a "miracle" that should be "prevented." As Helmer and Dr. Rank emerge from the study, she pleads with her husband not to open the mail in the letterbox, and persuades him instead to help her rehearse the Tarantella. Mrs. Linde returns, informing Nora that Krogstad is out of town. Nora tells herself she has "thirty-one hours to live," and rushes into Helmer's arms as *Act 2* ends and the curtain falls.

Act 3 opens with Mrs. Linde waiting in the foyer downstairs at the Helmer's house while the party is going on upstairs. Krogstad arrives. They speak about their former relationship. Still hurt, Krogstad complains that she left him as soon as she got a better offer. She explains that she ended their relationship because her marriage to a wealthier man enabled her to support her mother and brothers. Krogstad declares that his life is like a shipwreck, and that the only comfort he has known was the very job that he had just lost to her. Mrs. Linde immediately suggests they could "join forces," explaining that she wants to work and care for him and his children because she has faith in him. After a while he accepts her offer and proposes to take back his blackmailing letter against Nora. But Mrs. Linde prevents him from doing this, arguing that the truth should come out for the sake of Nora and Helmer.

Krogstad leaves as the Helmers enter. Helmer feels that Nora's performance of the Tarantella was a great success. After a slightly drunken lecture to Mrs. Linde about the merits of embroidery versus knitting, he is glad to show her out. He wants to make love to a troubled Nora, but they are interrupted by Dr. Rank, who has ostensibly come to get a cigar from Helmer. But in coded language, Dr. Rank informs Nora that his last test has confirmed that the final stage of his disease has begun. As he leaves, he puts two calling cards marked with a black cross in the letterbox.

Nora explains the meaning of the cards to her husband, who continues his unwelcome amorous attentions until she reproaches him for his insensitivity and tells him to read his letters. He reads the one from Krogstad and erupts in a rage. Their marriage is over, he proclaims—although they will preserve a front for the sake of respectability. Nora is shocked, for the miracle she has awaited and dreaded did not take place. The maid arrives with another letter. It is from Krogstad, who is returning the loan document with the forged signature and promising no further action. Helmer selfishly rejoices that he is saved now, but Nora is lost in profound disillusionment although Helmer lectures her about the depth of his forgiveness.

Shortly afterward, Nora has taken off her fancy dress and emerges not in her nightgown, but in day clothes, to demand the first serious talk of their marriage. She accuses Helmer and her father of denying her the chance to grow up, and announces her decision to leave their marriage to educate herself. This is a "duty," she says, higher than that of wife or mother. When Helmer realizes she has ceased to love him, Nora divulges the "miracle" she had hoped for: that he would step forward to take all the blame for her forgery. Since he has failed to step up in this way, Nora feels she is married to a stranger. Helmer pleads with her, but Nora insists she must go, adding that she could only return if they would both change and their relationship would become "a real marriage." As she exits, the door slams behind her.

Ibsen's Intent in Writing *A Doll's House*

Henrik Ibsen explicitly declared that he wanted the reader of *A Doll's House* to experience "a piece of reality."[5] He believed that women could not live a personal and dignified life in his time because they were obliged to follow social rules that in his opinion had nothing to do with the personal level, with emotions and love. Already before his marriage, Ibsen had stood up for women's rights. His wife, together with her friend Camille Collet and the painter Aasta Hansteen, were champions of the Norwegian feminist movement. All three women were well-educated, and Ibsen admired them for their opinions and emotional power. Within the Scandinavian artists' community in Rome, he himself officially pleaded for women's rights.[6] He did not support the so-called "Code Civil," which was the European code of laws devised by Napoleon.[7]

Undoubtedly, Ibsen wanted to write a socio-critical play against the legal suppression of women's rights.[8] We also know that the end of the play was very important to him: Nora leaves Helmer, and it is unclear if she will return to him later, after she has found her identity and an understanding of the difference between legal and moral justice. The end of the play, depicting a woman who walks out on her husband and children, was highly offensive to audiences when it was first performed. It was attacked by many reviewers. In a letter to a newspaper in 1880, Ibsen wrote that he could in some way understand the reviewers' rejection of the play's conclusion, but that it was for the sake of this end that he was wrote the play in the first place.

Ibsen was coming into in a tight spot, because the play was copyrighted in Norway only. This allowed theaters in Europe to deliberately change the play's conclusion. To prohibit these arbitrary changes, Ibsen reluctantly decided to propose a different ending. In this second version, Nora wants to leave the family, but Helmer forces her to watch her children first. The play ends with her saying: "Oh I sin against myself, but I cannot leave them."[9] In this second ending Nora is caught in the middle, between two kinds of love: her love as a mother of her children—and her love, her desire to find her own personal truth. Forced to choose, Nora must decide which "sin" she will commit by following one love instead of the other. In the original ending, Nora does not doubt her decision to leave her children, for she is convinced that she cannot be a good mother as long as she has not come to terms with herself. At first, audiences and critics favored the second ending, but, as the women's emancipation issue caught on with the public, Ibsen's original ending gradually gained acceptance.

EARLY AND CONTEMPORARY RECEPTIONS TO THE PLAY

A Doll's House was very successful as a play from the beginning. The first circulation of 8000 copies sold within two weeks of publication. The second and third printings also sold within a short time, and the premiere of the play at the Royal Theatre of Copenhagen created a sensation. Each premiere performance of the play evoked hot controversies in Europe, especially among male reviewers, who found it immoral. The question arose as to the nature of motherly love, as it seemed inconceivable that a mother could leave her children.

A Doll's House reveals the misogynistic code of law that obstructed the feminist movement of the 19th century, that is, it was largely embedded in the issues of its era. Yet in 2011 the play was performed 166 times in thirty-five countries, making it the most frequently staged play worldwide. The amazing popularity of the play today raises the question of whether the issues it presents are far broader than those reflecting the 19th century spirit. To find answers, I would like to go through the play again, following the development of the main characters: Nora, the protagonist; Helmer, her husband; Kristina Linde, her friend; and Krogstad, her money-lender and blackmailer. Hidden aspects of the story are also uncovered through Dr. Rank, the witty, cynical observer who, on the brink of death, has given up nearly all personal and social concerns. In this essay I do not explicitly interpret his role, but approach it implicitly in my reading.

Interpretation of the Play as a Masquerade and Love Story

In *Act 1*, we first witness a couple with ostensibly well-defined characteristics. Helmer is a man of honor, representative of law and order, a serious person, first and last. He is sober and industrious, overworking himself even to the point of illness in order to achieve promotion and provide for his family. Nora, on the other hand, appears as a scatter-brained woman without any sense of responsibility, following only her immediate desires.

One of the main issues between Nora and Helmer is money and debt: From Helmer's point of view, borrowing money is the "devil's cure." Nora counters that, given his future new income, they could easily waste money a bit or even borrow money until his new salary arrives. He replies:

> Nora! The same little scatterbrain. Just suppose I borrowed a thousand kroner today and you went and spent it all by Christmas, and then on New Year's Eve a tile fell on my head, and there I lay—.[10]

Later, when Helmer points out that, if such an accident occurred, the money-lenders would not get their money back, Nora argues that she would, in such a horrid case, not bother about them. This argument results in Helmer admonishing her again.

> Nora, Nora! Just like a woman! . . . No debts, no borrowing. There's something constrained, something ugly even, about a home that's founded on borrowing and debt.[11]

At the very beginning of the play—in prelude to the later discussions—Helmer emerges from his study, sees Nora's Christmas parcels on the table, and remarks, "Has my little featherbrain been out wasting money again?"[12]

Discourses of this kind might reveal Helmer's financial worries. In the 19th century there was almost no welfare system. Incomes were not secure. Industrial growth brought not only vast fortunes but also terrible losses.[13] On the other hand, Helmer's comments might be just playful exaggerations that belong to an intimate, teasing style of communication between the couple. From my point of view, the problem lies not so much in Helmer's resistance to spending money, but in his seizing any chance to call Nora a "spendthrift" and "featherbrained little girl." His epithets are not based on economic insecurities and are not part of a playful or amiable teasing. But (as later becomes clear) they are used to assert his dominance, and even reinforce and preserve Nora's infantile dependency. Helmer patronizes his wife, although he sincerely believes that he loves her and wants her to feel comfortable and secure.

Reading the play for the first time and not knowing how it ends, it is hard to bear Nora's behavior. Her acting as a naïve, flighty little girl makes no sense, and one wonders why she does not oppose Helmer's making her into a doll. The urgent question arises: why does she join in this demeaning game, thereby supporting, and maybe even provoking Helmer's treatment of her?

Already in the first act, for instance, as Helmer insults her for spending what he feels is too much money, Nora's answer makes the reader shake their head: "Oh, if you only knew what expenses we skylarks and squirrels have, Torvald."[14] During the conversation with Kristina Linde, her old friend, Nora behaves not like a wife and mother—but, whispering her story to Kristina, more like an overenthusiastic teenager in love. Nora talks in riddles, making it impossible for Kristina Linde to take her seriously, but instead, to look upon her as a spoiled girl. Nora's behavior gives Mrs. Linde reason to feel superior to her. Even when Nora agrees to help her get a job at Helmer's bank, Mrs. Linde patronizes her, echoing Torwald: "It *is* kind of you, Nora, to want to do this for me . . . especially when *you* know so little about the troubles and hardships of life."[15]

Many reviewers criticize the way Nora is characterized by Ibsen.[16] They note a discrepancy, arguing that the highly flighty Nora of the play's beginning could never become the Nora of the play's end—a calm and mature woman, who does not allow herself to become confused by her husband. This discrepancy between the two Noras is the most striking feature in the play. The interpretation of the whole plot largely depends on one's understanding of her transformation. That's why the question must be answered as to whether Nora's change can be psychologically understood, or if Ibsen actually failed with her character.

From my point of view Nora's annoying behavior until nearly the end of the play must be put into the context of what we gradually learn about Nora's illegal actions. At the end of the first act, we are informed that Nora is a woman who, seven years earlier, broke the law twice. First, she entered into a loan contract, which married women were not allowed to do in the 19th century; and secondly, she forged her father's signature.

Therefore, from the very beginning of the play, Nora is not an innocent child but a person who is aware of the severity of her former actions. Before signing the contract, she fruitlessly tried to convince Helmer to borrow money for the medically indicated travel to the south. However, he was too pigheaded to let this happen. This is why she had to find her own way to help him survive. Only by pretending the money came from her father could she convince Helmer to go on the trip.

In other words: Nora, who behaves so childishly—especially in relation to her husband—is the same woman who did everything to save her husband's life, even consciously taking on a debt and risking criminal liability. In addition to this, she has secretly worked hard for seven years to pay the loan back in installments. A first hint about her secret emerges in Helmer's (naïve) recollection of last year's pre-Christmas period, when Nora was frequently absent. He teases her:

> Helmer: Do you remember last Christmas? For three whole
>   weeks beforehand you shut yourself up every
>   evening till long after midnight, making flowers for
>   the Christmas tree, and all the other wonderful
>   surprises for us. Ugh, those were the most boring
>   three weeks I've ever had to live through.
> Nora: It wasn't the least bit boring for me.
> Helmer: But there was so little to show for it, Nora!
> Nora: Now, you mustn't tease me about that again. How
>   could I help it if the cat got in and tore everything
>   to bits?
> Helmer: Poor little Nora—of course you couldn't. You did
>   your best to please us—. . .[17]

Only in the later discussion between Nora and Kristina Linde does it emerge that Nora had not shut herself up in order to create Christmas decorations, but had been working to pay the loan installments.

To recapitulate: Nora is not stuck in childhood or adolescence. She is not a doll, but only pretends to be one. Her exaggerated behavior helps her hide her former illegal actions. With this, she deceives her husband and friends, and also herself. Her pretenses arise from her inability to stand up for her own deeds, done while Helmer was seriously ill. She manages to convince herself that Helmer will take the blame for her fraud, but deep down she knows this will never be the case. In other words, she is keenly aware of Helmer's need for social approval, but cannot accept the sad reality that he will inevitably protect his reputation at her expense. If Nora had been convinced of Helmut's support, she would have confessed the whole story to him, at least when they returned home from Italy.

Viewed psychologically, Nora is not only in conflict with the outer world, she is first of all in conflict with herself—one might even say she is in a state of pathological dissociation. For she is unable, within herself, to truly accept the moral justice of the illegal actions that saved her husband's life. At the same time she remains in denial of the fact that these very actions were destined to isolate her from him.

Nora's self-contradictory state can be observed again and again during the play. It reaches a painful point when Nora begins to speak of a dreadful miracle "that mustn't happen—not for anything in the world."[18] This "miracle" lies in her hope that Helmer will take the blame for her actions. This is a strange and absurd way to imagine a miracle. A miracle is defined as something that unexpectedly happens and affects us in a positive way, with the sense of superhuman forces being involved. Nora however expects a miracle that would obviously be more problematic than helpful, but it remains to be her profound hope nonetheless. Such inconsistent ideas reveal Nora's inner disunity, which lets her misjudge her husband's reality. She tries to keep herself on a happy neurotic island, but at the same time cannot avoid anticipating the moment in which her illusionary life will collapse.

Nora's self-contradiction reaches its peak at the fancy dress party while she dances the Tarantella. An Italian folkdance, the Tarantella is characterized by a fast, exuberant tempo with flirtatious movement, including spinning and much light foot tapping, and ruffling of skirts on the woman's part. The story behind it can be told in a few words: Historically, the frenzied Tarantella dancer was said to have been bitten by a wolf spider, the tarantula. The bite was believed to be highly poisonous and deadly, leading first to an hysterical condition known as tarantism. The 16th century folk belief was that only the dancing of the Tarantella could rid the victim of the spider's venom and prevent death.[19] Nora's performance of the dance is expressive of her own hysterical state and poisoning, caused by the discrepancy between her false conviction that Helmer will protect her and her repressed knowledge of the truth that he will never be capable of doing so. Generally speaking: She is poisoned by her own self-disownment.

As Nora's dance grows wilder and threatens to spin out of control, the family friend Dr. Rank is the only person in the play who can read her behavior and see through her masquerade. This is revealed at several points, especially after the fancy dress party when he announces his looming death. At next year's fancy dress party, he says, Nora shall be a mascot, "go[ing] dressed as she is in everyday life," and he himself "shall be invisible."[20] With this hint he points to the end of the masquerade, and, that is, to end of the whole play.

Indeed, shortly after Dr. Rank leaves the Helmer's house, Nora's self-contradiction or inner disunity comes to its end. It happens just as Helmer reads the letter in which Krogstad reveals Nora's forging of her father's signature. In that moment the play reaches its turning point, which coincides with ground zero of the couple's relationship: Nora is shocked because Helmer does not react the way she has hoped, but instead calls her a wretched woman and insults her:

> For these last eight years you've been my joy and my pride—and now I find that you're a liar, a hypocrite—even worse—a criminal! . . . You've completely wrecked my happiness, you've ruined my whole future! Oh, it doesn't bear thinking of. I'm in the power of a man without scruples; he can do what he likes with me—ask what he wants of me—order me about as he pleases, and I dare not refuse. And I'm brought so pitifully low all because of a shiftless woman! . . . It's so incredible that I can't grasp it.[21]

Helmer not only insults Nora, but then presents an outrageous solution:

> Somehow or other I must try to appease [Krogstad]—the thing must be hushed up at all costs. As for ourselves—we must seem to go on just as before . . . but only in the eyes of the world of course. You will remain here in my house—that goes without

> saying—but I shall not allow you to bring up the children . . .
> I shouldn't dare trust you with them. . . . [F]rom now on, there'll
> be no question of happiness, but only of saving the ruin of it—
> the fragments—the mere façade . . . [22]

Helmer's reaction throws Nora out of her inner disunity, instilling her with calm and self-confidence. This becomes obvious on the same evening, when Nora and Helmer have a serious conversation—from her point of view, the first such conversation in their married life. Nora explains to Helmer the miracle she has been awaiting, and expresses her sudden awareness that he is not the man she had always thought him to be:

> For eight years I'd waited so patiently—for, goodness knows, I
> realized that miracles don't happen every day. Then this disaster
> overtook me, and I was completely certain that now the miracle
> would happen. When Krogstad's letter was lying out there, I
> never imagined for a moment that you would submit to his
> conditions. I was completely certain that you would say to him
> "Go and publish it to the whole world!" And when that was
> done— . . . I thought—I was completely certain—that you
> would come forward and take all the blame—that you'd say "*I'm*
> the guilty one." . . . That was the miracle I hoped for . . . and
> dreaded. It was to prevent *that* that I was ready to kill myself. [23]

Helmer's answer again evidences his identity with the spirit of the time, for he says, "no man would sacrifice his *honor* for the one he loves." [24]

Let me turn now to the money-lender Krogstad and Mrs. Linde, Nora's friend. Mrs. Linde is proud of what she has done in her life. Having rejected Krogstad, she married a wealthy man she did not love to financially help her bedridden mother and two younger brothers. Furthermore, she tells Nora, her husband's "business wasn't sound," and so when he died "it went to pieces and there wasn't anything left." [25] She goes on to say that her mother has died, and her brothers can now look after themselves. When Nora supposes that Mrs. Linde must feel relieved, her friend gives a surprising answer:

> No . . . just unspeakably empty—I've no one to live for any
> more. That's why I couldn't bear to stay in that little backwater
> any longer. It must be easier to find some sort of work here that'll
> keep me busy and take my mind off things . . . [26]

We can easily deduce that Mrs. Linde will offer to become Nils Krogstad's wife. Indeed later, the two have a long discussion in which Krogstad confesses the disappointment he felt when Mrs. Linde left him for a wealthier man. When he expresses his feeling of having been "shipwrecked and clinging to a spar," Mrs. Linde seizes the chance to propose that they "join forces," because "two on one spar would be better off than each of [them] alone."[27] Note that Mrs. Linde does not respond with sentiments like: *I love you. I have always loved you. By leaving you I made the biggest sacrifice of my life.* To the contrary: shortly before her offer to join forces, she explains: "I had to break with you [when I married the other man], so it was up to me to kill any feelings that *you* might have had for me."[28]

At first glance we might assume that Mrs. Linde's situation is similar to Nora's. Both women have made sacrifices for the sake of others. Nora risks criminal liability to be able to afford the trip to Italy that will save her husband's life. Mrs. Linde foregoes a marriage of true love to Krogstad to marry a wealthier man who can take care of her mother and brothers. It might appear that both women were motivated by a kind of love that is related to charity, or, what in Christianity is called *agape*. But the story also shows that Mrs. Linde is actually quite interested in putting herself in service to a man. She worries too much about her social status and cannot be called an unselfish woman, with only charitable motives. We can hardly avoid thinking that she eagerly jumps at the chance to marry Nils Krogstad so that she can be received back into society.

Krogstad himself is in a similar situation. Already before colluding in Nora's crime, he had been flung out of society for committing forgery. There are some hints that he became a hack lawyer as a result of his disappointing experience with Mrs. Linde. However we might to choose to explain his actions, his post at the bank was his first step back into an honorable life. During the whole play he is willing to do anything to get his job back, even impudently blackmailing Nora. Mrs. Linde's offer of marriage is therefore highly attractive to him because it will allow him to remain in good standing within the community and this matters much more to him than the question of whether Mrs. Linde is still fond of him.

How the Four Characters Relate to Love

In order to compare the characters and their relationship to love, we can consider how they respond to their disappointing experiences.

Mrs. Linde, having lost her husband, mother, and brothers to work for, tries to improve her situation as soon as she can. She takes advantage of Krogstad's feeling shipwrecked and proposes to help him and herself, in her own words: to "join forces." Her actions seem to be motivated by love in terms of charity, but if we look at them more closely, we can see that her love is actually quite pragmatic, oriented toward fulfilling her own wishes: (1) She comes into town to ask Nora to put in a good word to Helmer to get her a job at the bank. (2) She arrives to mend Nora's fancy dress—but with the ulterior motive of exploring Krogstad's situation. (3) Finally, she finds the just right time to offer Krogstad a solution that will help both of them. Her behavior follows the motto: "One must live." This is what she says to Dr. Rank in *Act 1* when she explains to him why she looks for work in spite of the fact that she is overworked already.[29] The motto holds true for everything she decides. She neither reflects on the unconscious meaning of her actions, nor does she seem conflicted or aware that her actions could lead to self-division. She acts out her own psychological needs, tending to transfer to other people the cause and/or her source of fulfillment. Her rationale goes as follows: My mother was sick, therefore I had to marry a wealthy man. I feel empty, therefore Krogstad can fill me up.

In spite of his blackmailing Nora, Nils Krogstad is not a brutal person who wants to damage anyone's life. Nor does he claim that he is acting out of love. He is just figuring out his options. As soon as he feels that he has a chance to regain his reputation, he immediately withdraws the damning evidence against Nora.

Krogstad and Mrs. Linde have much in common: They have a clear idea of how life should be and grasp any opportunity to have their wishes fulfilled. Although Krogstad is called a "moral invalid," he shares the wish with Mrs. Linde to be a socially accepted person. This is a legitimate wish. The way he tries to reach his goal, however, is morally questionable. But in terms of psychology, he is an ordinary man who does not much care about others and does not pretend otherwise.

Helmer too has a clear idea of how life should work and tries to live according to his convictions. In his case this means he does everything he can to stay in a dominant position over others, and one of the ways he attempts to do this is by lecturing them, thereby placing himself in a superior position. He holds himself out as representing the established laws and societal order, and so avoids facing his own low self-esteem. Even at the end, when Nora tries to have a serious talk with him, he continues to patronize her by announcing: "Play-time's over, now comes lesson-time."[30] Thus Helmer himself is conflicted, for on one hand he expects women to be dutiful and fulfill their tasks without complaint—and on the other hand he is fascinated by overexcited women on the edge, as he perceives Nora to be. This is implicitly revealed when Nora instructs Mrs. Linde to stop sewing and to rapidly bundle up her dress because Helmer cannot bear to watch ordinary mending. Also later, when Helmer and Nora come back from the party, he presents Nora as his "lovely . . . *capricious* little Capri girl," and tells Mrs. Linde that she should do embroidery instead of knitting. He is a bit drunk and does not hesitate to demonstrate how much more graceful embroidering is compared to knitting.[31] Repeatedly, we experience Helmer's main desire, which is to have power over others. Although he believes himself to be a moral person, he does not argue in moral terms. His principles are guided rather by the social conventions of the day.

Like Krogstad and Mrs. Linde, Helmer questions neither his position, which he takes for granted—nor his actions, which he thinks are beyond reproach. Again similarly to Mrs. Linde, Helmer is convinced that his actions are motivated by love, in his case, his love for Nora and his children. He sincerely wants to take care of his family and enjoy his attractive little "Capri girl." At the end of the play, Nora realizes what he is really like, and asserts that he does not love her, but "only found it pleasant to be in love with" her.[32]

Helmer's and Mrs. Linde's "love" can be conceptualized as the desire to escape anxiety and inner insecurity. Helmer is afraid of being confronted by an equal partner; Kristina fears solitude. None of the three—Helmer, Mrs. Linde, or Krogstad—undergo any inner development but stay the same from the beginning to the end of the play. Remaining dependent on their own wishes and aims to uphold their social status and failing to develop their own subjectivity, they remain objects of the circumstances they are in.

Nora is the only person in the play who gradually develops self-awareness and consciousness of serious psychological problems in her life. She even reaches a point where she no longer needs to unfairly condemn Helmer's mode of behavior during the marriage. In spite of his betrayal, she acknowledges the positive aspects of her marriage. This emerges when, just before leaving, she says to him: "You have always been so kind to me. But our home has been nothing but a play-room."[33]

With such words, Nora finally arrives at a place where she can try to do justice to Helmer, society, and herself. After seven years of false pretenses, she is ready to transform self-contradiction into self-relation and thereby attain a more personal relationship to the world. To put it another way: Nora undergoes a time of inner disunity and reaches the complex but vital question of what her inner standpoint is. This is a courageous step in the world she lives in, and would have been unrealistic at that time. When critics say that such a step could only be taken in the story, not in reality, they appear to be correct. Although Ibsen wanted the reader to experience "a piece of reality," the figures are caricatures and the whole story is meticulously detailed, constructed in favor of Nora's leaving home.

Nora's development might explain why the play's message is not limited to the 19th century. What happens to her reflects a kind of psychological transformation that can take place at any time and in anyone's life. In order to reach a new level of consciousness, we human beings—men or women—must often endure a time of inner disunity, in which we try to preserve a form of life that is no longer valid. In spite of Nora's failures, or even because of them, her manner of coping with her difficulties can be taken as a model of transition from one psychological level to another. Nora's final trial—to honestly become aware of her inner conflicts and to bring them into relationship with the spirit of the time—clearly shows that she is reaching toward a new status and a new form of love. This love is not charity and not desire; it is not an interpersonal love and not a self-love. It is a love that wants to find the personal truth and thus can be called a love for truthfulness.

At the end of the play Nora can only recognize that she has lived in a doll's house and that she now must find out where her personal truth lies. Beyond this, she only knows that she was too dependent on Helmer, the family, and her social position—meaning that, as she departs, the best she can do is to negate her previous life. This state of not-knowing makes her tolerant, calm, and confident. She does not yet know what new identity she might discover, but rather she become fully aware of her inner disunity. Maybe this is another reason why the play is still so impressive today. It implicitly conceptualizes the love of truthfulness as the imperative to search for one's personal truth. Love of truthfulness means to dive into not-knowing and to question former perspectives.

Nora does not yet fully understand what it means to enter this process. She is still naively convinced that she can find out "which is right—the world or she."[34] After 150 years of psychoanalysis, we know that the task of questioning ourselves is an ongoing work, once it is begun. We also know that psychoanalysis can easily become destructive: It can be used to sabotage our wishes and actions or to feel superior to others. In pursuing the way of self-questioning we also risk becoming too isolated from society. But in spite of all the dangers, self-questioning might be the only effective antidote to dogmatism and fundamentalism. It prevents us from becoming blind to the spirit of the time and helps us explore our inner conflicts. And above all, it enables us to acquire a first-person perspective, thereby becoming a subject, i.e. a self-reflecting individual.

NOTES

[1] *A Doll's House* is the English translation of Ibsen's original title. In some other editions and/or languages the title has been changed to, *Nora: Or a Doll's House.*

[2] Frances Gray, "Notes," in Henrik Ibsen, *A Doll's House* (London: York Press, 3rd impression, 2010).

[3] Henrik Ibsen, *A Doll's House and Other Plays*, trans. Peter Watts (London: Penguin Books, first publication, 1965).

[4] For further explanations of the Tarantella, see *A Doll's House*, Notes by Frances Gray, p. 12.

[5] Henrik Ibsen, *Nora oder Ein Puppenheim. Schauspiel in drei Akten*, Hrsg. [ed.] Joachim Hintze, 2. Auflage [2nd edition] (Berlin: Cornelsen Verlag, 2011), p. 79.

[6] Hintze, in Henrik Ibsen, *Nora oder ein Puppenheim*, pp. 81-83.

[7] *A Doll's House*, Notes by Frances Gray, pp. 98-104. See also Hintze, in Ibsen, *Nora oder ein Puppenheim*, p. 91.

[8] Robert Fergusen, *Henrik Ibsen: A New Biography* (London: Richard Cohen Books, 1996).

[9] Hintze, in Henrik Ibsen, *Nora oder ein Puppenheim*, p. 84-85.

[10] Ibsen, *A Doll's House and Other Plays*, p. 148.

[11] *Ibid.*, p. 149.

[12] *Ibid.*, p. 148.

[13] *A Doll's House*, Notes by Frances Gray, pp. 98-104. See also: http://www.englihttp://www.english.uwosh.edu/roth/VictorianEngland.htm.

[14] Ibsen, *A Doll's House and Other Plays,* p. 151.

[15] *Ibid.*, p. 158.

[16] Hintze, in Ibsen, *Nora oder ein Puppenheim*, pp. 85-87; *A Doll's House,* Notes by Frances Gray, pp. 81-89.

[17] Ibsen, *A Doll's House and Other Plays,* p. 152.

[18] *Ibid.*, p. 201.

[19] Alfred Blatter, *Revisiting Music Theory: A Guide to the Practice* (New York and London: Routledge, 2007).

[20] Ibsen, *A Doll's House and Other Plays,* p. 217.

[21] *Ibid.*, pp. 220-221.

[22] *Ibid.*, p. 222.

[23] *Ibid.*, pp. 229-230.

[24] *Ibid.*, p. 230.

[25] *Ibid.*, p. 157.

[26] *Ibid.*, p. 157.

[27] *Ibid.*, p. 209.

[28] *Ibid.*, p. 208.

[29] *Ibid.*, p. 165.

[30] *Ibid.*, p. 226.

[31] *Ibid.*, pp. 213-214.

[32] *Ibid.*, p. 225.

[33] *Ibid.*, p. 226.

[34] *Ibid.*, p. 229.

9

Dante's Cosmogonic Love Moves The Stars: May It Move Me!

Brigitte Egger

THE *DIVINE COMEDY*: FROM DESPAIR TO BLISS

Dante composed his *Divine Comedy* with one intention: "to remove those living from their state of misery and to lead them to the state of bliss, in this lifetime," as he states in a letter to his friend and patron.[1] This jewel of a poem and dynamic map of the soul begins in the deepest valley of sorrow, at the very moment when it dawns on Dante that he has completely lost the true path. Now remarkably enough, just as he realizes that he needs a new orientation, he sees the mountain and the light of the sun, which he knows could lead him out of his despair. This moment is like a second birth, and brings to mind the corresponding moment when we decide to enter analysis, ready to change. Dante has made the journey successfully himself, and he lets us know from the start that recounting his ordeal is entirely for our benefit. We may retrace his steps alongside him and he will offer each of us individually what we need to find our own right path.

Dante's poem opens with these lines:

> In the middle of the journey of our life
> I found myself within a dark forest,
> for the straight way was lost.
>
> Ah, how hard it is to say what it was,
> this forest, savage and harsh and strong,
> the very thought of it renews my fear!
>
> It is so bitter that death is hardly more;
> but to report the good I found there
> I will speak of the other things I saw.
>
> I cannot well retell how I entered there,
> for I was so full of sleep at the time
> I abandoned the true way.
>
> But when I had reached the foot of a hill
> where the valley ended
> that had afflicted my heart with fear,
>
> I looked up and saw its shoulders
> already vested by the rays of the planet
> which leads men straight by every road.
>
> At this was a little quieted the fear
> that I had endured in the lake of my heart,
> during the night I had passed in such misery.[2]

In these few verses, Dante outlines the whole of the journey he is going to unfold for us, already focused on the central Light. In this first scene the light is described with the image of the sun, "the planet that leads straight." But gradually it will intensify into an ever brighter light, well beyond what human eyes can normally endure. And as we proceed from the dark wood to Hell, Purgatory, and finally to Paradise, we find that Light will reveal itself as being identical to Love, functioning both as an "attractor" and leading to the source of healing, that is, to the prime mover. Thus, asserts Dante, light and love together, as common experiences and evocative images, carry us through the life-changing process from despair to bliss.

MAY LOVE MOVE ME!

In the course of his long quest, sustained by the dual exertion of empathy and reflection, Dante concentrates more and more on this node of light and love, and his seeing improves accordingly. In fact "eye," "sight," and "vision" count among the most frequently occurring words in the poem. No wonder, for the eye is the organ of both love and knowledge. Thus eye and sight, as well as light, are the best symbols for awareness and consciousness. Moreover, seeing and being seen through the eyes of love has a transforming effect: is not the essence of love to bring the deepest and best into being? Dante is truly a visionary seer who, through the power of love given and received, experienced the healing power of wholeness.

> I believe, for the acuteness I experienced
> from the living ray, I would have been lost
> had my eyes turned away from it.
>
> And it reminds me that I was bolder
> because of this to sustain my gaze, until I joined
> my sight with the infinite value.
>
> O abundant grace by which I presumed
> to fix my eyes upon the eternal light,
> so much that I spent my seeing on it!
>
> In its depth I saw gathered
> and bound with love in one volume,
> the pages that scatter through the universe:
>
> substances and accidents and their interactions
> as if conflated together in such ways
> that what I tell is but a simple light.
>
> The universal form of this node
> I believe I saw, since, saying this,
> I feel my bliss grow wider.[3]

Dante's quest culminates in a transforming experience of becoming one with cosmic Light and Love and with the Node wherein they are joined. In other words, he has an experience of uniting with the primordial Mover, or melting of ego with Self. This peak experience brings bliss and fulfillment. Of course, the last step occurs not through an act of conscious doing and imagining, but through an act of grace. Here, desire and will, love and reason, become one. Here, dancing transforms into being danced, moving into being moved. The "olé¡" in Flamenco captures this moment of grace, when the divine sparks can be felt.

As the last verse of the *Comedy* shows, the whole journey is centered on Cosmogonic Love. And as such, it carries a message of astonishing timeliness, a teaching about integrating love and reason, and provides precisely what is needed to resolve our modern ecological and psychic problems.

> but my own wings were not up to this,
> except that my mind got struck
> by a lightning, which brought what I had wished.
>
> Here the high fantasy lost power;
> but already did revolve my desire and my will,
> as one wheel which equally is moved,
>
> the love that moves the sun and the other stars.[4]

DANTE'S LIFE AND TIME

Dante Alighieri lived from 1265 to 1321. He is renowned as the greatest Italian poet but, curiously enough, not as a visionary or mystic. He acquired an encyclopedic knowledge and, as well as poetry, wrote on political philosophy, language, and even physics. Born into an important Florentine family, he was an engaged politician and ambassador. Dante lost his mother when still a child and seems to have had a rather lonely youth. His father remarried and had two more children, but died before Dante's coming to manhood. As was the custom in those days, he was promised in marriage at age twelve. He married at about age twenty, and with his wife had at least four children. We know nearly nothing of her and she appears nowhere in his works.

Dante lived in a troubled and harsh time. Along with an increase in population and competition for resources, not to say greed for power and material possessions, came the fragmentation of the Holy Roman Empire. The powerful tension between Pope and Emperor brought enmities on all levels, between and even inside cities. When the opposing faction came to power in Florence in 1302, Dante was condemned to death and had to remain in exile ever after. He found shelter in various cities and in the courts of northern Italian princes. He died in Ravenna, after twenty years of exile.

The unity of the medieval world was irreversibly breaking up. Fear of the Antichrist and of the end of the world were widespread, but likewise was a longing for peace and justice. Thus, a counter-movement developed, especially expressed in courtly love, obviously influenced by contact with Arabic culture during the crusades. In Florence this emergence of feminine values and veneration of the woman gave birth to the literary movement *Dolce Stil Novo*, or the *Sweet New Style*, entirely centered on love. Dante joined it around the age of eighteen and was to give it a profound and innovative turn. Through him we can witness the dawn of the awesome revolution known as the Renaissance with its cascade of enduring geniuses.

There is at least one portrait, considered to be Dante's, by someone who knew him: a moving fresco by his friend Giotto (1267–1337). He painted it a dozen years after Dante's death, between 1334 and 1337. Dante appears as a crowd member in Paradise in the scene of the Universal Judgment.[5] He has a long thin nose, an intense inward and contemplative look, and the determined expression of a man of reflected action.

THE *VITA NOVA* AND THE LOVE FOR BEATRICE: *METANOIA*

Dante offers us insight into the beginning of his spiritual and poetic journey, his transformation by love, with his *Vita Nova* or *New Life*. This work, written several years before the *Comedy*, is an extraordinary and moving confession of the slowly growing, guiding and inspiring impact of his encounter with Beatrice and his love for her, and how it brought him to a thoroughly new sense of life. He composed it between 1292 and 1295, a few years after Beatrice's death when both were in their mid-twenties. Like Dante, Beatrice was married.

Formally the book is organized around a series of thirty-one poems, accompanied by the autobiographical events that prompted the poems and a structural analysis of them. The subject is the development of Dante's emotional life and how it transformed the content and the form of his art. The deeper content is a series of visions and dreams about Beatrice, whose name means, appropriately, "she who makes happy, blessed," that is, offers beatitude or bliss. These and other events suggest that Dante must have experienced amazing synchronicities.

Most impressive is the turn towards discovering the subjective soul significance of his beloved. When the women in Beatrice's circle made him realize that in his poems he was speaking more of himself than of her, Dante went through a deep spiritual crisis which led him to invent a totally new narrative and a new poetic expression. His turn towards an introverted reflection finds parallel in the mythical horn of the impetuous bull which, torn from the animal and turned upright, becomes the horn of plenty. It is a true *metanoia,* in Jung's sense of the self-healing of an unbearable conflict, which occurs through a process of melting down and being reborn into a larger dimension. It is no wonder that such an inversion is so central to the process of individuation described by Jung, for he himself went through an astoundingly similar soul-transforming experience that led him to write his *Red Book*, six hundred years later. The original title of Jung's book is *Liber Novus* or the *New Book*.

Dante's *metanoia* was all the more intensified by Beatrice's death. The *Vita Nova* ends with reference to an unshared vision prompting him to stop writing poems about her until he had created a totally new way of expressing and communicating his startling experience. He was determined to show adequately the transforming power of feminine wisdom and its power to lead to transcendence. The first poem after his discovery begins thus:

> Ladies who have understanding of love,
> I want to speak with you of my lady,
> not because I believe her praise may be exhausted,
> but to express and thus relieve my mind.
> Thinking of her worthiness, dare I say,
> love makes me feel so sweet,
> that should I not lose courage,
> I would by speaking make people fall in love.[6]

To accomplish his task Dante started studying all the disciplines and cultural expressions he could access and he prepared a breathtaking synthesis of his time, bursting with new concepts, reflections, insights, and even language: the *Commedia*. He chose vernacular Italian rather than Latin, so that even uneducated people could benefit from it. If engaging in human love may lead ordinary people to catch a glimpse of the divine love described by mystics and theologians, then the value of earthly human life is clearly elevated. This was a radical shift from traditional thought. We can read this amazing development as a part of the larger movement of his time towards assigning a greater value to the individual in contrast to the collective, and to the earthly human realm in contrast to the beyond or archetypal realm. Like Giotto in his paintings, Dante in his poems describes the first fully real human characters in European art.

Dante, like Jung when his vision of war became reality, realized how much his personal subjective experience tapped into an objective reality, into timeless patterns that give meaning both to the individual and to humanity. This awareness brought each of these men to feel an obligation towards the collective of their time. They both devoted the rest of their lives to translating their inner experience for the benefit of humankind: Dante with his poetic work, the *Comedy*, and Jung with his scientific work, Analytical Psychology.

THE *DIVINE COMEDY*: A MANDALA FOR INDIVIDUATION

The *Divine Comedy* is a most elaborate, far-reaching, and powerfully conveyed map of the soul. Structured as a true mandala, with a remarkable geometry, this extraordinary work of active imagination consists predominantly of conversations with dozens of inner figures, usually in the form of known historical or mythological characters. It amounts to a personal guide to individuation, like a modern self-help manual: all that is needed is there, in the form of a book you can keep tucked in your pocket.

Dante began the *Comedy* after some years of exile. He first finished "Hell," a few years later "Purgatory," and he completed "Paradise" only a couple of months before his death in 1321. The seven days of his initiation journey take place at Easter 1300 when he was thirty-five, then considered to be the mid-point of life. His masterpiece must have been born out of his deepest creative core, for it is thoroughly composed and consistent in minutest detail, with innumerable cross-references, each part mirroring and containing the whole, and yet there are no signs that the poet ever modified anything. Its effect on the reader is to feel like sinking into an experience of totality, reminiscent of an experience of the transcendent function, which contains all points of view at once. Or like listening to Bach's compositions, which are rooted in this mysterious core where feeling and structure are utterly melted into one.

The *Comedy* consists of three canticles, "Hell," "Purgatory," and "Paradise," each comprising thirty-three songs, plus one preamble, amounting thus to one hundred songs. Each song is composed of an average of one hundred forty-two verses. The verses, with eleven to thirteen syllables each, are organized in tercines of the type aba bcb cdc, forming a chain pattern and making it easy to remember.

While the poet called his poem simply *Comedy*, the epithet "Divine" was added two and a half centuries later with the published versions. It is a comedy because it ends well: a true poem of hope and an ode to love. Dante considered four levels of meaning, from the more superficial to the deepest: literal, allegoric, moral, and anagogic.[7] It is this latter we could name symbolic, and it is the one considered here exclusively. Dante shows a remarkable mental agility, lucidity, and energy, posing a constant intellectual and emotional challenge by shifting among many formal perspectives: emotional narratives, dialogues, comparisons, commentaries, prayers, teaching, and dreams. He manages simultaneously to draw the reader into the emotion of events and to provide a reflective distance from them. It has an effect similar to an analyst's reflecting what is happening in the moment while keeping the emotion alive without drying it out. And, lastly, as a true poem, it is built on a vivifying musical and rhythmical framework of echoes and reverberations.

HUMAN PURGATORY BETWEEN HELL AND PARADISE

Dante's *Comedy* invites us, if I may boldly sum up, to consciously climb down the circles of Hell in order to realize the deadly consequences of being possessed by drives without considering a larger context; next, to dare a radical turning towards introspection, or *metanoia*, and thus be able to climb the mountain of Purgatory, working at finding the right dialogue with all opposing forces and balancing them out; and finally to enter Paradise to unify all these experiences corresponding to a peaceful acceptance of life, revivified and focused on eternal values—in short, to find bliss.

Dante's guide through Hell and Purgatory is the wonderful poet Virgil. He clearly represents a conscious function, traditionally described as reason, but with a warm heart. In my eyes he also represents the exceptional talent of putting every kind of experience into words. In this part of the journey, Dante is mainly focused on observation and empathy and holds illuminating dialogues with the figures he encounters. This again reminds us strongly of the situation in analysis.

His second masterful guide, who leads him through Paradise, is Beatrice, divine love, who uses a vast range of registers, from scolding, challenging, and endlessly teaching him much more rigorously and wisely than Virgil, yet essentially offering him deepest compassion. With her, Dante is confronted more painfully with his own shortcomings and has to enter the work much more directly. Beatrice evokes thus the decisive experience, the one we undergo when we are really alone in the intimate recesses of our own soul and confront ourselves honestly and ethically, for example, with the help of active imagination.

Dante's genius is, firstly, to have dared giving such a central place to Purgatory, in keeping with his acknowledgement of the value of human life on earth; and, secondly, to have been able to give such a differentiated picture of Paradise and Hell, reflecting his exceptional spiritual breadth and ethical depth. Hell and Paradise are non-human, archetypal realms; only Purgatory is a human realm. Moreover, Dante introduces the noteworthy conception of the mountain of Purgatory created by the fall of Lucifer from Heaven and its impact on Earth. For Dante, it was Lucifer who brought about the breaking of the original symmetry and created the axis of Hell-Purgatory-Paradise. And it is on the body of Lucifer himself that Dante and Virgil perform the heroic *metanoia* that brings them from Hell to Purgatory, that is, to the realm of conscious integration of instinctual drives. Indeed, the question of good and evil was as central to Dante as to Jung, and these two have in common their enormous efforts to build a human bridge between hell and paradise.

COSMOGONIC LOVE AND ARCHETYPAL DRIVE

Love, as organizing principle or as fundamental mover, is a universal perception, and it plays a central role in holistic expressions such as creation myths or mystical literature: for instance, the myth of cosmogonic Eros in Hesiod from ancient Greece and the poignant love poems by the Islamic mystics, Rumi and Ibn Arabi, a mere generation before Dante. Jung too confers to love a central place, as testified in his *Mysterium Coniunctionis*, and he ends his biographic late thoughts on the "cosmogonic love" that seizes us:

. . . we are in the deepest sense the victims and the instruments
of cosmogonic "love" . . . as something superior to the individual,
a unified and undivided whole.[8]

Love is closely associated to other fundamental forces, such as
relationship, creation, transformation, movement, energy, all forming
a whole and interrelated field, but love is certainly the most poetic
and inviting expression of them all. Dante often uses the image of the
bow and the drive that moves it to speak of love, on one hand on a
cosmic level, as the primordial mover, on the other hand in the human
realm, as the urge toward individuation, all embedded in the larger
frame of the universe.

Moreover, his poetic descriptions reveal a surprising version of a
theory of archetypes, as presented here by Beatrice:

And she began: "All things whatever they are
have an order among themselves, and this is the form
that makes the universe resemble God.

Here the high creatures see the imprint
of the eternal value, which is the aim
for which the order aforementioned is made.

In the order I speak of, all natures
are inclined, according to their different destinies,
more or less close to their origin;

Hence they move toward different ports
over the great sea of being, and each one
carried according to the instinct it received.

This carries the fire towards the moon;
this is the moving force in mortal hearts
this binds the earth together and unites it.

Not only the creatures that are without
intelligence this bow shoots forth,
but also those that have both intellect and love.

The providence, which assesses all this,
makes with its light the heaven forever quiet,
wherein revolves what has greater speed.

And there now, as to a site decreed,
the power of that bow carries us,
which aims all its arrows at a joyous mark.

Yet it is true that oftentimes the form does not
accord to art's intention,
for matter is deaf in answering,

so likewise does the creature sometimes deviate
from its straight course, for it has the power,
thus impelled, to turn towards elsewhere.

And as one may see fire fall
from a cloud, so the primal impulse
falls to earth, distorted by false pleasure.

You should no more wonder, if I judge well,
at your ascending, than at a rivulet
descending from a high mountain to the lowland.

It would be a marvel if, deprived
of impediment, you remained seated below,
as if on earth a living fire kept still."[9]

In other words, we humans, who have the power and liberty to choose our path, carry therefore the responsibility to make our choices by considering a wider perspective and a higher purpose: put simply, we carry the responsibility to channel love adequately. And we know we do so by the deep bliss that fills us.

PURGATORY OR LOVE AND FREE WILL

Thus, for Dante, love is the basic driving force: on one side it inspires and drives us, and on the other side it is our goal and dignity to aim at reuniting with it. He makes no essential difference between human and divine love. This follows the line of Saint Francis of Assisi (1182–1226) who lived a century before and is legendary for his love of nature and for all creatures whom he called "brothers" and "sisters."

As a consequence Dante gives free will a central place in the human realm, mainly influenced by Thomas Aquinas (1225–1274), a theologian who, half a century before, reflected philosophically about the relationship between faith and reason. Indeed, Dante perceives love and reason as natural dispositions, both, as all movements, being initiated by "heaven." Love, he conceives, and as we commonly experience it first, as an instinctual drive, desire, or attraction, a primordial seeking for pleasure. Reason he describes as the capacity that counsels us about good and evil, and more specifically, enables us to restrain our instinctual drives and orient them towards the good. This amounts to a teaching of ethics, briefly defined as the way to behave best with regard to the whole. Hence it is the very tension between love and reason that creates the space for free will. For heaven cannot be made responsible for all iniquities. As a consequence, all revolves around achieving dynamically the right synthesis between love and reason:

> And although her image, which remained constantly with me, was the boldness of love in holding sovereignty over me, it was of such noble virtue that it never allowed me to be ruled by love without the faithful counsel of reason, in those things where such advice would be useful to hear.[10]

This can be achieved by remaining related to the Self as the organizing principle of the psyche, or expressed in poetic images, by keeping the eyes fixed on the light, on the central point, or keeping the heart turned toward the Celestial Rose.

The main dynamic line of the *Comedy* is, on the cosmic level, the primordial distortion of cosmic love by Lucifer who crashes down from Heaven into Earth, creating in reaction the funnel of Hell *inside* the Earth as well as the mountain of Purgatory *on* the Earth. Lucifer appears here as a dark counterpart to Christ, accompanied by reversed rituals and attributes. Likewise human sinners distort this original Love by being seduced by love in the form of instinctual drives for their egoistic purposes, without considering the larger dimension, nor aiming at reaching any higher expression of love. Dante classifies all the possible distortions of Love producing manifold sins. This differentiated classification corresponds to his differentiated map of Hell, itself mirrored in Purgatory, where sins can accordingly be redeemed. Thus both free will and the possible development in Purgatory prove cardinal for the dignity of humankind.

Meaningfully, the instinctual drives are illustrated by beasts of prey, taking different roles according to their place in the *Comedy*'s mandala. For Dante recognizes them as natural, archetypal energies, expressed either in the material or in the spiritual realm, that is either in Hell or in Heaven, depending on the attitudes of the human beings with whom they are associated. Thus, in Hell, the three beasts— leopard, lion, and she-wolf—stand for the sins of unbridled passion, violence, and fraud. Their respective distortions of love consist in excessive or defective love, perverted love, and betrayed love. However, in Paradise, the three beasts simply provide different types of creative impulses, energies all necessary to accomplish the journey.[11]

Actually, Dante's plan of the *Comedy* offers a suggestive illustration of Jung's theory of neurosis. Aiming at becoming one with primordial love or primal life flow corresponds to finding the source of bliss, peace, and creativity within free human relationships. On the contrary a neurosis or a neurotic symptom corresponds to a reversal or distortion of the life flow which freezes into fixed and sterile rituals, in Dante's world the deadly sufferings of Hell. As the adage says: "destiny carries the willing person but drags the unwilling."

COSMOGONIC LOVE IN BOTTICELLI'S *PRIMAVERA*

One of the most stunning visual interpretations of the *Comedy* was created by Sandro Botticelli (1445–1510) in the same Florence, two centuries later, during the full blossoming of Renaissance humanism. He worked nearly fifteen years (1480–1495) on illustrating the whole drama, distilling each song into a drawing, with the written text on the back of the page. Most are pencil and ink drawings, a few are colored miniatures—a breath-taking achievement.[12] Botticelli's compositions are laden with spiritual meaning and daring formal abstraction, in strong contrast to the empirical and realistic sketches by his contemporary, Leonardo da Vinci (1459–1519):[13] the unity of the medieval world is definitely lost, but the exaltation of the human realm, so dear to Dante's heart, is flowering.

One painting in particular seems to me to sum up in an original way Dante's cosmogonic understanding of love: Botticelli's *La Primavera* or *Spring*. Under the aegis of Venus, the Goddess of Love, standing here for *Humanitas*, we see the full expression of the highest quality of the human mind. It offers a wonderful amplification of Dante's emphasis on human achievement and the role of love in this lifetime.

La Primavera (Figure 1), painted around 1482, more than merely illustrating a season, expresses a profound message finding no better symbol than spring. This masterpiece indeed proves to be a genuine key with which to meditate on the archetype of Cosmic Love through the lens of the motif of Spring: it offers a moving synthesis of human insight about creativity and happiness, the three being synonyms at

Fig. 1: Sandro Botticelli, *La Primavera*, ca. 1482 (Uffizi Gallery, Florence, Italy).[14]

their core. A subtle dance, with an inner rhythm, develops from right to left, in accordance with its introspective message.

On the right, Zephyr, the god of spring wind, ravishes the nymph Chloris, the green one, who makes flowers grow: thus the world spirit fertilizes vegetative nature. (Elsewhere, Zephyr carries Psyche to Eros, or Soul to Love). This marriage transforms Chloris into Flora, goddess of spring and nature in its power of blossoming and renewal, and illustrates the natural creative drive animated by the breath of the spirit. Flora's glance comes to seek us. Her apron is a horn of plenty and spreads the joy of living. Overlooking the scene, Venus leads this process toward spiritualization and consciousness. Goddess of amorous desire, beauty, and fecundity, both physical and spiritual—and to whom spring and the color green are dedicated—Venus is identified here with *Humanitas*, the full expression of the highest quality of the human mind. She is assisted by the Three Graces, venerated for their generous influence on mind, work, and art. The path ends at Mercury, the god who mediates between humans and gods, and thus symbolizes knowledge. Guide of the souls toward the beyond and toward the accomplishment of the work, he points with his caduceus beyond the clouds. His staff with its two winged dragons in equilibrium symbolizes peace and prosperity reached by a creativity integrating opposing forces such as spirit and matter, human and divine, conscious and unconscious, love and reason. The whole unfolding takes place under the sign of Love, depicted as Cupid, son of Venus and Mercury. Cupid, assisting his mother, aims his arrow at the Grace who turns her back to the world and fixes her eyes on Mercury, confirming the introversion of the process and emphasizing the act of reflection.

This initiatory path invites us to choose the very essence of spring—love, desire, generosity, joy of heart—as a basic spiritual attitude and to transform the breath of instinctive drives, in Dante's words, Love, into the conscious accomplishment of the mind. True creativity, nurtured by and dedicated to the eternal dimension, is an attitude leading to harmony, renewal, and healing. And this means nothing less than the joyous blossoming of human dignity.

REHABILITATING THE LOVE PRINCIPLE

Love moves us to the core, to the heart—as does the absence of love. Love is a powerful energy, implicitly of highest value. Explicitly however, in our present culture, love receives little acknowledgement and still less teaching, compared to the complementary values of reason, science, or technology. Yet to resolve the crucial problems of our time—in the realms of ecology, of economics, of psyche—is not Love, as an essential principle, exactly the elixir bitterly needed? Therefore, everything that encourages a higher regard offered to Love represents a basic contribution to these issues: here a field of truly meaningful growth and development lies ahead of us.

As we have seen, Dante and Jung share strikingly similar values. And both offer Love a central place in their worldview. Von Franz goes so far as to recognize one of Jung's greatest achievements as the rehabilitation of the feminine principle of Eros, that is, of personal differentiated relatedness and empathy, along with the rehabilitation of the feeling function—all different forms of Love.[15] Truly, human love and relationship prove unique in challenging us to open our heart to otherness and transcendence. And, understanding ethics as the best possible way to behave with regard to the whole, it is vital that an ethical standpoint be informed by a personal, loving relationship to something beyond our limitations, be it the planet or a divine spirit.

To resolve deep problems, deep insights are required. Thus, to foster lasting transformation of behavior, for example ecological or economic behavior, it is wise to search for inspiration in the greatest and timeless teachings of humankind, involving the whole human being with intellect, spirit, soul, and heart. Dante's *Comedy*, with its powerful mystic poetry, belongs to the treasury of guides and testimonies about the journey to transformation. These recount journeys of "death and rebirth," whether symbolic or real, at the verges of the unknown, journeys to the beyond, and to death. They form the large family of individuation journeys describing mystic, shamanistic, initiatory, or near-death experiences, and may take the shape of the "Books of the dead" or their medieval correspondents, the "Ars moriendi" or Art of dying. The *Comedy* shares the main archetypal features of these experiences: first, a struggle through hellish and dark suffering, imprisonment, and dismemberment; second, a passage through a narrow turning point bringing radical transformation; and, third, an emergence, a rebirth into light, bliss, and love, being at one with the world. They all express the search for the treasure so difficult to reach, the nodal place of wholeness and love, where creativity, healing, and communication flow. In more abstract terms, this journey to transformation leads to the source of all energy; or, from Dante's perspective, to being moved by the cosmogonic love that moves the sun and the other stars.

Discovering the *Divine Comedy* counts among the most precious gifts received in my life.[16] Learning and reciting verses by heart offers a sustaining teaching and presence. As for the world at large, I believe Dante's message about integrating love and reason is of utmost timeliness.

NOTES

[1] Dante, § 15 in his letter to his young friend and patron Cangrande della Scala, ca. 1316-1317, in *Dante Alighieri. Tutte le opere*, ed. Borzi I (Roma: Newton Compton, 2010). All translations of Dante in this essay are my own.

[2] Dante, "Hell," 1:1-21, in *Dante Alighieri*.

[3] *Ibid.*, "Paradise," 33:76-93, in *Dante Alighieri*.

[4] *Ibid.*, 33:139-145.

[5] Fresco in the Capella del Podestà, Palazzo del Bargello, Florence.

[6] Dante, "Vita Nova," § 19, in *Dante Alighieri.*

[7] *Ibid.*, § 8, letter to Cangrande della Scala, in *Dante Alighieri.*

[8] C.G. Jung, *Memories, Dreams, Reflections*, ed., Aniela Jaffé, trans. Richard and Clara Winston (London: Fontana, 1993), p. 354.

[9] Dante, "Paradise," 1:103-141, in *Dante Alighieri.*

[10] *Ibid.*, "Vita Nova," § 2, in *Dante Alighieri.*

[11] Adriana Mazzarella, *In Search of Beatrice. Dante's Journey and Modern Man* (Milano: In/Out—Vivarium, 2001), p. 386.

[12] See for instance, Hein-Thomas Schulze Altcappenberg, ed. *Sandro Botticelli, The Drawings for Dante's Divine Comedy* (London: Thames & Hudson, 2000).

[13] *Ibid.*, p. 282.

[14] Sandro Botticelli, *La Primavera*, ca. 1482, tempera on wood, 79.9×123.6 inches, provenance, Lorenzo and Giovanni di Pierfrancesco de' Medici family collections, Uffizi Gallery, Florence, Italy. Digital image by *Art Project Powered by Google*, at http://www.googleartproject.com/collection/uffizi-gallery/artwork/la-primavera-spring-botticelli-filipepi/331460/(accessed December 14, 2012).

[15] Marie-Louise von Franz, "C.G. Jung's Rehabilitation of the Feeling Function in Our Civilization," in *Jung Journal: Culture & Psyche*, Vol. 2, No. 2 (2008), pp. 9-20.

[16] My heartfelt gratitude goes to Adriana Mazzarella, cited above, for generously sharing her deep (Jungian) understanding of the *Divine Comedy.* My warmest thanks also to Alison Vida for her skills and empathy in reworking my English; and to Luca Vetterli for his shared love of Dante and for his critical support.

10

Compassion In Buddhism: Practices And Images

Dariane Pictet

s I reflected on compassion, I was reminded of a recent event, when I witnessed two young children being informed that their father had been lost at sea. I felt such a spontaneous outpouring of love and sadness that any attempts to repress it would have caused a far deeper suffering. Something in us dies when we bear the unbearable: narcissistic feelings melt away; we attune to the anguish around us and respond with compassion. In this field of shared being, we become infused with presence and separation dissolves. Compassion is the flowering of love, effortless and natural as a water flowing out to sea.

Compassion is rooted in suffering (the word comes from the Latin, *compati,* and means literally "with passion;" it is composed of *com* "together" and *pati* "to suffer.")[1] To be able to suffer with a person means that one's individual concerns are no longer central and that we participate in the suffering of others. In Buddhism, compassion stems from knowing that we are not separate from one another. As there is no divide, loving another is an extension of loving oneself and we are united in the flow of existence.

Non-duality

In the Buddhist view, a state of consciousness exists which is beyond duality, where subjectivity expands into oneness and affirms a state of unity that can be consciously apprehended. Listen to Zen master Son-o, from the 17th century:

> I came to realize clearly that Mind is no other than mountains and rivers and the great wide earth, the sun and the moon and the stars.[2]

Jung says:

> At times I feel as if I am spread out over the landscape and inside things, and am myself living in every tree, in the splashing of the waves, in the clouds and the animals that come and go, in the procession of the seasons.[3]

Jung postulated an objective or autonomous psyche, and felt that we are in the psyche, the psyche is not in us. This experience is constellated when the tight edges of our identity are loosened and awareness expands into boundlessness. In this *unio mystica*, we are interwoven with our ancestors, our culture, the air, and nature, and so share the suffering and the joy of all forms of life.

In Buddhist terms, this kind of experience reflects the true nature of reality, which is beyond concepts that may lead to the delusion of separateness, like self and other, inside and outside, past and future. All of existence is one. The world doesn't exist in itself; it is not separate from us, and is constructed by and reflects the projections of our own state of consciousness. Although for Jung, the Self represents a *coincidentia oppositorum*, the archetype that reconciles opposites such as conscious and unconscious, he also writes:

> I have just finished reading a book by a Chinese Zen Buddhist. I felt as if we were talking about one and the same thing and were simply using different words for it. The use of the word "unconscious" is not the decisive thing; what counts is the Idea that lies behind this word.[4]

Although the formulation by Jung and Chinese Zen Buddhism is different, the experience of mystical oneness they each describe may be very similar. For instance the Zenrin allows that, "From of old there were not two paths; 'those who have arrived' all walked the same road."[5]

Buddhism is traditionally described as a non-theistic religion. Even though statues and artistic depictions of the Buddha abound, and people may even kneel to them in devotion, they are not worshipping Siddhartha Gautama as a god; they are honoring Buddha for the teachings he received and the wisdom he shared with them after he was enlightened under the Bodhi tree. By showing respect to these images, they are reminding themselves of the qualities of the "buddha" state, such as concentration, generosity, compassion, patience, and morality, and are inspired to develop them. As the Dalai Lama says:

> The great white whale a Buddhist seeks is Buddhahood—a complete awakening from limitation, a complete awakening from the hallucination of an independent, eternal self. And it can be achieved only through a motivation of selfless compassion for all beings without exception.[6]

DHARMA

To become a Buddhist, one takes refuge in the Three Jewels, which are the Buddha (the state of enlightenment that the Buddha represents), the Dharma (the teachings of Buddhism), and the Sangha (the community of practitioners).

> Taking refuge in the Buddha, we learn to transform anger into compassion; taking refuge in the Dharma, we learn to transform delusion into wisdom; taking refuge in the Sangha, we learn to transform desire into generosity.[7]

Dharma, the teachings and doctrines of the Buddha, include careful examination of the nature of reality; the Four Noble Truths. The first Noble Truth is that we are subject to change; suffering is created by impermanence.

The second Noble Truth is that attachment to transient things is at the origin of suffering. We try to grasp what is forever changing, or we crave something that is not there, gone. Life is an open stream of change, and like the weather, brings storms and harvest moons, thunder and cooling breezes. We suffer when we get attached to a season, and rage and protest and cry when the winds carry us to a different reality. When we accept what is and stay open and related, we are naturally responsive. When we dam the natural stream of life with our resistance to the changing world, life loses its sense of vitality and becomes a source of misery.

The third Noble Truth is that we can end suffering, essentially by letting go of the sense of self that causes it. We can discover that, we too, are as fluid as the winds of life which stream through us. No hardness, no sedimentation, no need to reclaim yesterday's identity and imagine how to force tomorrow to be what we want it to be. We can be with what is, or what is no longer, suffering the lost father at sea, observe it, befriend it, be still, and thus live fully the present moment.

The fourth Noble Truth is expressed in the Eight-Fold Path, the steps that lead us to free ourselves from attachment and delusions. It announces that all of our faculties and attitudes can be focused and directed to the discovery of the unity of all things.

> Thus the transformation of the world is brought about by the transformation of oneself…To transform oneself, self-knowledge is essential; without knowing what you are, there is no basis for right thought, and without knowing yourself there cannot be transformation.[8]

Buddha is called "the Intelligent Heart,"[9] and Buddhist practices encompass self-examination. "Right Thought" is one of the steps in the Eight-Fold Path, which is a practical guide given by Siddhartha Gautama to aid in the development of wisdom, ethical conduct, and mental discipline. It shows us where we imprison ourselves in self-perpetuating narratives and self-defeating statements that contribute vastly to feelings of alienation and dissatisfaction.

Byron Katie tells us that, "A thought is harmless unless we believe it. It's not our thoughts but the attachment to our thoughts that causes suffering."[10] Let's be attentive to the consequences that derive from unexamined thoughts or from the way we can be tricked by language. Take, for example, the statement, "My father is selfish." This assertion implies that he loves himself more than me and this places me in a victimized position. It constellates the wish that "today, maybe, he will be different," which leads to a cycle of thwarted expectation and disappointment. Furthermore, my father probably perceives he is being judged, that somehow he is failing me, which puts him in a defensive stance.

If I imagine what it would feel like not to have the thought, "my father is selfish," a door opens and lightness enters, in this new space I can ask myself what makes him behave as if he didn't care for me? Perhaps he has not opened his heart because of the way he was raised? Perhaps in his culture, in his time, parenting was viewed very differently? Now, I am beginning to understand him instead of judging him. I may then begin to feel sorry for a man who has never been able to be spontaneous and playful with his children. Sadness for a person who has been cut off from the loving intimacy of relationship with his own kin begins to soften me.

Another way to unblock the flow of compassion is to turn around the assumption made in the above example ("my father is selfish") and ask, "how am I selfish?" Finding that kernel of egotism in oneself evokes resonances between our own flawed attitudes and those we experience in others. Perhaps I want my father's attention for myself and am not open to him in a loving way. Perhaps, I am, in my behavior, just as selfish as he supposedly is. It is not so easy to impart blame when we find the same attitudes in ourselves. This insight enables us to respond with an understanding that arises from a sense of common ground that we share with one another.

We recognize our parents in ourselves; we share DNA strands with them and thus carry them in every cell of our body. In this shared identity, we can get caught in a loop of suffering; when we are angry with them, we are angry with ourselves. And when projecting anger outwards, we sense that we are inflicting pain to loved ones, which in turn perpetuates suffering. We may also barricade ourselves from closeness by thinking unkind thoughts such as: "I don't have time for this, we all have problems, this person is always complaining, or their attitude is wrong." These moralistic undertones mask our difficulty with engaging with someone else's pain. It throws us back to our own undigested hurt, and areas in ourselves that we have encapsulated and hidden away somewhere on the frontiers of consciousness. To unknot these situations, we have to engage with our own shadow material.

Suffering is part of existence; we all know it. However, Buddhist doctrine distinguishes neurotic suffering from selfless suffering. The former is egocentric and attached to our so-called history, our past, or rather our interpretation and clinging to the past. When we are tied down by the heavy baggage of our expectations, of how things should be, we create separation within ourselves. This damming up of the stream of life contracts us and we curl up in avoidance of what actually is, huddled in fear of our own emotions.

Selfless suffering is dynamic and expansive, as we accept it and become one with it. Then we take care of the hurt with appropriate, healing action. This requires a shift in the way we understand time, a succession of moments, none of which we get attached to. The suffering child of the past is present in our awareness, together with all the other memories of our childhood; all are alive simultaneously, side by side, all still there, there is no frozen experience isolated in trauma. We don't have to cure any one; we can allow all those children to be. Freed from the desire to single out particular moments, fluid memories add their particular vibrancy to a continuum of existence.

There is a vertical movement of consciousness that is directed towards one's inner world: an active listening, attentive, accepting, and non-judgmental. As we develop concern and empathy for our own wounds and abandoned potentials, we extend horizontally towards the other. Similarly, as we attend to another with openness and care, this relatedness also unfolds its gentleness within us. Whether the primary impulse is constellated by an outer or inner object depends on whether one's predominant orientation is introverted or extraverted.

> . . . wisdom and compassion are the two sides of the same coin, one representing personal and the other transpersonal consciousness and both are equally indispensable for the attainment of enlightenment.[11]

The Intelligence or "wisdom" side of the coin is to examine our beliefs, with simplicity and directness, and question fearlessly and courageously all the ways we interpret reality. In the analytical encounter, the analysand describes his world, his experience or her memories. It is in the weaving and retelling of the narrative, the exploration and the being-with of the story that healing perspectives emerge. We do no attempt to change the experience with another interpretation of it, but to dwell in it until it transforms all of itself. We metabolize undigested experiences by giving them our attention, our lovingkindness, without the judgments that inevitably bring us back into duality, into the affect that screams that something was good, or bad, or unjust—even when acceptance of what is can appear as passivity or even as a lack of compassion.

To develop compassion, we need to examine reality and our assumptions about it, in order to see things as they are. Wisdom is differentiated and finely attuned, and compassion cannot operate from an inauthentic ground. If we say yes to something without being authentic, we deny the ground of our being and our reactions will be tinged with resentments and bereft of love. Compassion is also distinct from the feeling of being pulled in by an emotional response to someone's situation. In this case, attachment may come from the negative pole of the relational complex and lead to fusion.

The Vietnamese Zen teacher, poet, and activist Thich Nhat Hanh speaks beautifully about compassion as a result of the understanding of what he calls "Interbeing," the ability to see beyond the tight envelope of personal identity and feel the oneness that lies beyond it. He describes Interbeing as the ability to see "you in me and me in you." This deep level of interconnectedness, which Jung calls the collective unconscious, links us to our parents, our ancestors, and all forms of life. As we are all interdependent, we cannot exist by ourselves, we "inter-be" with our surroundings, our culture, the air we breathe, and the sun which gives us existence. Hanh's poem is called, "Please Call Me by My True Names:"

> Don't say that I will depart tomorrow—
> even today I am still arriving.
> Look deeply: every second I am arriving
> to be a bud on a Spring branch,
> to be a tiny bird, with still-fragile wings,
> learning to sing in my new nest,
> to be a caterpillar in the heart of a flower,
> to be a jewel hiding itself in a stone.
> I still arrive, in order to laugh and to cry,
> to fear and to hope.
> The rhythm of my heart is the birth and death
> of all that is alive.
> I am the mayfly metamorphosing
> on the surface of the river.
> And I am the bird
> that swoops down to swallow the mayfly.
>
> I am the frog swimming happily
> in the clear water of a pond.
> And I am the grass-snake
> that silently feeds itself on the frog.

I am the child in Uganda, all skin and bones,
my legs as thin as bamboo sticks.
And I am the arms merchant,
selling deadly weapons to Uganda.
I am the twelve-year-old girl,
refugee on a small boat,
who throws herself into the ocean
after being raped by a sea pirate.
And I am the pirate,
my heart not yet capable
of seeing and loving.
I am a member of the politburo,
with plenty of power in my hands.
And I am the man who has to pay
his "debt of blood" to my people
dying slowly in a forced-labor camp.

My joy is like Spring, so warm
it makes flowers bloom all over the Earth.
My pain is like a river of tears,
so vast it fills the four oceans.
Please call me by my true names,
so I can hear all my cries and my laughter at once,
so I can see that my joy and pain are one.
Please call me by my true names,
so I can wake up,
and so the door of my heart
can be left open,
the door of compassion.[12]

The idea of Interbeing is that life is a continuous process of transformation and interconnectedness; the mayfly eaten by the bird changes into a new life form. This also applies to our deeds; every action has a consequence on our environment. In a Jungian sense, the poem illustrates how our shadow functions. We participate in collective suffering because we are all part of the long chain of being. Like the pirate who rapes the girl, we too have hearts "not yet capable of seeing and loving." We too feed on other life forms, like "grass-snakes that silently feeds itself on the frog." We do this by ignorance, in buying clothes made in a sweatshop, by investing in arms or any other business which creates suffering at the end of the industrial chain. There is nothing we can do that doesn't impact, in some way, the world around us. These conscious or unconscious forces are continually at work in us and in the universe. Jung asks us to be attentive to how the shadow functions in us, but in Zen, there is no separate "I" that commits foul deeds.

Thich Nhat Hanh's Interbeing also reminds me of intersubjectivity; the intimately shared relational field created in the analytical *temenos*. The Self there is experienced as a unifying Third, an objective, mutual field beyond the personal conscious spheres yet encompassing subjectivity.

> When two appropriated worlds have dissolved into an encompassing realm of profound and disturbingly alien mutuality, "my" concerns are also "yours."[13]

Buddhist practices endeavor to stop the mind from dualistic thinking. When consciousness is directed towards what is, suspending judgments and identifications, then awareness opens into boundlessness.

MINDFULNESS AND LOVINGKINDNESS

Mindfulness is concerned with awakening to the present moment. Our mind constantly goes toward reliving the past or elaborating on the future. The practice of mindfulness aims at developing a witnessing attitude to the sensations, feelings, and thoughts that stream through our consciousness, an attitude that leads to non-attachment to them. To be mindful is to be truly alive, present, and open to what is happening right now. As we breathe, consciously in and out, we become immersed in the present moment. A non-critical hovering awareness helps us to become aware of a source out of which all mental activities emerge. This ground of being is described as pure and luminous and experienced as lovingkindness.

Pema Chodron, a Tibetan Buddhist, tells us that to awaken lovingkindness, we need to develop curiosity about who we are, to be interested, inquisitive, and befriend ourselves without the desire to change anything. She describes the thought that we need to change or improve ourselves as "a subtle form of aggression against who we really are."[14]

This being with what is, as opposed to nurturing a desire to improve ourselves, finds its culmination in Zen Buddhism. The stance there is that we are already enlightened; we sit (practice meditation) because we are enlightened. If we haven't reached this level of consciousness, fear creates the three poisons of ignorance, greed, and anger. The notion that we lack anything stems from ignorance of what is, which breeds greed, the desire for something other than what is, which in turns generates anger.

> If we are rid of the self, the three poisons become transmuted into the three virtues of the bodhisattva. Ignorance becomes the state of total discrimination, so we no longer discriminate between what is good and what is bad; instead we deal with it in the appropriate way. Similarly anger becomes determination and greed becomes the selfless compassionate desire of the bodhisattva to help all beings realize the enlightened way.[15]

The qualities required for this examination of our ground are gentleness, openness, and precision—and the medium is meditation. Joan Halifax, who works with the dying, says:

> Loving-kindness allows us to transform our sense of separation and alienation into love. It is helpful to see that we are part of a greater whole and a contemplative practice like loving-kindness can remind us that we are part of a continuum. We are more than our bodies, more than our thoughts, more than our feelings. Every time we identify with a fixed point in space or time, we close our hearts to the vastness of our being. Every time we narrow the vision of what we really are, we fall into fear.[16]

In compassion meditation we initially focus on extending compassion to someone for whom we feel genuine love. Then, as we learn to enlarge this field, the practice expands to include people in our close circle, until we can include the whole world. Many Buddhist compassion meditations begin with basking in the memory of mother's love. This practice can only begin when the ego can evoke a primordial experience of security and containment.

A borderline patient comes to mind for whom the energy of the mother complex evoked only anguish and rage, again and again in an endless circle of pain. Her deep deprivation of good-enough mothering led her to self-medication and the turmoil of heroin addiction for long and painful decades. No one can survive very long a total absence of love. Love was there somewhere, hidden in the subtext of her constructed reality. One day, she described to me a full sense of containment when lying on the grass on a summer's day. Her recovered memory of being sustained by nature, by the warmth of the sun, by the strength of gravity and the smell of soil and earth under her body laid the ground for our work to constellate the positive pole of the mother archetype.

In Buddhism, meditation expands the field of consciousness; and, as we periodically touch the luminous source, the buddha nature, lovingkindness, and compassion become increasingly part of our relational attitude. The challenge is to make this transitory mood permanent and all-encompassing. And this requires practice, daily practice in letting go of the attachment to our ideas about things, as opposed to what is. As lovingkindness matures, it expands into compassion.

BODHISATTVA

Great compassion is the very essence of the Buddha mind and is released in service to mankind. A *bodhisattva* is a being who takes the vow of coming back to this realm of existence, life after life, until every single sentient being has been liberated from delusion. It describes the extraordinary willingness to be present, life after life, until everyone has awakened from the shackles of suffering. The vow is four-fold: However innumerable sentient beings are, I vow to save them. However inexhaustible the defilements are, I vow to extinguish them. However immeasurable the *dharmas* are, I vow to master them. However incomparable enlightenment is, I vow to attain it.

The figure of the *bodhisattva* emerged from Mahayana Buddhism, the school of the "Great Vehicle" (which includes Tibetan Buddhism and Zen Buddhism), and it lies at the very center of the *Dharma*. (The word *bodhisattva* comes from the Sanskrit, and literally means "one whose essence is perfect knowledge." It is composed of *bodhi* "perfect knowledge" and *sattva* "reality, being.")[17] In these traditions, enlightenment is inextricably linked to compassion. In other traditions, like Theravada Buddhism, the adept seeks nirvana, or liberation for himself.

> The bodhisattva, (is) the archetypal social worker, who is not primarily concerned with his or her enlightenment, not with ascending but descending the mountain, going into the world to help everyone become enlightened.[18]

Compassion is not a feeling but an activity. We don't just accept what is; we take care of things, we deal with the situation. *Karuna* is the movement of compassion in the world. When we practice compassion, we renounce the self and we become the hands and the arms of the *bodhisattva*, or the workings of compassion.

> The goal of Eastern religious practice is the same as that of Western mysticism: the shifting of the center of gravity from the ego to the Self, from man to God. This means that the ego disappears in the Self, and man in God.[19]

In the West, we may think of Michelangelo's *Pieta*, where Mary holds in her outstretched arms the body of her crucified son, lying on her open lap. Her gaze evokes compassion, her right hand open in acceptance.

In the East, Buddhists turn to the *Bodhisattva*, who hears the cries of the world and has thousands of eyes to perceive suffering. The most exalted image of compassion is *Avalokiteshvara*, the *bodhisattva* of Infinite Compassion. His name is said to mean "he who observes the sounds of the world" and "lord of all that is seen." It is said that the ambrosia of his compassion drips from the tip of his fingers into the deepest crevices of hell; and, he has renounced bliss until we all awaken.

Here, in Figure 1, *Avalokiteshvara* dwells in innermost silence. His joined hands support a seated, meditating Buddha. This image symbolizes both an eternal source and its manifestation, lovingly embraced and contained. *Avalokiteshvara* wears serenely a double strand of the pearls of illumination and joy. This necklace of souls can also refer to the pearls of past experiences: a purified, realized, and atoned life, remembered pearl by pearl. The Buddha

Fig. 1: *Avalokiteshvara*, jade carving height, 20 cm, photographed by Dariane Pictet.

on his lap offers continuity, the transmission of knowledge for future generations, revealing that out of Being springs forth the dharma, the teachings which lead to wisdom. He displays the *kapala*, the skull bowl of wisdom containing *amrita*, the elixir of immortality.

Avalokiteshvara also takes the form of *Tara*, who is said to have been born from a lotus that grew in a lake formed by the tears he shed as he gazed at the infinite sufferings of the world. Some also say that from his left eye White Tara was born, and from his left, Green Tara. In the Far East he changes form, into *Gwan Yin* in China, and *Kannon* in Japan. Like *Avalokitesvara, Gwan Yin* is often depicted with a thousand arms. In this form she represents the great mother, extending herself to alleviate suffering with infinite expressions of her mercy.

Bodhisattvas are not so much worshipped as they are invoked so that their qualities can be integrated through contemplation. Buddhist practices are designed to slowly help us expand our limited consciousness into the fullness of Being, which the Bodhisattva embodies. "Every sentient being has the potential to be a Buddha."[20]

East/West Formulations

Western research involving MRI (magnetic resonance imaging) indicates that lovingkindness and compassion can be learned. "The scans revealed that brain circuits used to detect emotions and feelings were dramatically changed in subjects who had extensive experience practicing compassion meditation."[21] Another study, from Emory University's Department of Psychiatry and Behavioral Sciences, focused on the effects of compassion meditation on inflammatory, neuroendocrine, and behavioral responses to psychosocial stress. The "findings suggest that meditation practices designed to foster compassion may impact physiological pathways that are modulated by stress and are relevant to disease."[22] A further study of MRI scanning during Zen meditation concluded that,

> current research is suggestive of a current stage of mind, which may have resemblances with the experience of an enlightened state, where time and place limits may have disappeared, and a great feeling of love/unity is experienced.[23]

For Jung, there is a great difference between the Eastern and Western outlooks. There is what Claude Lévi-Strauss called *participation mystique*, a tribal shared Self, in which personal identity is merged with the collective. There is also the individuating self, distinct from this collective oneness, in which Jung stresses the importance of a relational axis between ego and Self as the way through which Westerners can apprehend the transcendent and still retain a witnessing consciousness. He describes the transcendent function as the third that holds both states of consciousness in their shared essence of Unity:

> Between the Christian and the Buddhist mandala there is a subtle but enormous difference. The Christian during contemplation would never say, "I am Christ," but will confess with Paul: "Not I, but Christ liveth in me" (Gal. 2: 20). Our sutra, however, says: "Thou wilt know that *thou* art the Buddha." At bottom the two confessions are identical, in that the Buddhist only attains this knowledge when he is *aniitman*, "without self." But there is an immeasurable difference in the formulation. The Christian attains his end *in Christ*, the Buddhist knows *he* is the Buddha. The Christian gets *out of* the transitory and ego bound world of consciousness, but the Buddhist *still* reposes on the eternal ground of his inner nature, whose oneness with Deity, or with universal Being, is confirmed in other Indian testimonies.[24]

In the mystical experience, individuality dissolves temporarily into the eternal, returning to the field of time and a sense of personal identity after the experience of oneness. For Jung, the *unio oppositorum* is a transient experience, a moment of wholeness, and we fall back into duality. This movement from unity back into duality describes the individuation process. The timeless wisdom of the Self, whose wisdom the ego surrenders to, supports us and gives us a sense of trust, what Jung described as being "in Christ." The symbol for this is the cross. The vertical axis represents the transcendent or eternal field of time. The horizontal axis is historical and human. At the center of the cross, both experiences of time merge and we experience "now time," *kairos*, where we are present, utterly in the moment, held secure in the trust that everything passes.

Enlightenment, for a realized *bodhisattva* such as *Avalokiteshvara* who holds the Buddha in his arms, "the Buddhist *still* reposes on the eternal ground of his inner nature." Here, the center of the cross describes two simultaneous ways of apprehending time: the awareness of the eternal dimension co-existing within the field of time. Being present to the eternal means that all is well, whilst holding in compassion the suffering, transient human experience.

Acting from this place, the center of the cross is spontaneous and free from egoic differentiation such as good or bad. The concern that we may not react ethically stems from a dualistic standpoint and lack of trust. When we know all things are one, that what we do to others we do to ourselves, we can only be compassionate in our response.

In Zen, some practices involve Koans, which are short, paradoxical statements that shock the mind out of its normal habitual thought patterns so that the adept can experience both fields of time simultaneously. These turning words induce a vertigo that silence the mind's chatter. For example: "You cannot get it by taking thought; you cannot seek it by not taking thought."[25]

Buddhism is also attentive to inflation, and humility is practiced daily. The Dalai Lama says: "As for myself, ever since I became a Buddhist monk, that has been my real destiny—for usually I think of myself as just one simple Buddhist monk, no more and no less."[26] Jung is also very attentive to ego inflation, identifying with an archetype, such as saying "I am Christ," can be a psychotic statement.

> Every human being has the same potential for compassion; the only question is whether we really take any care of that potential, and develop and implement it in our daily life.[27]

A Buddhist will say that the ground of one's nature is identical to the ground of Being; there is nothing to escape to or to develop into, and cultivating non-violence and non-attachment ensue. As we wake up from the illusion of separateness, we are in resonance with the free, the boundless, the unconditioned. Self care and care for the community of beings, the *sangha*, becomes a dialectical process, and concerns for the planet, the environment, and all living creatures unfold naturally. When we accept the suffering that accompanies all crisis, it naturally opens the heart, which in turn, expands beyond itself to an all-enfolding sense of presence, of Being. I could do nothing but bear the suffering of the two children I discussed at the beginning of this article, and let it travel through me in compassionate waves.

Finally, "Crowned Compassion," speaks for itself in this poem by Zayra Yves:

I rise on this plateau from another world,
from the world beyond, from the roots of virtue
and noble intention. I rise from a prayer
part land, part stone, part divine imagination and clay.

I am carved from the human life here in this world,
from hands that have known sorrow, innocence, loss,
from hands that have known drunkenness and love lust.

I am formed simultaneous as all movement, motion, aware:
born as a Bodhisattva, as a friend, as the Eternal Mother,
as embodiment of attributes both strong and slender.

I grow from the roots of non-attachment as Bodhicitta,[28]
as the relief from torment and suffering I grow up
out of the dirt, mud, rock toward the sun, rain, sky.
I evolve as porcelain insight, blue as the universe
unfolding brilliant white, glowing constellation
star by star, blossoming consciousness petal by petal,
crystal as the lotus from the pure land I emerge.[29]

NOTES

[1] *Online Etymology Dictionary* (© 2001-2012 Douglas Harper), hereafter abbreviated to OED, s.v. "to suffer," retrieved Dec 7, 2011 at http://www.etymonline.com/index.php?term=compassion&allowed_in_frame=0.

[2] Son-o, quoted by Yamada-Roshi, in Michael Gellert, "Zen and Death: Jung's Final Experience"(A lecture delivered at the C.G. Jung Institute of Los Angeles, Los Angeles, CA 2003), PDF, p. 5, retrieved November 10, 2012 at *The Website of Michael Gellert, Author and Jungian Analyst*, http://www.michaelgellert.com.

[3] C.G. Jung, *Memories, Dreams, Reflections*, ed. Marie-Louise von Franz (London: Fontana Press, 1993), p. 252.

[4] Jung, quoted in Gerhard Wehr, *Jung: A Biography*, trans. David M. Weeks (Boston/London: Shambhala, 2001), p. 449.

[5] The Zenrin, quoted in *The Gospel According to Zen: Beyond the Death of God*, eds. Robert Stohl, Audrey Carr (New York: Mentor, 1970), p. 29.

[6] His Holiness the Dalai Lama, *A Profound Mind: Cultivating Wisdom in Everyday Life*, eds. Nicholas Vreeland and Richard Gere (New York: Harmony, 2011), p. 146.

[7] Red Pine, *The Heart Sutra: The Womb of Buddhas* (Berkeley: Shoemaker & Hoard, 2005), p. 132.

[8] Jiddu Krishnamurti, *The First and Last Freedom* (New York: Harper & Row, 1975), p. 44.

[9] Alistair Shearer, *Buddha: The Intelligent Heart (Art and Imagination)* (London: Thames & Hudson, 1992).

[10] Byron Katie, *Loving What Is: Four Questions That Can Change Your Life* (New York: Three Rivers Press, 2003), p. 5.

[11] Radmilla Moacanin, *Jung's Psychology and Tibetan Buddhism: Western and Eastern Paths to the Heart* (Somerville, MA: Wisdom Publications, Inc., 2003), p. 47.

[12] Thich Nhat Hanh, *Call Me By My True Names: The Collected Poems of Thich Nhat Hanh* (Berkeley, CA: Parallax Press, 1999), p. 72, reprinted by permission of Parallax Press, Berkeley, California, www.parallax.org.

[13] John Ryan Haule, "Analyzing From the Self: A Phenomenology of the 'Third' in Analysis," in *Pathways into the Jungian World: Phenomenology and Analytical Psychology*, ed. Roger Brooke (London: Routledge, 1999), p. 266.

[14] Pema Chödrön, *Awakening Loving Kindness* (Boston/London: Shambhala, 1996).

[15] Bernie Glassman, *Infinite Circle: Teachings in Zen* (Boston: Shambhala, 2002), p. 60.

[16] Joan Halifax, *Being with Dying: Cultivating Compassion and Fearlessness in the Presence of Death* (Boston: Shambhala, 2008), p. 39.

[17] OED, s.v. "bodhisattva," retrieved Jan 12, 2012 at http://www.etymonline.com/index.php?allowed_in_frame=0&search=bodhisattva&searchmode=none.

[18] Glassman, *Infinite Circle*, p. 82.

[19] C.G. Jung, "The Holy Men of India," in the *Collected Works of C.G. Jung, vol. 11, Psychology and Religion: West and East,* trans. R.F.C. Hull (Princeton, NJ: Princeton University Press, 1990), § 958.

[20] The Dalai Lama, quoted from *Dalai Lama: Discourse on the Heart Sutra* [a film documentary], director Kazuo Kikuchi (Beckmann Visual Publishing, 2006), DVD.

[21] "Compassion Meditation Changes The Brain" (University of Madison-Wisconsin, March 26, 2008), retrieved May 11, 2012 from *Science Daily*, at http://www.sciencedaily.com/releases/2008/03/080326204236.htm.

²² "Compassion Meditation May Improve Physical and Emotional Responses To Psychological Stress" (Emory University, October 7, 2008), retrieved Jan 15, 2013 from *Science Daily*, at http://www.sciencedaily.com/releases/2008/10/081007172902.htm.

²³ Rients Ritskes, Merel Ritskes-Hoitinga, Hans Støkilde-Jøgensen, Klaus and Hartman Bærentsen, "MRI Scanning During Zen Meditation: The Picture of Enlightenment?" in *Constructivism in the Human Sciences*, Vol. 8 (1), 2003, p. 86.

²⁴ Jung, "The Psychology of Eastern Meditation," CW 11, § 949.

²⁵ Zenrin, in *The Gospel According to Zen: Beyond the Death of God*, eds. Robert Stohl, Audrey Carr (New York: Mentor, 1970), p. 30.

²⁶ The Dalai Lama, *Dzogchen: Heart Essence of the Great Perfection* (Ithaca, NY: Snow Lion Publications, 2000), p. 122.

²⁷ The Dalai Lama, as quoted in *Buddhist Wisdom: The Path of Enlightenment,* ed. Gerald Benedict (London: Watkins, 2008), p. 37.

²⁸ *Bodhicitta* is sometimes simply defined as "the mind of enlightenment," "the fundamentally empty nature of all things."

²⁹ Zayra Yves, "Crowned Compassion," Track 3, in *Crowned Compassion: Poetry Collection by Zayra Yves* (Label unsigned, 2006, © Zayra Yves), Audio CD, reprinted by kind permission of Zayra Yves.

11

Brother Klaus
and His Love of God

Isabelle Meier

INTRODUCTION

Even though he has been dead for over six hundred years, I met Brother Klaus for the first time in my childhood. A stained glass image of him hung in a window of our house in Uri, Switzerland where I grew up. The light shone through the glass in many colors. I would stand before the window, amazed at the light, the colors, and the image of the gaunt Brother Klaus, his hand raised in protective benediction. I was awed by the numinosity and devotion expressed through this figure.

My fascination was like a distant echo of the emotions triggered in others by Brother Klaus during his own lifetime in the 16th century.[1] Even though he could neither read nor write, he had an energizing and healing effect on the people and culture around him. Many priests, princes, and politicians turned to him for wisdom and guidance. The yearning for the Absolute, the longing for the One, connecting to the "one essence" was the impetus and passion which drove him. He was willing to give up his ego in order to open himself to mystical experience and revelation. His prayer was:

> My Lord and my God, take from me everything
> that distances me from you.
> My Lord and my God, give me everything that
> brings me closer to you.
> My Lord and my God, detach me from myself to
> give my all to you.[2]

For C.G. Jung, Brother Klaus was "the only outstanding Swiss mystic ... by God's grace, [who had] unorthodox visions and was permitted to look with an unerring eye into the depths of the divine soul, where all the creeds of humanity which dogma has divided are united in *one* symbolic archetype."[3]

WHO WAS BROTHER KLAUS?

Brother Klaus, depicted in Figure 1, was originally called Nicholas of Flüe, and was born in 1417 to a respectable family. His father was Henry of Flüe, a mountain farmer and citizen of the village Sachseln. Nicholas of Flüe learned early how to keep cows and bring them across the Alps into Italy to market. One of his earliest biographers, Henry Wölflin, wrote that even as a child, Nicholas of Flüe often prayed and fasted. At the age of sixteen, he performed his military duty and fought with his fellow Swiss in a war. When he was thirty, he married Dorothea and built a house for his family that we visited during the Odyssey week. Dorothea gave birth to five girls and five boys. Nicholas of Flüe was later a councilman in Sachseln and, as such, an arbitrator in ecclesiastical disputes. He was also a respected farmer, whose advice was actively sought in agricultural matters.

At the age of forty-eight, Nicholas reached the pinnacle of success in his public life and political career. He had achieved everything he might have wanted in the public sphere: family happiness, economic success, and social advancement as a judge, councilman, and as the leader of a group of soldiers. Yet despite these outer accomplishments, he was not satisfied. For in his function as judge, he had all too often witnessed and become disturbed by the propensity of his countrymen to make false

Einsidels zu Underwalden. 159
Diß ist Nicolaus / der in dem Wald/
Untrund en und Ungessen/
Allen bey zwanzig Jahren bald
Einsidlerisch gesessen.
Die Berg und Felsen im Schweizerland/
Die haben gehört sein Klagen/

ℛ ƒ   Ein

Fig. 1: Artist Unknown, "Nicholas of Flüe," Woodcut 10 x 6.8 cm, Print 14.8 x 8.3 cm, first published by Petrus Hugo (1684).[4]

accusations, to lie, steal, and generally to overindulge their materialistic desires. His longing for the "one essence," something he had sought in his younger years, came back powerfully.

Consequently, Nicholas of Flüe withdrew from all functions and activities. (Let us recall here another Swiss figure who went through a similar experience: Jung, after leading an extraverted life and achieving international fame, suddenly withdrew from his positions at the University, at the University Psychiatric Clinic, and the International Psychoanalytic Association, started his own search for the soul, and began writing the Red Book.) Thus Nicholas began a painful period of introspection, disappearing for days in the mountains to be alone. Yet his familial responsibilities still called. He had ten children, some of them very young. Should he abandon them? He was angry, depressed, and despairing, and often confided in Heimo Amgrund, a pastor and priest in the village of Kriens, later of the village of Stans, a few kilometers away from Sachseln. Finally, Nicholas of Flüe decided to leave his family, with the apparent acceptance of his wife, to seek God. In the end he didn't go far, but remained in the area of Flüeli-Ranft, where it seems that his wife and children often visited him. So began Nicholas of Flüe's search for peace and love of God.

And, although Brother Klaus was more and more overwhelmed by his experiences and visions of the glory of God, he still remained open to the concerns of his fellow countrymen. His reputation as a "living saint" spread through the Swiss Confederation and soon throughout Europe. Men and women came from far and near seeking his advice. Simple people came as well as councilors and envoys facing difficult problems and conflicts. The latter included representatives of the Archduke Sigismund of Austria, of the city of Constance, and the Duke of Milan.[5]

Fig. 2: Diebold Schilling the Younger, "[E]vents of the *Tagsatzung* [Assembly] at Stans in 1481," plate in the illuminated manuscript, *Amtliche Luzerner Chronik* (1531) [*Official Chronicle of Luzerne*].[6]

It is said that Brother Klaus used his wisdom in a dispute in the Swiss Confederation. He is still today mentioned in Swiss school books as a peacemaker par excellence: On December 21, 1481, Switzerland stood on the brink of civil war. In the night, the priest Heimo Amgrund hurried to a meeting and, presenting some unknown advice of Brother Klaus, urged the council members to continue their discussions. Two hours later, they came to a unanimous resolution of their differences.

This not only eliminated the threat of civil war, but also resulted in two new cantons, Fribourg and Solothurn, being added to the Confederation. Between the city and country compromises were found. An image of Brother Klaus in this advisory role can be seen in Figure 2. It is possible that Brother Klaus's advice brought peace, because the official closing speech to the Assembly (*Tagsatzung*) of December 22, 1481, stated: "First, bring home the news of the loyalty, effort and work that Brother Klaus has shown in these matters! To him we owe truly truth."[7]

I would now like to focus on three of Brother Klaus's visions: the Liestal Vision, the Fountain Vision, and the Pilatus Vision. These three visions, as well as the symbolism found in the image of the wheel, reflect the inner path that Brother Klaus took in his search for the love of God.

THE LIESTAL VISION AT THE BORDER OF SWITZERLAND

On October 16, 1467, Nicholas put on a pilgrim's habit and set out from his home in Flüeli-Ranft, heading for the village of Liestal, which, at that time, lay on the northern border of Switzerland. Here, he was overcome by a terrifying vision. He was shocked to see everything in red: the village and everything around it. He then went to a nearby farmer and asked him for advice. The farmer said that he should go back home to his family and serve God there. Here is a report of what happened, from Brother Klaus's friend and neighbor Emil Rorer:

> So that night he left the farmer's house, went to the field and lay down near a fence to sleep. Suddenly he saw a light shining in the sky. This light opened up his stomach, which he experienced as painfully as though being sliced open with a knife. It showed him that he should go back home and then to the gorge, which he did when morning came.[8]

According to Marie-Louise von Franz, when Nicholas saw red in this vision, he may have fallen into a destructive rage. (Red is the color of war and bloodshed, among other things.) Von Franz believed that Nicholas had a fierce temper, a "very deep passion,"[9] like the many central Swiss soldiers who were eagerly hired from abroad because of their savagery and brutality. These so-called *Reisläufer*, or mercenaries, resembled berserkers who stormed wildly into battle without protective clothing, like armor and chain mail. Nicholas's vocation was, however, to go inward. As indicated at the end of the vision, it was an emotional decision, for the light pierced his stomach, not his head. Von Franz suggests that in order to go inward, he had to accept his shadow—his aggression.[10] In other words Nicholas may have found true inner peace by following the unconsious—that is, by entering into seclusion and going ever more inward, to come to terms with the "berserker" within himself.

(I would like to point out another parallel between Nicholas and C.G. Jung. Like Nicholas, Jung also made a stop at the northern border of Switzerland in Schaffhausen, where he too had a terrifying vision. Jung saw Europe full of blood. It seems as if these two Swiss suffered a similar fate, Jung's vision like a distant echo of Nicholas's. Both men envisioned the destruction and violence that waited outside Swiss borders.)

But where should Nicholas go after Leistal? Nicholas remembered that he once had a vision of a tower in the gorge near his home. So he retired to the gorge in Flüe Ranft and started to live in accord with the natural world, in deep meditation, to search for the "one essence." (I recall here another tower, Jung's tower in Bollingen.) Brother Klaus spent the last twenty years of his life living in the Flüe Ranft gorge as a hermit and a mystic in a cell. According to legend, he fasted for twenty years, surviving only on the Holy Sacrament. He lived in this place of peace and power, the place where he expressed his love for God and found his inner spark of soul (*scintilla animae*), as the mystics called it. The eminent mystic Meister Eckhart said that it was with this inner spark of soul that the human can commune with God.[11]

Fig. 3: Brother Klaus's Meditation Wheel, Artist Unknown, untitled drawing, first printed by Peter Berger of Augsburg (ca. 1488).[12]

It was Brother Klaus's deepest conviction that peace can only be created by the love of God. In his meditations he used the image of a wheel, like that depicted in Figure 3, to help him in his concentration and contemplation.[13]

The wheel image is reflected in the sun wheels that have been widespread for millenia, having their origins in pre-Christian sun cults. In Switzerland, sun wheels are still burned as fireworks on New Year's or on the Swiss National Day (1st of August). As noted by C.G. Jung:

> Brother Klaus' elucidation of his vision with the help of the three circles (the so-called "wheel") is in keeping with age old human practice, which goes back to the Bronze Age sun wheels (often found in Switzerland) and to the mandalas depicted in the Rodesian rock-drawings.[14]

The Jungian analyst, Franz-Xaver Jans, leader of the *Via Cordis* retreat center in Flüe-Ranft today, points out that the center of the wheel represents the divinity. The three spokes of the wheel pointing outward toward the circumference of the circle can be seen as an indication that God remains not in Himself, alone at the center. Rather, he goes outward in relatedness, toward a You and then back to the center as illustrated in the other three spokes of the wheel that point toward the center. The You, the creatures of creation, respond to this offer of relationship with God. Jans describes this process:

> The people taken by the love of God answer with love. The offer of love of God returns from the creation back to the Creator: in an eternal cycle of receiving and passing on, as love of movement in the whole creation.[15]

When a person trusts in God, he or she can be carried away by this love and let go of everything non-essential.

THE FOUNTAIN VISION: THE SOURCE OF THE LOVE OF GOD

Brother Klaus compared the source of the love of God with a fountain that appeared to him in another vision, known as the "Fountain Vision."[16] In this vision, he saw in a village square a large number of hard-working people. It surprised him that despite their prolonged labor, they were so poor. Suddenly he saw on his right an open door and went inside. He found himself in the village communal kitchen, where he saw a fountain springing from within a square basin, which was "crafted on all four sides with iron plates." Brother Klaus's grandson Caspar am Büel describes further:

> Approaching the basin, [Brother Klaus] began to sink, as if walking in a swamp. . . . As the fountain sprang from the basin and flowed on through a canal, it sang so beautifully that it filled him with astonishment. So clear was the water that even at the source, a single human hair could have been seen. And it gushed so mightily that the basin was always filled to the brim and overflowing. It seemed to him that no matter how much [water] flowed forth, there was always more.[17]

Brother Klaus went to investigate why the people in the community did not fetch water from this overflowing fountain. He saw that some were demanding money from the poor to enter the kitchen where the fountain was. Since the poor had no money, they could not draw from the well. Yet, as Isaiah says, "Lo, every one that thirsteth, come ye to the waters, and he that hath no money, come ye, buy, and eat, yea, come, buy wine and milk without money and without price."[18] Brother Klaus's vision seems to have revealed how some people try to profit by selling the precious nourishment of God—a practice that Brother Klaus criticized, making him a forerunner of later-born Protestant reformers, such as Martin Luther and Ulrich Zwingli.

MT. PILATUS: THE MOST IMPRESSIVE VISION

Perhaps Brother Klaus's most impressive vision was influenced by the high mountain, Mount Pilatus (about 2,000 meters /6,561 feet), which dominants the region around Flüeli-Gorge. A record of this vision was not discovered until 1928 in a Lucerne Capuchin monastery, which housed some of the oldest writings about Brother Klaus. In this vision, Brother Klaus saw a pilgrim approaching from the east, dressed in a hat and coat, singing songs and shouting hallelujah. It was as if everything between heaven and earth, all of creation, resounded in harmony.

Brother Klaus was delighted and gave the man a coin, which he accepted in a dignified manner and placed in his hat. Brother Klaus asked him curiously where he was from, but the man answered evasively. Suddenly Brother Klaus saw Mt. Pilatus sink into the ground. The pilgrim transformed too, now wearing a bearskin that was sprinkled with gold and wrapped completely around him, shining like a halo. Brother Klaus could not look away, so beautiful was this sight. "Where are you going?" he asked. The pilgrim replied that he wanted to go up to the mountains. As he walked away, Brother Klaus watched him in amazement.

> As the gold on the bearskin sparkled, sometimes more, sometimes less, it looked as if [the pilgrim] bore upon his shoulder a shiny weapon that flashed with his every step in the sun . . . . In the distance the pilgrim turned around and bowed down in gratitude to all of humankind. Thus Brother Klaus apprehended [the pilgrim's] great gift of love, and was stunned.[19]

The singing of the pilgrim, in his sparkling bearskin, left the whole of creation resonating in melodious, all-encompassing harmony. One can suggest that as Mount Pilatus trembled and sank, the sinfulness of greed was revealed as a truth that would prevail. The pilgrim in the shining bearskin can be seen to symbolize the transformation of the warrior, or the berserker, by the spark of soul or divine light. I imagine that this mystical experience must have filled Brother Klaus with an indescribable feeling of happiness and connection to the creation and the cosmos.

CONCLUSION

Brother Klaus was canonized in 1947 by Pope Pius XII. Marie-Louise von Franz has said that Brother Klaus was not only a typical Christian saint, but also embodied both "the old archetype of the primitive medicine man, the shaman of the Nordic with the archetype of the prophets."[20] The Mt. Pilatus vision especially shows the connection of Brother Klaus to nature. In that vision, the pilgrim changes into a divine figure wearing a shimmering bear cape, perhaps signifying one who has embraced his animal nature and redeemed his aggressive-animal side. If Brother Klaus redeemed his own shadow, which von Franz suggests was aggressive, this vision of the pilgrim wearing the bear cape indicates that this aspect of Brother Klaus's shadow also has been integrated or acknowledged, with him neither displacing nor denying it.

The longing for the "one essence," or for the self, for psychological wholeness, is an experience that many of us strive for in a variety of ways.[21] Many pilgrims continue to come to the Gorge here at Flüeli Ranft seeking Brother Klaus's blessing and healing. May your thirst be quenched at the fountain. May our longing for the One, for the "one essence," bring to us the love of God, which brings peace and harmony.

NOTES

[1] See for instance, Robert Durrer, *Bruder Klaus: Die ältesten Quellen über den seligen Nikolaus von Flüe, sein Leben und seinen Einfluss*, ed. Regierungsrat des Kantons Obwalden, 3 Vols. (Sarnen: Louis Ehrli, 1917-1987). See also, *Quellen: Bruder Klaus und Dorothea, Verzeichnis der Quellen*, at www.nvf.ch/quellen.asp; and *Im Herzen Europa: Bruder Klaus*, sources compiled and published by Werner T. Huber © 1998-2003, at www.nvf.ch (both accessed December 10, 2011).

[2] Heinrich Wölflin, *Die älteste Biographie über Bruder Klaus* (1501), trans. from Latin by Josef Konrad Scheuber (Malters, Switzerland: Lothar E. Kaiser, 1955), p. 56, standard English translation. To create this volume, Wölflin collected years of eye-witnesses' oral reports, written notes, and studied the *Church Book of Sachseln* (1488) [*Sachsler Kirchenbuch*].

[3] C.G. Jung, "Brother Klaus" (1933), in *Psychology and Religion: West and East*, Vol. 11 of *The Collected Works of C.G. Jung*, eds. Sir Herbert Read, Michael Fordham, Gerhard Adler, William McGuire, trans. R.F.C. Hull (Princeton, N.J.: Princeton University Press, 1977), § 487. All further references to Jung's *Collected Works* will be by chapter title followed by volume and paragraph numbers.

[4] "Nicholas of Flüe," Woodcut, Artist Unknown, in Petrus Hugo, *Nicolai von der Flüe Leben dess weitberühmten Br. Clausens, Einsidels und Landtmans zu Vnderwalden, Leben und Wandel* (Luzern: [publisher not named], 1684/1705), p. 159, digital image provided and reproduced by the kind permission of the Graphics Collection of the Zentralbibliothek Zürich.

[5] See Durrer, *Bruder Klaus*, Vol. 1. Volume one contains many reports of encounters with Brother Klaus by simple peasants, priests, princes, ambassadors, and other townspeople.

⁶ Diebold Schilling, "[E]events of the *Tagsatzung* [Assembly] at Stans in 1481," top section of plate in the illuminated manuscript, *Amtliche Luzerner Chronik 1531*, in Franz Meyer, *Schweizergeschichte von der Bundesgründung bis Marignano* (Frauenfeld, Switzerland: Lehrmittelverlag des Kantons Thurgau: 1976), digital image downloaded and cropped from *Wikimedia Commons*, at http://en.wikipedia.org/wiki/File:Tagsatzung_Stans_1481.jpg (accessed November 22, 2011).

⁷ "Quelle Nr. 024," in *Quellen zum Stanser Verkommnis*, in Huber, at www.nvf.ch/qnr024.asp#anf (accessed Nov 23, 2011). For further information about the Treaty of Stans [*Stanser Verkommnis*] and Brother Klaus, see Durrer, *Bruder Klaus*, Vol. 1, pp. 115-171.

⁸ Nicholas von Flüe, "Liestal Vision," reported by Emil Rorer, friend and neighbor of Nicholas, in "Sachsler Kirchenbuch 1488," cited in Durrer, *Bruder Klaus*, Vol. 1, p. 463, my translation with support from Katy Remark.

⁹ Marie-Louise von Franz, *Die Visionen des Nikolaus von Flüe*, 6ᵗʰ Ed. (Einsiedeln: Daimon, 1980/2010), p. 44.

¹⁰ *Ibid.*, p. 44.

¹¹ *Dtv-Atlas Philosophie*, eds. Peter Kunzmann, Franz-Peter Burkard, and Franz Wiedman (München: dtv, 2005), p. 87.

¹² Some historians suppose that, having visited and learned of it from Nicholas, an unknown pilgrim drew the wheel vision and wrote down the related text. In Augsburg, ca. 1488, Peter Berger published a print of the wheel with the text, attributing these to Brother Klaus under the title, "Pilgrim's Tract." See more about the origin of the wheel image: Durrer, Vol. 3, "Ergänzungsband," pp. 229-236.

¹³ Brother Klaus's Meditation Wheel, Artist Unknown, untitled drawing, first printed by Peter Berger (ca. 1488), reprinted in Durrer, *Bruder Klaus*, Vol. 2, p. 363, digital image scanned from this volume.

¹⁴ C.G. Jung, "Brother Klaus," CW 11, § 484.

¹⁵ Franz-Xaver Jans, "Das Tor zur Rückseite des Herzens," in *Schriften zur Kontemplation*, Vol. 9 (Münserschwarzach, Germany: Vier Türme Verlag, 1994), p. 47, my translation with support from Katy Remark.

¹⁶ There are two accounts of the fountain vision. Caspar am Büel, Brother Klaus's grandson, passed on his version orally before 1500, and it was probably written down first in Engelberg. The written

version was discovered in 1928 in the Capuchin monastery Wesemlin in Lucerne. A second version was recorded in 1501, in Heinrich Wölflin's biography of Brother Klaus. Wölflin's version was based on another oral source that he had heard in Sachseln. In this paper, I rely upon Caspar am Büel in Durrer, "Aber ein Gesicht," in *Bruder Klaus,* Vol. 3, *Ergänzungsband,* pp. 29-30.

[17] Nicholas von Flüe, "Fountain Vision," reported in *ibid.,* p. 29, my translation with support from Katy Remark.

[18] Isaiah, 55:1, *The Holy Bible* (Revised Standard Version).

[19] Niklaus von Flüe, "Pilatus Vision," recorded by the Capuchin Father Caspar am Büel, discovered in the library of the Wesemlin Monastery and published by Father Adalbert Wagner, in "Ein Beitrag zur Bruder Klausen-Forschung," in *Der Geschichtsfreund,* Vol. 83 (Einsiedeln: Historischen Verein Zentralschweiz, 1928), pp. 104-116, my translation with support from Katy Remark.

[20] von Franz, *Die Visionen,* p. 130.

[21] See for instance Franz-Xaver Jans-Scheidegger, "Brother Klaus of Flüe and the Prayer of the Heart: A Map of Individuation," in *Unwrapping Swiss Culture, Spring: A Journal of Archetype and Culture,* Vol. 86, guest eds. Stacy Wirth and Isabelle Meier (New Orleans, Louisiana: Spring Journal Books, 2011), pp. 97-109.

About AGAP, ISAPZURICH, and the Jungian Odyssey

A GAP, the Association of Graduate Analytical Psychologists, was established as a Swiss-domiciled professional association in 1954 by the American Mary Briner and several other international graduates of the C.G. Jung Institute Zürich. AGAP is a founding member of the International Association for Analytical Psychology (IAAP, 1955). In 2004, AGAP delegated its IAAP training right to a sub-group of some ninety members who in turn founded the International School of Analytical Psychology Zürich (ISAPZURICH). Thus, since 2004, ISAPZURICH has been conducting postgraduate training in Analytical Psychology under the auspice of AGAP.

Since 2006 the Jungian Odyssey has taken place each semester as an off-campus week-long retreat, open not only to the students of ISAPZURICH, but also to all with interest in C.G. Jung. In keeping with the Homeric journey, the Odyssey travels from year to year, finding "harbor" in different Swiss "ports." A hallmark of the Jungian Odyssey is its thematic inspiration from the *genius loci*, the spirit of the place.

ISAPZURICH was honored to begin collaborating with Spring Journal Books in 2008, when Nancy Cater proposed the publication of an annual series based upon each year's Odyssey lectures. The inaugural volume, *Intimacy: Venturing the Ambiguities of the Heart*, was published in 2009, ensuing from the Jungian Odyssey 2008.

The Jungian Odyssey Annual Conference and Retreat		Venue	JO Series
2006	Jungian Psychology Today: Traditions and Innovations & The Quest for Vision in a Troubled World: Exploring the Healing Dimensions of Religious Experience	Flüeli-Ranft	
2007	Exploring the Other Side: The Reality of Soul in a World of Prescribed Meanings	Gersau	
2008	Intimacy: Venturing the Uncertainties of the Heart	Beatenberg	Vol. I, 2009
2009	Destruction and Creation: Facing the Ambiguities of Power	Sils Maria	Vol. II, 2010
2010	Trust and Betrayal: Dawnings of Consciousness	Gersau	Vol. III, 2011
2011	The Playful Psyche: Entering Chaos, Coincidence, Creation	Monte Verità	Vol. IV, 2012
2012	Love: Traversing Its Peaks and Valleys	Flüeli-Ranft	Vol. V, 2013
2013	Echoes of Silence: Listening to Soul, Self, Other	Kartause Ittingen	*Forthcoming* Vol. VI, 2014

All published volumes of the Jungian Odyssey Series can be
ordered online at www.springjournalandbooks.com.

Editors

Series Editors

Stacy Wirth, MA, graduated from the C.G. Jung Institute Zürich (2003) after earning her MA in the psychology of art from Antioch University (1997). Her bachelor's studies in dance and anthropology were completed at Mills College (1977). As a choreographer and the co-founder of the Zürich foundation, *Seefeld-Tanzprojekt*, she shared the Zürich Mayor's Counsel Prize for dance in 1991. She is a former vice-president and secretary of ISAPZURICH, where she is a training analyst and co-chair of the Jungian Odyssey Committee. Since 2004 she has served on the AGAP Executive Committee, and became co-president in 2010. She is a member of the Advisory Board of *Spring Journal*, and together with Isabelle Meier co-edited *Unwrapping Swiss Culture, Spring: A Journal of Archetype and Culture, Vol. 86, 2011.*

Isabelle Meier, Dr. phil., is a graduate of the C.G. Jung Institute Zürich and maintains a private practice in Zürich. She is further trained as a Guided Affective Imagery therapist. She was recently elected co-president of ISAPZURICH, where she previously served as co-chair of the Jungian Odyssey Committee, and is presently a training analyst and supervisor. She co-edited *Seele und Forschung* [*Soul and Research*] (Bern: Karger Verlag, 2006) and is the Swiss editor for the German edition of the *Journal of Analytical Psychology*. Her special area of interest is the link between imagination, complex, and archetype.

John Hill, MA, received his degrees in philosophy at the University of Dublin and Catholic University of America. He trained at the C.G. Jung Institute Zürich, has practiced as a Jungian analyst since 1973, and is a training analyst and supervisor at ISAPZURICH. He has published articles on the Association Experiment, Celtic myth, James Joyce, dreams, and Christian mysticism, and is the author of the book, *At Home in the World: Sounds and Symmetries of Belonging* (Spring Journal Books, 2010).

Consulting Editor

Nancy Cater, JD, PhD, is the editor (since 2003) of *Spring: A Journal of Archetype and Culture,* the oldest Jungian psychology journal in the world, and the author of the book *Electra: Tracing a Feminine Myth through the Western Imagination.* She is the publisher of Spring Journal Books, which specializes in books by leading scholars in depth psychology, the humanities, and cultural studies. She is an Affiliate Member of the Inter-Regional Society of Jungian Analysts, and a former appellate court attorney.

Contributors

Brigitte Egger, Dr. sc. nat. ETH, is a Jungian training analyst at ISAPZURICH with a private practice in Zürich. As both an ecologist and analyst, she concentrates her research on the psychic and symbolic dimensions of collective issues and works at introducing this dimension into practical environmental protection, especially in areas concerning energy and water, animals, landscape, and market globalization, thus building up the field of psychecology. She is interested in creative ways to communicate depth psychological insights.

Mark Hederman, PhD, is a philosopher, monk, and the Abbot of Glenstal Abbey. He studied in Paris under Emmanuel Levinas and has lectured worldwide, including Flüeli-Ranft at the first Jungian Odyssey in 2006 and at the C.G. Jung Institute Zürich. He is a founding editor of the cultural journal, *The Crane Bag*, and has written ten books, including the best-seller *Kissing the Dark,* as well as *Manikin Eros, The Haunted Inkwell, Tarot: Talisman or Taboo, Walkabout, Symbolism, Underground Cathedrals,* and *Dancing with Dinosaurs.*

John Hill, MA, received his degrees in philosophy at the University of Dublin and the Catholic University of America. He trained at the C.G. Jung Institute Zürich, and has practiced as a Jungian analyst since 1973. He is a training analyst at ISAPZURICH, where he also served as Academic Chair of the Jungian Odyssey from its inception in 2005 until 2012, when he stepped down to concentrate on other projects. His publications have focused on the association experiment, Celtic myth, James Joyce, dreams, the significance of home, and Christian mysticism. His book, *At Home in the World: Sounds and Symmetries of Belonging,* was published by Spring Journal Books in 2010.

James Hollis, PhD, graduated thirty years ago from the C.G. Jung Institute Zürich and is an analyst in private practice in Houston, Texas. In addition, he is Director Emeritus of the Houston Jung Center, Vice President Emeritus of the Philemon Foundation, and the author of fourteen books, most recently, *What Matters Most: Living a More Considered Life* and *Hauntings: Dispelling the Ghosts Who Run Our Lives.*

Doris Lier, lic. phil., studied history at the University of Zürich and subsequently received her training in Analytical Psychology at the C.G. Jung Institute Zürich. Since her graduation in 1988 she has maintained her own therapy practice in Zürich. In addition she works as a training analyst, supervisor, and lecturer at ISAPZURICH. Her publications are in the areas of analytical psychology, the history of symbols, and epistemology.

Lucienne Marguerat, lic. phil., was born in 1943 in Lausanne. She received her degree in sociology from the University of Geneva. Having worked for over ten years as a computer specialist in Zürich, she finally returned to her interest in the human condition and started her training at the C.G. Jung Institute Zürich, Küsnacht. She has a private practice in Zürich, and is a training analyst and supervisor at ISAPZURICH and chair of the Promotions Committee. She has lectured and held workshops at the C.G. Jung Institute Zürich, ISAPZURICH, the Jungian Odyssey, and at the *Antenne Romande* in Lausanne. Her areas of interest include time, the archetypal feminine, the cultural complex in relation to Swiss history, and *Art Brut.*

Isabelle Meier, Dr. phil., is a graduate of the C.G. Jung Institute Zürich, and has been Co-President of ISAPZURICH since March 2012. She was co-chair of the Jungian Odyssey Committee through June 2012, when she stepped down after six years of service to this project. She is a training analyst and supervisor at ISAPZURICH, and maintains a private practice in Zürich. She has further trained as a Guided Affective Imagery therapist (GAI). She co-edited *Seele und Forschung* (Karger Verlag, 2006), and is on the editorial staff for the German edition of the *Journal of Analytical Psychology.* Her special area of interest lies in the links of imagination, complexes and archetypes.

Dariane Pictet received her degree in Comparative Religion from Columbia University. She is a graduate of the C.G. Jung Institute Zürich, Küsnacht and a training analyst at ISAPZURICH, the Guild of Analytical Psychology, and the Independent Group of Analytical Psychologists in London. Since 2004 she has served on the Executive Committee of the Association of Graduate Analytical Psychologists (AGAP). She delights in poetry and practices Yoga.

Bernard Sartorious, lic. theol., received his degree in theology from Geneva University in 1965 and worked for several years as a protestant minister, first in a parish and then in youth work. He graduated from the C.G. Jung Institute Zürich in 1974, maintaining his private analytical practice first in Geneva, and since 1997 in Lucerne and Zürich. He is a training analyst at ISAPZURICH. His publications include a book on the Orthodox Church, and many papers (in *Vouivre*, Lausanne) on symbolical subjects, such as, "A Pilgrimage to Mecca."

Regine Schweizer-Vüllers, Dr. phil., is a psychotherapist and Jungian analyst in private practice in Zürich. She was one of the founders and a board member of The Research and Training Centre in Depth Psychology According to C.G. Jung and Marie-Louise von Franz for many years. She is also a training analyst and regular lecturer at ISAPZURICH. In addition, she has published psychological interpretations of legends, fairy tales, and historical works. Her book, *Die Heilige am Kreuz* [*The Feminine on the Cross*] explores the feminine aspects of the Christian God image during the Middle Ages and the following centuries.

Ann Ulanov, PhD, LHD, is a member of the Jungian Psychoanalytic Association and has a private practice in New York City. Besides serving on the Editorial Advisory Board of the *Journal of Analytical Psychology*, she is the Christiane Brooks Johnson Professor of Psychiatry and Religion at Union Theological Seminary. She is also the author of many books and articles, among which are, with her late husband Barry Ulanov: *Cinderella and Her Sisters: The Envied and the Envying* and *The Healing Imagination*; she herself authored *Spiritual Aspects of Clinical Work* and *The Unshuttered Heart: Opening to Aliveness and Deadness in the Self*. She is recipient of the Oskar Pfister Award from the American Psychiatric Association and the Gradiva Award from the National Association for the Advancement of Psychoanalysis for her book, *Finding Space: Winnicott, God, and Psychic Reality*.

Lightning Source UK Ltd.
Milton Keynes UK
UKOW031142240513

211207UK00003B/24/P